Popular Spanish Film under Franco

Popular Spanish Film under Franco

Comedy and the Weakening of the State

Steven Marsh

First published 2006 by
PALGRAVE MACMILLAN
Houndmills, Basingstoke, Hampshire RG21 6XS and
175 Fifth Avenue, New York, N.Y. 10010
Companies and representatives throughout the world

PALGRAVE MACMILLAN is the global academic imprint of the Palgrave
Macmillan division of St. Martin's Press, LLC and of Palgrave Macmillan Ltd.
Macmillan® is a registered trademark in the United States, United Kingdom
and other countries. Palgrave is a registered trademark in the European
Union and other countries.

ISBN-13: 978–1–4039–4117–6 hardback
ISBN-10: 1–4039–4117–3 hardback

This book is printed on paper suitable for recycling and made from fully
managed and sustained forest sources.

A catalogue record for this book is available from the British Library.

Library of Congress Cataloging-in-Publication Data
Marsh, Steven, 1963–
    Popular Spanish film under Franco : comedy and the weakening of the
state / Steven Marsh.
        p.   cm.
    Filmography: p.
    Includes bibliographical references and index.
    ISBN 1–4039–4117–3 (cloth)
    1. Motion pictures—Spain—History.   2. Fascism and motion
pictures—Spain.   3. Comedy films—Spain—History and
criticism.   I. Title.
    PN1993.5.S7M2939 2005
    791.43′658—dc22   2005049204

10   9   8   7   6   5   4   3   2   1
15   14   13   12   11   10   09   08   07   06

Printed and bound in Great Britain by
Antony Rowe Ltd, Chippenham and Eastbourne

This book is dedicated to my daughter Jana

Almost everything in Spanish Cinema is incongruent.

Fernando Fernán Gómez in Cobos *et al.*, 1997: 75

Spain is the country with the least sense of humour on the planet, although paradoxically we are always game for a lark. Just about anybody loves to laugh at somebody else but if you mess with him he is capable of killing you. We have an exacerbated sense of the ridiculous. Spain is full of dickheads, the problem is that we do not realize it.

José Miguel Monzón 'El Gran Wyoming' in Rigalt, 1997: 32

A list of 'populist' tendencies and an analysis of each of them would be interesting: one might discover one of Vico's 'ruses of nature' – how a social impulse, tending towards one end, brings about its opposite.

Antonio Gramsci, 1985: 364

Contents

List of Figures

Acknowledgements

I would like to take advantage of the opportunity to thank first and foremost Jo Labanyi without whose rigorous criteria, enthusiasm and constant encouragement I would never have finished the research on which this book is based. I am grateful to Paul Julian Smith and Peter Evans who were among the first to see the publication potential of the original research. I thank colleagues Anja Louis, Tatjana Pavlovic, Parvati Nair, Celia Martín Pérez, Susan Larson and Michael Ugarte for the ongoing dialogue and debate that we have maintained now for several years on Spanish culture and politics. Kathleen Vernon, Susan Martin Márquez and Tatjana Gajic very kindly read and commented on extracts from the original text. My students at the University of Missouri and at the University of South Carolina provided a fresh insight into a number of aspects of Spanish film that familiarity had inured me against. I would also like to acknowledge the cultural and sentimental debt I owe Esther Alonso, Heinrich Dening, Mila Lasaosa, Jan Eidersson Posada, Pepe Roldán, Amparo Perdomo Feo, Anna Gimein, Santiago Aguilera and Analía Beltrán i Janés. These are people who have accompanied me throughout the time that followed my impromptu arrival in Madrid where I lived between 1989 and 2003; genuine organic intellectuals who taught me the humility from which dominant academic discourse on Spain would do well to learn. Gratitude too is due to my sister, Jenny Peachey. A final word must go to my parents, Walter Marsh (1931–1995) and Jo Aplin, who met in a low-life language academy on Madrid's Gran Via *circa* 1959 and began it all.

Sections of this book, albeit in very different form, have been published in the following journals and books: a section from Chapter 1 appeared in *The Journal of Iberian and Latin American Studies* (5.1, 1999: 65–75), an earlier version of Chapter 2 appeared in *La herida de las sombras: El cine español de los años cuarenta* (2001: 99–113). Part of Chapter 3 was published in the journal *Studies in Hispanic Cinemas* (1.1, 2004: 27–41). Chapter 4 first saw the light of day in the *Bulletin of Hispanic Studies* (2004: 25–41). An abridged section of Chapter 5 was published in the collective volume *Spanish Popular Cinema* (2004: 113–128) and part of Chapter 7 appeared in the *Journal of Hispanic Research* (2003: 133–149).

Introduction

The emergence in 1950 of the first promotion of graduates from the Madrid film school, the *Institute of Cinematic Investigation and Experience* (IIEC), marked a major event in Spanish cultural history. This generation of future filmmakers most famously included Luis García Berlanga and Juan Antonio Bardem who would in time become the key figures in shaping the cinema of their day. Under the influence of the Spanish Communist Party (PCE), of which Bardem was a member, they would form *Uninci* – the production company behind such films as *Welcome Mister Marshall!* (*¡Bienvenido Mister Marshall!* Berlanga, 1952) and *Viridiana* (Luis Buñuel, 1961) – and found the film magazine *Objetivo* in July 1953.[1] They would also be present and decisive at the 1955 Salamanca Conference organized by the future director and critic Basilio Martín Patino as an attempt to refocus the direction Spanish cinema was taking and to coordinate a dialogue between liberal elements within the state machinery (most notably the erstwhile head of cinema and theater in the Ministry of Tourism and Information, José María García Escudero, who would hold the position on two different occasions in 1951 and 1962) and the leftish opposition. It was Bardem's searing intervention in the course of the conference that has defined (and in my view misdefined) the entire generation. Bardem declared that Spanish cinema was 'politically ineffectual, socially false, intellectually poverty-stricken, aesthetically void and industrially stunted' (Gubern *et al.*, 1995: 283).

It is both a commonplace and a falsehood – and one founded, among other sources, upon Bardem's celebrated phrase – that Spanish cinema of the early Francoist period comprised exclusively nation-building propaganda exercises in the form of rewritten history and religious epic. Of the more than five hundred films made in Spain between 1939 and 1951 – the so-called period of *autarky* – less than twenty conform to this

1

particular caricature. The vast majority of Spain's filmic production of the period consists of popular comedies, melodramas, costume dramas that are often set in the 19th century, and musicals. It is, nonetheless, true that in the aftermath of the Civil War, the Nationalist victors were conscious of the necessity of incorporating the bulk of the losing masses into their project. To this end, the horrors of the post-war repression were coupled with cultural initiatives designed to elicit popular consent. However, it will be my contention in this book that these efforts also opened up ideological spaces that enabled critical elements to work with relative freedom while, simultaneously, witnessing the appropriation of the cinematic legacy of the defeated Second Republic (1931–1939).

Two connected and interrelated things can be said at the outset with regard to comedy: that it is often held to be Spain's distinguishing national genre – from the picaresque novel to the cinema of Pedro Almodóvar – and secondly that there is no consensus of opinion on whether it is subversive or conservative. Indeed, frequently it is considered more conventional than not and many of those directors discussed in this book have been accused, precisely, of conservatism. It is interesting then – and engagement with this issue is one of the objectives of the text that follows – that comedy should be conceived of as *the* genre that links 'nation' and 'people' and that its allegedly conservative nature is attributable to its conventional pursuit of a resolution of conflicts. It is, indeed, undeniably the case that traditionally comedies, filmic and otherwise, end in marriage and that there is both a sense of 'togetherness' in the very content of the genre and a much commented element of what is generally referred to as escapism in the anticipated relation between screen and spectator.

Tradition, then, is what is at stake in this book. My aim is to interrogate the premises upon which such traditions are constructed and how they come to form the basis of the cinematic canon. More importantly, however, it is in the spirit of Italian Communist Party leader Antonio Gramsci that I seek to contextualize the persistence of residual 'national' traditions and analyze how they might intersect with popular culture. My purpose, moreover, is to investigate how such an articulation can sometimes lead to the popular reinscription of national tradition. Rather than regarding film exclusively as an artform, I will argue that cinema (both in and outside the screen text) mediates experiences of everyday life. To this end, much of this research revolves around a notion of the non-discursive. It starts from the basis that there is a significant difference between discourse and practice, that non-discursive practices are not only the building material of comedy but that they provide effective means by which to subvert normative regulation. And, fundamentally, this book is an attempt to identify the meaning of subversion. Practices elude discourse in the same way as customs are not the same thing as traditions. Traditions strive to bind customs into their totalizing web just as discourses strive to incorporate practice. Much of this book seeks both to demonstrate the failure of this totalizing determinant and to analyze non-discursive practices as the key to understanding subversion. By non-discursive practices I refer to those activities of consumption (often very real consumption: eating and drinking are among the distinctive elements of comedy) in which the consumer participates actively in a series of negotiations whereby power relations are mediated and occasionally transformed. Dining of course, particularly in the form of the banquet, has a long history in classical and Christian traditions as is testified to in Plato's *The Symposium* or The Last Supper. Indeed Aristophanes, the most important of the Old Attic Comedians, began his career as a comic dramatist in the year 427 BC with *The Banqueters*.

Any study of popular culture must sooner or later address the question: what *is* the people? A number of cultural critics have sought to celebrate 'the people' in an uncritical and unproblematic way. 'The people' is reduced to an idealization permanently initiating resistance to power in myriad forms. Such a caricature is not too far removed from the position of the influential John Fiske whose work in the field I think is flawed by his failure to contemplate 'the people' as nuanced and multifarious. On the other hand, much of the criticism leveled at a pioneer in this area, Mikhail Bakhtin, is similar to my disagreement with Fiske. In this instance, however, I depart from those who attack Bakhtin's work as utopian populism, an exaltation of 'the people' and their practices or, in the same vein, a celebration of resistance that provides no more than 'a safety valve' with which to let off of steam, thus enabling dissent to be aired without consequences for real power (Matthews, 2000: 31; Dentith, 1995: 73–79). To a degree, this book is an attempt to respond to such criticism and to politicize Bakhtin's insights.

Coincidentally, soon after I commenced this research Roberto Benigni's Oscar-winning film *Life is Beautiful* (1997) came under attack for being a comedy about the Holocaust. One of Benigni's critics was Steven Spielberg whose own *Schindler's List* (1993) had also dealt with the subject of the Shoah and Nazi concentration camps. There are, of course, several comic antecedents – Ernst Lubitsch (*To Be or Not to Be*), Mel Brookes (*The Producers*), Billy Wilder (*Stalag 17*) and various references in Woody Allen films for example – with regard to the atrocities of World War II. Spielberg's critique recalled Bardem's earlier attack on Berlanga for having trivialized the death penalty in *The Executioner* (*El verdugo*, 1963) (Cañique and Grau, 1993: 195). Comedy that deals with horror and morbidity – what is often termed 'black comedy' – is not in any case a recent or modern concept. Bakhtin comments, in his classic work on Rabelais, on the age-old tradition of laughing at death or indeed death by laughter that stretches back to antiquity (Bakhtin cites Pliny and Aulus Gellius) and reaches contemporary cinema (see, for instance, Alex de la Iglesias's 1999 *Dying of Laughter* [*Muertos de risa*]). As we shall see in the course of this essay, death appears in almost all the films discussed. There are shades and degrees of death and these are debated through and within comedy. Indeed comedy itself is debated. As we shall see, reading some critics one would have thought that black comedy was something invented by that trio of 1950s pioneers Berlanga, Marco Ferreri and their screenwriter, Rafael Azcona, or indeed that it was an exclusively Spanish phenomenon. By beginning in the 1940s I hope to refute such assertions and show that there is an evolutionary process at work. In both Bardem and Spielberg's cases there seems to be an element of ideological possessiveness, a confusion between propriety and property. Both claim ownership of what others have done better and it is my view that Berlanga's films are more subversive than those of that professional figure of opposition, Bardem.

Gramsci, jailed by Mussolini in 1926, proposed a means of analyzing culture that neither unconditionally celebrated 'the people' nor underestimated the resistive potential of popular cultural practices. For Gramsci, 'the people themselves are not a homogenous cultural collectivity but present numerous and variously combined cultural stratifications which, in their pure form, cannot always be identified within specific historical popular collectivities' (1985: 189).

It is difficult, in light of this quote, to sustain the accusations of populism that were leveled at Gramsci during the 1960s. His analysis of Italian fascism (in many ways the model for early Francoism) led Gramsci to conclude that culture was an important field of struggle in the conquest of hegemony, that molecular structure of domination distinguished by its dependency on popular consent rather than coercion. Gramsci's interest is in how what he terms the 'humus of popular culture' (1985: 102) – including that with no apparent revolutionary content – can be reinscribed and politicized by subaltern groups. Gramsci maintains that 'man' has two consciousnesses or 'one contradictory consciousness' (1971: 333) that, on one level, relates to the realities of his active life and, on another, is 'inherited from the past and uncritically absorbed' (1971: 333). Gramsci's term 'the national-popular' was coined partly as a response to the failure of bourgeois revolution in Italy (often also cited to explain Spain's Civil War, and the country's failure to become fully modern and to embrace democracy). It expresses the desired means by which subaltern groups could match and, in a certain manner of speaking, mimic – within the territorial confines of the nation and precisely by use of populism – Mussolini's success in securing leadership of the hegemonic process which witnessed a hitherto unknown unity between the industrialists of northern Italy and their land-owning counterparts in the rural, underdeveloped south (again not dissimilar to the contemporaneous situation in Spain). When Gramsci speaks of 'the national-popular' he refers to subaltern reinscriptions within the interstices of existing dominant culture (and it is important to the thesis of this book that it be framed spatially). This is particularly the case when that dominant culture employs populism as an instrument and is thus made more vulnerable to subaltern intervention. Indicative of this is Gramsci's citing of 'common sense' and 'folklore' as inherited from previous periods of dominant culture that has become sedimented in the popular consciousness. The Gramscian view of culture implies a two-way relationship, a field of engagement between ruling and subaltern groups, that modifies the view of the subaltern class as duped into passive acceptance of dominant ideology that characterizes classical Marxism. What determines resistance in Gramscian thinking is the complex relation and proximity between consent and contestation; the primacy (as in all Marxism) of agency. It is important to bear in mind thus that Gramsci's 'critical sociology of culture' (Harris, 1992: 195) is inseparable from his revolutionary political project and this book seeks to avoid the pitfalls produced of disarticulating the two; contrary to what is often thought 'the national popular' is not an aesthetic style or school; nor, as Forgacs and Nowell-Smith point out, can it be conflated with neorealism as it often was in Italy during the 1950s.

In recent years, and in the wake of what might be termed 'the Almodóvar phenomenon', Spanish cinema has attracted the attention of a number of Anglo-American critics, of which Marsha Kinder has provided the most influential yet controversial theoretical framework. Kinder's contribution is a valuable one that has gone a long way towards relocating scholarship on Spanish cinema within mainstream film studies. Nonetheless, her Lacanian reading of an entire national population is, in my view, problematic; in essence, it amounts to psychoanalysis put to the service of Orientalism. She seeks, moreover, to position Spanish cinema as a hybrid sandwiched in a permanent dialogue between

Italian neorealism and Hollywood, to which reductive end she applies the label of neorealism to Berlanga and Bardem. In spite of the consensus in academic writing on such classification, I find little evidence for the claim. Such a convention is ironically similar to Hobsbawm's description of how traditions are invented (1984: 1–2).

Kinder's books, on the other hand, although dealing only briefly with the period I analyze, have come under attack from Spanish defenders of an authentic 'native' tradition that does indeed foreground the filmmakers I discuss. Santos Zunzunegui's onslaught on North American criticism dismisses what have come to be known as 'transnational' approaches to Spanish cinema (most notably defended by Marvin D'Lugo and Kinder herself) and locates a specific tradition running from Edgar Neville to Pedro Almodóvar. Other work has sought to mediate between these two positions but this one does not. I disagree with both of them and this book is in part a response to them. It is my belief that both have more in common with one another than they do with me. In due course, I shall argue that these two apparent polar opposites represent distinct and competing strands of the discourse that prevails in contemporary Hispanic film studies. Significantly, in my view, both sides in this particular debate employ the terminology of progressive discourse for ends that are, at the very least, questionable. Zunzunegui wilfully misinterprets sophisticated theoretical approaches to cinema and resorts to a tradition of Spanish liberalism, the key figure of which is José Ortega y Gasset, to argue in favor of a form of cultural nationalism, while Kinder's subjection of Spain – combined with a cavalier indifference to the specificity of the country, its history, its politics and its languages – to the disciplinary surveillance of the North American academy comes close to cultural imperialism.

By appeal to Gramsci's theorization of hegemony I seek both to undo the discourse of the nation without departing from the local reality that constitutes Spain. The Spanish liberal tradition, in my view, is indeed pertinent to the filmmakers studied in this book. While a number of significant liberals initially supported the Nationalist uprising, their support sat uneasily with the regime. Humor and, above, all, irony is a characteristic of liberalism and the Gramscian model seems particularly apt when it comes to analysis of a cinema that had little option but to work within the constraints of its political and social circumstances, by surviving on its wits and the incomprehension of those who established and marshalled its limits.

Much writing, both that of Spaniards and foreigners, on Spanish cinema revolves around a curiously conflictual employment of 'stereotypes';

curious because stereotypes are usually indicative of the attempts by dominant groups to simplify subaltern groups in fixed representation.

While Zunzunegui has attacked North American critics (and Kinder is particularly exercised by this point) for focusing upon the Spanish 'Black Legend' of cruelty and violence, his compatriot José Enrique Monterde – in specific reference to Berlanga's *Plácido* (1961) – distinguishes between the latter director and those efforts to connect his work to Italian neorealism by claiming 'black comedy' exclusively for the national patrimony. By the same token, as we will see, the painter José Gutiérrez Solana who collaborated with Edgar Neville on *Carnival Sunday* (*Domingo de carnaval*, 1945) – a film discussed in this book – actually wrote a treatise on the subject of *España negra*. 'Blackness', it seems, is a contested concept, one that – like religion, the family or comedy itself – provides a non-discursive field that dominant discourse strives to colonize. It is in this welding of popular practice to discourse that stereotypes such as 'Black Legend', 'black comedy' and 'black Spain' prove vulnerable to subaltern intervention. The locus of factors that cluster around the national stereotype both destabilizes the intended fixity of the stereotype itself and has repercussions that inflect and refract other perspectives, whether those that seek to maintain the purity of Spanish tradition or those involved in the current trend of transnationalism.

This book examines a period that stretches from 1942 to 1964. The choice of years that mark these boundaries is fortuitous, one based more on the directors that originally interested me than for the purposes of marking out a defined historical epoch with precision. Nonetheless, the period is rich in historical and cultural changes and the years that initiate and terminate it have symbolic weight. The year 1942 was when Franco abandoned hopes of an Axis victory in World War II and the resulting policy change brought consequences within Spain, particularly with regard to the pro-German faction in the Spanish fascist organization, the Falange. The year 1964 witnessed the culmination of Spain's long post-war transition towards recovery and modernization, signified most spectacularly by the celebrations held to commemorate the '25 years of Peace', organized by Manuel Fraga Iribarne the then Minister of Tourism and Information and still, at the time of writing, an active politician. It also heralded the consolidation of Spain as a holiday resort for tourists from northern Europe – a fact that brought with it a panoply of prosperity and disruption of the Catholic-inspired mores that had governed human relations since the end of the war. Ironically, this was partly the consequence of the revamping of the Spanish economy produced by the consolidation of the influence of tecnocrats associated with the right-wing Catholic grouping Opus Dei who had entered government in 1957. 1964 was, additionally, the year in which the Asturian miners' strike was savagely repressed by the forces of the state. Among those intellectuals who suffered reprisals for protesting the ill-treatment of the miners was Fernando Fernán Gómez whose masterpiece *The Strange Journey* (*El extraño viaje*), made the same year, constitutes the final film discussed in this book.

Political and historical signifiers aside, the choice of temporal parameters also has much to do with placing Berlanga's generation of cineastes within a cultural context with regard to their filmic precursors and successors. It is generally held that the school of filmakers known as the New Spanish Cinema originated in the early 1960s and occasionally it has been suggested that Berlanga represents a precedent for this school (see, for example, Rolph, 1999: 16; Kinder, 1993: 6). I am skeptical of this claim which I think goes a long way to construct Berlanga as an *auteur* and to distance him from popular cinema. I do, however, believe that Berlanga cannot be seen in isolation from those who followed him. Suffice it to say, for the moment, that it is of some significance that his favored scriptwriter, Rafael Azcona, and one of his preferred actors, José Luis López Vázquez, both went on to pursue lengthy and fruitful collaborations with that darling of art-house cinema, Carlos Saura, in the years following the successes of *Plácido* and *The Executioner* (1963). That said, and while it is indeed interesting and a feature of this book to map the historical progression of Spanish cinema, its primary concern is with the political implications of that evolution.

Berlanga's friend and immediate predecessor Edgar Neville represents one of the most significant figures of a previous generation of humorists that has been buried beneath the discriminating weight of critical taste. What has been occasionally been termed the 'other generation of 1927' (in the typically classificatory vein which this volume seeks to critique) constitutes an extraordinary group of comic writers who were marked by cinema and particularly Hollywood. Neville was perhaps the most prominent of those Spaniards, that included Enrique Jardiel Poncela, Miguel Mihura and Antonio de Lara 'Tono', who in the late 1920s and early 1930s travelled to Los Angeles to work either as scriptwriters or directors of Spanish language versions of Hollywood studio movies. Not only does the experience of this group leave its imprint on successive generations but directors such as Berlanga counted on their collaboration in several of his projects and their humor, particularly marked by involvement in the satyrical magazine *La Codorniz* founded by Mihura in 1941, permeates this book. Moreover, the rival comic strains (pioneers of a kind of Theatre of the Absurd a decade before Ionesco) forged by Jardiel Poncela on the one hand, and Mihura on the other, while lying beyond the scope of this study, await serious scholarly treatment. Mihura, one of the scriptwriters on *Welcome Mister Marshall!*, commences his memoirs with a sentence that proves significant to the thrust of this book's argument.

When I was on the point of being born, Madrid still wasn't invented, and had to be invented quickly so that I could be born and so that another short gentleman whose name I can't remember at this precise moment and who also wanted to be a Madrilenian, could also be born. (17)

One thing is clear; popular culture of post-war Spain not only emerges from the shadows of the nation's civil conflict, it itself *shadows* an official culture. The notion of 'the double' pervades this book and seeks to link the caricature of the 'two Spains' (that of foreign-influenced cosmopolitanism that lost the war versus National Catholicism with values that hark back to rural, provincial traditions) to Gramsci's contradictory consciousness, to mimicry, to the popular carnavalesque employment of masquerade and comic couples and to establish a connection with the substitute and the *ersatz* economy that so distinguished the post-war period. While this analysis of the 'double' does not draw on psychoanalytical theory other than incidentally, it does seek to explore the complexities of comic ambivalence, that which Joseph Roach describes as 'the surrogated double's uncanny suspension between life and death, strength and vulnerability, body politic and body natural' (1996: 79). The particular experience of loss and absence points suggestively to the means by which comedy might come to mediate discursive relations of national history and historiography. The customary criticism (as in Bakhtin) that comedy simply masks crude reality thus becomes a more complex analysis of how to deal with the unsutured wounds of Spain's Civil War.

The chapters of this book roughly follow a chronological order. Chapters 1 and 2 provide an outline of its theoretical parameters and offer analysis of a number of films from the 1940s that, in my view, are not only exemplary with respect to the postulations I advance in the rest of the book but also suggest a continuum – establishing themselves as both predecessors to that generation of the 1950s and heirs to the cinema produced in the Second Republic. Chapter 1 ends with a detailed analysis of the 1940s films of Jerónimo Mihura while Chapter 2 introduces the work of Neville and the theories of Michel de Certeau concerning the possibilities of non-discursiveness, which are questions that will be followed up in greater depth in the latter part of the book. The discussions deal with cineastes who almost universally supported the Nationalist uprising and interrogates the relationship of comedy with the state. My aim is to subvert the cliché that caricatures Spanish film production of the time as Francoist propaganda. The films discussed in this section not only pre-date the Spanish screening of the classics of Italian neorealism (and indeed have little in common with such cinema) but are clearly influenced by North American screwball comedy, by George Cukor, Ernst Lubitsch, Frank Capra, Gregory La Cava and those starring the Marx brothers. Likewise there is a correspondence in these films with the European millennial popular comic traditions of carnival, travesty, the circus and *commedia dell'arte* – and in this there is indeed a similarity with Italian cinema. Additionally, I agree with Zunzunegui (though only superficially) that the Spanish filmic tradition that starts with the films of Neville (and in reality begins in the 1930s) leads to Almodóvar and the 'Madrid comedies' of the 1980s.

Chapters 3 to 5 represent the core of the book. In this section study is limited to those two directors who I consider among the most important of the period: Neville and Luis García Berlanga. While the initial discussion of Neville in Chapter 2 focuses upon *Life on a Thread* (*La vida en un hilo*, 1945) as a film that destabilizes the configuration of national space by playing upon itself as an allegory of the 'two Spains', Chapter 3 revolves around the significance of Neville's view of the city of Madrid. In discussing *The Tower of the Seven Hunchbacks* (*La torre de los siete jorobados*, 1944), *Carnival Sunday* (1945) and *The Bordadores Street Murder* (*El crimen de la calle de Bordadores*, 1946) I will argue that, in what could loosely be described as a trilogy linked by location and form, Neville undermines unitary notions of the city of Madrid as capital of nation and empire and does so by resort to the city's most typical customs and popular traditions. Although the more extensive treatment of Neville and of Berlanga – and their placing in consecutive chapters – is based on their significance and close cinematic relationship, it is also based upon the divergences between the two filmmakers. Berlanga's work, commencing for the purposes of this study in Chapter 4 with *Welcome Mister Marshall!* (1952), does indeed mark a break with the past, albeit an evolutionary one. Chapter 5 involves detailed analysis of Berlanga's other two masterpieces *Plácido* (1961) and *The Executioner* (1963) as films in which the nation and the popular coincide. I consider Berlanga to have been treated unfairly by history. He has often been rejected by foreign critics as untranslatable, misogynistic (an accusation fostered by his own unfortunate declarations in interviews) and politically ambiguous (he remains fully unforgiven for having served as a volunteer in the *División Azul*, the unit of Spanish soldiers sent by Franco to the Eastern Front in support of Germany during World War II). And yet, equally well, as if to compensate for such neglect outside of Spain, he has been turned by national critics into a sacred cow of Spanishness. In many ways Berlanga embodies the issues discussed in this book. It is, in part, desire to rescue Berlanga from official appropriation and re-evaluate his subversive cinema that motivates the entire text.

The final two chapters offer fuller discussions of the meaning of non-discursive practices, particularly those concerning consumption, perform-ance and dressing up, as destabilizing of tradition. In Chapter 6, by means of an analysis of the Spanish films of Marco Ferreri (Spain is where Ferreri commenced his long and distinguished career as a filmmaker), I will discuss the parodic possibilities afforded by the preponderance of tawdry surrogates that I venture comes to represent an *ersatz* economy, and how this proves disruptive of both elements of the Spanish literary tradition and social relations. Ferreri worked in Spain as a director from 1958 to 1960 and it is apposite that his films, which make so much of home-spun improvized substitutions, should coincide in history with the 1959 Stabilization Plan that ignited the subsequent economic boom. It is this attempt to politicize the non-discursive and the performative (in the context of the dystopic body) that determines the chapter. In Chapter 7, the final chapter of the book, I analyze how the traditional and utopian function of the village, the *pueblo*, as substitute for and symbol of the nation, is undermined in Fernán Gómez's *The Strange Journey*.

de Certeau provides a panoply of terms ('tactics', 'strategy', 'making use', 'in-betweenness') that have enriched the vocabulary of the theory of resistance. Throughout the book I incorporate these terms within my own analysis. This is particularly the case in these later chapters, in which two loci of Spanish traditionalism converge. The Spanish *pueblo* and the streets of central Madrid – focal points where almost all the elements discussed in the book cluster – might appear unlikely sites for subversive activity. Nonetheless both represent arenas where dominant and subaltern groups congregate and where traditions are spawned. The central Madrid of popular operetta (*zarzuela*) and theater (*sainete*) vies in the popular imagination with the unchanging stasis of the village square which at least three of the filmmakers I discuss here choose quite literally to embellish and transform through a process of 'dressing up'.

This book attempts to defend comedy as a source of potential subversion and aims to identify those 'commonsensical' (in the Gramscian sense) elements which form the basic substance of comedic coherence: popular celebrations, dress, music and food. I will try to establish that it is precisely by use of the same elements that power is organized, that state legitimacy 'coheres' around incursions into the realm of the popular, but that therein also lies the seed of excess that threatens its own project. This is not something, of course, limited to Spain or to Francoism. The operations of clowns exceed temporal and spatial boundaries in all comedy, everywhere, outside of regulated time.

1
Comedy and the Weakening of the State

Leo Bassi springs onto the stage, picks up a mallet and smashes it into a row of watermelons splattering the audience in the front rows. Bassi is fifty-ish, bald, tightly besuited over his paunch and wears thick framed glasses. His show is physical in the extreme, punctuated with jerky movements, gymnastics, face pulling elasticity. He is highly scatological, fascinatedly celebratory of faeces and bodily fluids, which he happily consumes in the course of his performance. This reassertion of physicality is further reinforced by a constant dialectical relationship with his public, at times confrontational, on other occasions complicitous.[1] Invited onto Canal Plus' flagship TV program *Lo más plus*, whose smart alec interviewers specialize in smirking condescension to undermine their guests, Bassi took red paint to the spruce, pristine whiteness of the studio.[2] Born in New York, resident of Mallorca and Madrid and an Italian national, Bassi is geographically rootless and apparently ageless. A rather feeble attempt to explain this away has been to attribute it to parentage. Bassi comes from a family of comics and his father worked with Groucho Marx and Laurel and Hardy. Whereas all this is indeed of interest, I hope to demonstrate that there is rather more to people like Leo Bassi than that.

In comedy there is a constant interweaving between the outrageous and the acceptable, between autonomy and appropriation, between foolishness and danger, between civil society and the state. Bakhtin, on language, identifies 'centripetal forces' that, in the words of Michael Holquist, 'strive to make things cohere' (Bakhtin, 1996: xviii) and the disruptive 'centrifugal forces' of real utterance. Among these centrifugal forces, Bakhtin singles out rogues, clowns and fools as important in the creation of disturbance. In Bakhtin, what is originally a linguistic formulation is extended into an examination of social relationships within the matrix of power.

13

The verb 'cohere', as used here by Holquist is rich in implication. Homi K. Bhabha uses it to describe the way in which colonial mimicry functions (1994: 86) and Gramsci employs it to imbue political projects with ideological 'good sense' (1971: 327). In all three instances what is clear is that the relationship between subaltern and dominant elements in society is not simply one of opposition but of compliance, alliance and overlap. José Ortega y Gasset, with a rather different idea in mind to the three previously mentioned thinkers, nonetheless conceives of the nation-state in similarly dynamic terms when he writes the following:

> [T]he unifying, central energy of *totalization* – call it what you will – needs, so as not to been weakened, the opposite force, that of dispersion, of the centrifugal impulse that survives in collectives. Without this stimulant, cohesion atrophies, national unity dissolves, the parts come unstuck, they float away and have to live in isolation as independent entities. (1957: 29)

As we shall see, it is Ortega y Gasset who provides the theoretical framework for those who most fervently defend the Spanish native tradition and it is noteworthy that in such a framework the containing and freezing of oppositions, such as that described above, is an important factor. Hybridization is not always progressive; it often belies an impulse to subsume and absorb difference within a totality such as the nation itself.

As mentioned in the introduction, Gramsci describes state legitimacy as being dependent upon dominant groups securing the consent of subaltern groups. While this was true of Francoism, the post-Franco consensus has been established on the basis of quite literal negotiations. Its fragility was – and remains – such that it has had to reaffirm itself in written and highly ritualized form. The democratic process associated with the 1978 Constitution, the Moncloa Pacts[3] and even entry into the European Union and NATO has been combined with the exaltation – to the point of mythology – of personages like Adolfo Suárez, Santiago Carrillo and Juan Carlos de Borbón.[4] This has brought with it cultural repercussions.

Whereas the degree of coercion employed by the regime is undeniable, many of the manichean concerns of early Francoism floundered in the face of having to incorporate the popular masses, including those who had participated on the losing side during the Civil War, into the national project. Even before the war had ended Franco recognized the necessity of consolidating a cross-class consensus in an interview with Falangist journalist Manuel Aznar on 31 December 1938, in which he stated: 'I want my policy to have the profound popular character that politics has always had in the history of the Great Spain. Our work [...] will be orientated towards a constant concern for the popular classes' (Preston, 1997: 114–115).

Such notions of the 'popular' are suggestive of the influence of Mussolini's fascism on early Francoism; and Francoism itself was an uneasy coalition of different right-wing interests competing within the same set of constituencies. It was faced with Mussolini's success that Gramsci from his prison cell developed his analysis of hegemony which, in turn, led him to speculate on the nature and composition of subaltern groups both as a strategy for survival under fascism and a means of building the Communist Party. What is interesting in Gramsci is that he consistently rejects systematizing distinctions between high and low culture. Engaging with Bukharin's *Theory of Historical Materialism: A Popular Manual of Marxist Sociology*, he writes:

> The first mistake of the Popular Manual is that it starts, at least implicitly, from the assumption that the elaboration of an original philosophy of the popular masses is to be opposed to the great systems of traditional philosophy and the religion of the leaders of the clergy – i.e. the conception of the world of the intellectuals and of high culture. (1971: 419)

For Gramsci high and low cultures feed off each other; subaltern thinking is encapsulated within the concept of common sense, a kind of popular philosophy formed of the residual structures of previous dominant cultures, which is neither automatically critical nor is it homogenous; it is 'an ambiguous, contradictory and multiform concept' historically specific and ideologically susceptible to intervention (Gramsci, 1971: 422). Common sense involves 'borrowing' (1971: 327) from other groups' discourses and contains within it insights that are often more useful than those of 'official' experts, who Gramsci terms traditional intellectuals. The point is to weld the 'good' elements of common sense into an organic/Jacobin organization to make it 'ideologically coherent', to make it good sense. The objective for Gramsci therefore was the formation of organic intellectuals to direct the contestatory energies of subaltern groups within the molecular structures of hegemony in the production of a kind of reflection, an internally organized parody (in its non-comic sense) – a doubling – aimed at moving beyond formal unity to dialectical unity.[5] And here Gramsci introduces the concept of 'becoming' ('man "becomes", he changes continuously with the changing of social relations' [1971: 355]). 'When an individual from the masses succeeds in criticizing and going beyond common sense, he by this very fact accepts a new philosophy' (1971: 420–421).

Gramsci, then, is useful in analyzing early Francoism because he draws attention to the importance of consent in the construction of unity (particularly in his writings on Italian history and on the Catholic Church) and in showing how subaltern groups, by borrowing, resignify everyday life through language, customs, dress and performance and by doing so can come to speak for themselves.

The grotesque

Grotesque realism is a constant presence in Spanish cultural production – particularly in literature and painting, and film is no exception. It is perhaps worth dwelling upon if only because it has proved to be a singular field of contention. The grotesque is generally accepted to be non-naturalistic, often camp, theatrical and fluid, involving cross-dressing and identity confusion. It almost always emerges from the depths of popular consciousness in processions, popular song, costume, laughter and eating. More than anything else the grotesque reveals itself through the human body; that is, in signifying practice. It is central to this book's argument that uneven and partial development, the post-war characteristic customarily associated with Spain's failure to fully modernize is reproduced culturally. Indeed, the grotesque is an acute expression of Gramsci's idea of sedimented ideas of previous epochs that are residual in the popular consciousness. Discordance between the 'popular' and the 'dominant' is often manifested through the grotesque and, in its purported specificity, it both exacerbates concepts of a distinctive 'Spanishness' while simultaneously undoing the very same concepts. In this way the 'small wounds' or 'functional stimulants' that Ortega speaks of as a necessary element in the survival of national unity can exceed established boundaries, threatening them from within. The proliferation of celebratory, profane and often riotous humor in Spanish traditions is striking: from the figure of the *caganer* (defecator) in the Catalan nativity scene – a figure that emerges in several films to be discussed in this book – to the Vallecas *Naval Battle*, the annual water fight in the streets of a working class Madrid suburb, or the *Tomatina* in Buñol in the south-eastern region of Valencia, which involves huge crowds smothering themselves in tomatoes. Such celebrations are suggestive of the multihued fabric of popular culture and vie for protagonism with dominant culture's attempts to impose a single national identity as an instrument of order.[6] Even football and bullfighting (to cite two activities in which the national and popular coincide) frequently evoke and invoke carnivalesque inversion, a loosening of hierarchical ties, the imminence and menace of the crowd.

The subaltern voices that emerge hesitantly, in fits and starts, as if reflecting the unevenness of Spain's own historical evolution, in turn produce particular narratives of their own (as the films of Pedro Almodóvar graphically demonstrate). *Esperpento*, the term invented by Ramón María del Valle Inclán to denote a particularly nationally tinted literary grotesque realism, is greatly cited as evidence of a unique Spanish form; and yet it constitutes the kind of twisted subaltern diegesis to be found almost anywhere in a world undergoing perpetual modernization. Hybridization is a consequence of this process. Bakhtin's definition of hybridization is once more phrased in linguistic terms and one that is powerfully reminiscent of Gramsci's view of hegemonic relations:

> It is a mixture of two social languages within the limits of a single utterance, an encounter, within the arena of an utterance, between two different linguistic consciousnesses, separated from one another by an epoch, by social differentiation or by some other factor. (1996: 358)

In the 1990s it became almost a convention in Spanish cinema to contrast the super-modern diagonally positioned office buildings – the Kuwaiti Investment Organization (KIO) Towers – in the north of Madrid with the shanty town and the neo-Georgian mansions close to their base.[7] Yet what is often presented as postmodernist irony proves to be little more than a reflection of the tensions produced by modernity that marks Spain's cinematic history. In this vein, it is telling that the KIO Towers have been officially named 'The Gate to Europe' (*Puerta de Europa*), thereby attributing in a name a 'democratic' quality to the modernity by which entry in the European Union has been consistently associated and ideologically articulated, and fusing that in an echo of the traditional historical boundaries – they were literally gates – of Madrid in which certain key points that once limited the city's geography were called *Puerta de ....*[8]

Just as hybridization provides the narrative framework for cultural production, it also marks subaltern characters. Rogues, clowns and tricksters inhabit a kind of twilight zone, constantly flitting in and out of regulated order and, in the words of Bakhtin, 'possess their own special rights and privileges' (1996: 159). Often this type of character is a foreigner, a fool who is 'not of this world' (Bakhtin, 1996: 159) and as a result has a certain license to act and to say the unsayable beneath the alibi of foolishness, or is otherwise dangerous, a spy and a 'fifth columnist' from beyond national frontiers. Leo Bassi's 'foreignness' comes close to being dangerous. Such an ambiguity is a constant and contradictory – presence in Spain. While on the one hand the clownish figure of fun is considered a standard classic of Spanish *alegría*, on the other there exists an abundant xenophobic lexicon that has entered everyday life, much of which derives from Spain's past imperial conflicts, particularly with France and England. Once more, this is not attributable either to ideological affiliation or to popular prejudice. Indeed, it frequently emanates from above; both Franco and the Socialist prime minister from 1982 to 1996, Felipe González, spoke mysteriously of foreign conspiracies and identified themselves with the nation, as did González's successor in office, José María Aznar.

Stratification, the subaltern and the state

The politicization of Bakhtin's thought is just one of many coincidences with Gramsci. Just as Gramsci observes that 'the popular' is marked by different and 'variously combined cultural stratifications', Bakhtin also makes much of a highly personal notion of 'stratification' that Holquist describes in his glossary of Bakhtinian terminology as 'a cheerful war, the Tower of Babel as maypole' (Bakhtin, 1996: 433). By this Holquist means to stress the centrifugal, creative quality of art as the refracting and splintering element of 'an abstractly unitary national language' which, in turn, produces combinations otherwise known as genres. Bakhtin writes:

> Certain features of language (lexicological, semantic, syntactic) will knit together with the intentional aim and with the overall accentual system inherent in one or another genre: oratorical, publicistic, news-paper and journalistic genres, the genres of low literature (penny dreadfuls, for instance) or finally, the various genres of high litera-ture. (1996: 288–289)

Alternatively, stratification also creates professional jargons. Bakhtin's notion of *heteroglossia* closely parallels Gramsci's theorizing of hegemony. Just as hegemony, as the site of struggle, is the ideological battleground for the control of institutions within civil society, *heteroglossia* is Bakhtin's term for socially stratified language in which an 'official' dialect has established dominance but this dominance vies, in permanent dialogue, with alternative or opposing languages in what Jo Labanyi has described as 'a contest of voices' (2002: 211). Craig Brandist outlines a particularly rewarding parallel between hegemony and heteroglossia when he describes how Gramsci's Jacobin (and hypothetical, Gramsci envisages a future situation, albeit one based on existing realities) political party secures its dominance over other subordinate forces in a similar relation to that by which voices compete freely in the polyphonic novel that Bakhtin finds in Dostoevsky (Brandist, 1996: 103). In Gramsci this is a consequence of his highly sophisticated notion of 'democratic centralism' in which leadership is established by consent. According to Brandist:

> Discourses seek to bind other discourses to themselves according to two basic principles: by establishing a relation of authority between the enclosing and target discourses or by facilitating the further advancement of the target discourse *through* the enclosing discourse. (1996: 103)

This is to say that hegemonic relations consist of absorption or appropriation not only of 'the people' but also of the competing ideologies (at least in classical Marxist analysis) by which their world view is shaped. Securing of hegemony is achieved when one world view succeeds in being accepted by subordinate groups, but such a 'democratic' situation also involves reciprocal 'borrowings', imitations and reinscriptions of dominant discourses that occasionally threaten to exceed the parameters of the original discourses.

The nature of democracy lies in the realignment of regulatory power, not its abolition. In fact what is interesting about Spain is the similarity of the democratic period to that of the dictatorship particularly with regard to the way in which the ruling caste seeks to intervene and mobilize the popular masses when it suits its interests to do so. By stressing this I refer to the widely acknowledged process of continuity and evolution that has characterized the Spanish transition to democracy. I do not mean by this to suggest that the post-Franco period has not brought with it significant changes and improvements on the past but that, if the uneven composition of subaltern groups persists, then equally consistent is the way in which power operates.

The state is as much a construct as the nation. The nation, moreover, might be seen as the political construct of the interests of the state, its *raison d' être*, its territorial area of operations. The ongoing contemporary crisis besetting the Spanish state in the context of the northern Basque region has provided in recent years a clear set of examples in which the state has sought successfully to secure a popular consensus for its project and thereby justify a military solution to the conflict. Fundamental to this is the combination of popular mobilization, cultural activity and the role of intellectuals.

Following the massive street demonstrations convoked to condemn the killing of the then ruling Popular Party (PP) councillor Miguel Angel Blanco by the Basque separatist organization Euskadi Ta Askatasuna (Basque Land and Liberty) (ETA), in June 1997, the state, in the form of the public television company Televisión Española (TVE), organized a commemorative concert at the Madrid bullring that September.[9] To this end the 1970s pop group *Jarcha* was disinterred from retirement to provide the anthem for the event, the emblematic oppositional song of the latter days of Francoism 'Libertad sin ira' ('Freedom without Anger').[10] *Jarcha* shared the stage that evening with crooners whose anti-Francoism had hitherto been unknown, such as Julio Iglesias and Raphael. What was manifestly designed as a show of popular and national unity, however, fell apart when the legendary anti-Francoist singer Raimon was prevented from finishing his set by the audience who protested his singing in Catalan. Similar treatment was meted out to actor José Sacristán for his membership of the Communist Party. Such incidents provide salutory reminders of the dangers of populism when employed by the state; as Gramsci observes, while popular spontaneity always runs the risk of weakening the state's control over civil society (1971: 196–200) it is – like 'common sense' – by no means in any way 'intrinsically' progressive.

Bringing about this set of uneasy alliances has concomitantly weakened intellectual activity. By a happy coincidence the great Italian clown Dario Fo was awarded the Nobel Prize for Literature the same week the entire leadership of radical Basque nationalist coalition Herri Batasuna (HB) was jailed for a crime of opinion.[11] Fo condemned the sentences in an interview with Madrid daily *El Mundo* (Neila, 1997: 17). Rapidly, the country's most public professor of ethics, Fernando Savater, who hails from the Basque city of Bilbao, was wheeled out to respond in the rival newspaper, *El País* (Savater, 1997: 13), and did so by suggesting that Fo had been misinformed of the realities of the Basque country by fellow dramatist Alfonso Sastre. Two months later Savater signed a manifesto of Basque 'intellectuals' in which HB was deemed to be a 'fascist' organization. The irony of victims of Francoism, such as Sastre or erstwhile HB member José Bergamín, being deemed fascists is not something that Savater has addressed. However, such has been the success of the state's populist initiative with regards to the Basque conflict that practically anyone who dares question it is condemned as a supporter of ETA and a fascist. The list of public figures of the Left thus slandered is long and growing; from Sastre to Fo to veteran republicans like Eduardo Haro Tegclen.[12]

Cannibalism and cross-fertilization

What we can see from these examples is that rather than the state imposing its own agenda on civil society, civil society provides the slogans that are subsequently appropriated by the state. This appropriation extends beyond popular expression to often incorporate leftist discourse and vice versa. As journalist Francisco Umbral observed from his column in *El Mundo* (1998: 64), Felipe González, now distanced from public life, took to echoing José María Pemán's cliched vision of Andalusia.[13] In the same vein, Savater appears as simply the latest in a lengthy tradition of Basques providing ideological succur to Spanish nationalism – such as Ramiro de Maeztu and Miguel de Unamuno – in a peculiarly Spanish expression of the contradictory function of the traditional intellectual in nation formation; the double at its heart.

In one of his daily opinion pieces in *El País*, Haro Tecglen compared the fluidity between dominant political groups in terms of cannibalism, writing, 'And the good anthropophagi consumed their enemies to obtain their strength' (1998: 35). He was explicitly referring to the discursive overlap between the then Prime Minister, José María Aznar, and his predecessor, Felipe González, just as previously the PSOE (the party responsible for GAL) had adopted certain characteristics of Francoism. Similarly, Marcia Landy describes the Gramscian concept of the relationship between the state and civil society as a 'cannibalization' (1994: 236). What for Landy is the incursion of the state into civil society in the form of populism and appropriation is graphically illustrated in Bakhtin's carnival banquet:

> The encounter of man with the world, which takes place inside the open, biting, rending, chewing mouth, is one of the most ancient, and most important objects of human thought and imagery. Here man tastes the world, introduces it into his body, makes it a part of himself. (Bakhtin, 1984: 281)

This image of consumption connects carnival with borrowing; that is, with the making of one's own a previously 'alien' concept and resignifying it.

Encroachment into areas of the popular terrain by the state opens up a field of ideological space within which subaltern voices can come to be heard. Two things can be said at this juncture: first, that such incursions are two-fold, subaltern groups also insinuate within the space of dominant groups, albeit in different guise; and secondly, that such a cannibalization is, as the very term suggests, brought about by non-discursive activity, by means of consumption, popular song or dress, among other things. I will return to these aspects in the later discussion of the work of Fernando Fernán Gómez; for the moment, however, I will illustrate the prevalence of the idea in broad terms.

Many Spanish filmmakers of the 1940s came from a variety of ideological backgrounds. Ignacio Iquino, who produced and directed many of the comedies of the 1940s, had previously made propaganda films for the Iberian Anarchist Federation (FAI) during the war, while others like Edgar Neville, Jerónimo Mihura and Franco's favorite director, José Luis Sáenz de Heredia – all of whom backed the 1936 military uprising – had established their professional reputations during the Second Republic and some of them would produce films that clashed with the ideas of the regime.[14]

In his recent memoirs cinema historian Román Gubern recalls post-war Barcelona as a carnivalesque and cacophonic *mélange* of cultures; of officious policemen and transvestites in the central Barrio Chino, the turbaned Moroccan Guard and the skewed cosmopolitanism of the Catalan bourgeoisie. (Gubern himself was taught German and English from a very early age but rues the poverty of his Catalan). He describes the influence of North American cinema in competition with the teachings of the Catholic Church and the resulting sexual tensions produced by such conflictual cultural information. It is striking that Gubern should resort with such frequency to dress, hair style and appearance as symbolic of these tensions as they manifested themselves on the street. Clothing is a constant and fluid metaphor throughout his book and one that contains within it a relation to cannibalism and appropriation. Gubern's description of the Falangists, for example, is illustrative: 'uniformed with the blue shirt (of the workers' overalls), the black tie (of the anarchists) and the red beret (color of the proletariat and the Carlists.What a coincidence!)' (1997: 35).

Later Gubern returns to dress reference when dealing with the transition following the death of Franco and particularly with regard to the person with whom the period is most frequently and closely associated, the recycled Adolfo Suárez:

For someone like me, who could recall perfectly well the blue shirt of the Minister General Secretary of the 'Movimiento', this transformation was strange and went some way towards confirming the pessimism I felt towards the ideological coherence and ethics of professional politicians. (1997: 324)

Coincidentally Eduardo Mendoza's novel, *Una comedia ligera* (*A Light Comedy*), published the same year as Gubern's memoirs, is also set in 1940s Barcelona and returns to the same images of dress, cinema and popular culture. These elements are precisely the means that Mendoza employs to parody national difference and history. His novel also traces the social disruption produced of the supplantation of theater by cinema in the affections of popular urban audiences. In both Mendoza's and Gubern's books what is particularly well reflected is the complex and nuanced quality of civil society.

Actors and fools

Although writing from a non-academic perspective, Carlos Colón repeats a common and authoritative assertion that cinematic comedy can be divided between realism and escapism (1996: 214). This is a classification that enables illustrious figures like Berlanga and Almodóvar to be claimed for the Academy while permitting critical dismissal of a great deal of remaining popular comedy. Such an easy dichotomy ignores the Republican tradition of comedy (although Colón himself acknowledges the influence of *sainete* in the realist films he mentions and which connects the work of Benito Perojo and Florian Rey during the Second Republic to that of Bardem and Berlanga in the 1950s). More importantly, however, such an analysis disregards the welter of secondary actors that appear in both types of films and have an enormous effect on the nature of comedy. Actors like José Isbert, Manolo Morán, Tony Leblanc, Concha Velasco, José Luis López Vázquez, Alfredo Landa and Julia Lajos, among many others, are figures who, if only for their ubiquity, undo Colón's binary opposition. They are a constant group in both sets of film with performances that vary little irrespective of the movies in which they appear and in their typecasting – to employ a term that is generally used pejoratively – they conform to Bakhtin's description of carnivalesque clowns.

Above all, they defy preconceived notions of what an actor is. The performances of their characters demonstrate that an actor is not simply a vehicle at the service of a text and a director. Within the localized context of Spanish cinema, their pervasive presence crosses all the previously established boundaries of film genre. Spanish cinema has been particularly harnessed by historians in a way that is almost anti-historical. The list of clearly defined heroes of Spanish cinema, from Buñuel to Bardem and Berlanga to Saura to Almodóvar (a much invoked, almost Leavisite 'great tradition'), has been repeated with such frequency that it is almost a heresy to suggest closer connections either between them or to pursue other paths that spread beyond the scope of the orthodox pantheon. Just as Leo Bassi is ageless and rootless so too are these actors. José Luis López Vázquez, whose reputation was made with Marco Ferreri and Berlanga (generically similar directors) also appears in many of the early films of Carlos Saura, which have been neatly defined as 'art-house' productions. This is not a matter of actorial versatility; the repressed and solitary performances of the perennially middle-aged López Vázquez in Saura's *Peppermint frappé* (1967) and *La prima Angélica* (1973) are markedly similar to his more 'comic' roles in *Plácido* (1960) or *The Little Apartment* (*El pisito*, 1958).

In all these instances López Vázquez plays the perplexed, timid, other-worldly fool and provides an example of the discursive parallels that exist between Gramsci and Bakhtin discussed above. Just as Gramsci describes a subaltern group that has 'for reasons of submission and intellectual subordination, adopted a conception that is not its own but is borrowed from another group' (1971: 327), Bakhtin on fools writes:

> their existence is a reflection of some other's mode of being – and even then, not a direct reflection. They are life's maskers; their being coincides with their role, and outside this role they simply do not exist. (1996: 159)

Interestingly, as figures so closely identified with the national discourse, occasionally these actors also provoke disturbance within the very same discourse. Berlanga speaking at the 2001 Malaga Film Festival's celebration of the actor, described López Vázquez as being Spain's very own Groucho Marx (2001), while cinema critic Julio Pérez Perucha recently paid tribute to the actor's everyman like qualities by labeling him 'a Spaniard for everyone' (Pérez Perucha, 1999b). At the very moment that López Vázquez and others like him are claimed for the nation, a paradox emerges to interrogate the premises upon which such claims are based.

Bakhtin identifies the fool's chronotope as being 'closely connected with that highly specific, extremely important area of the square where the common people congregate' (1996: 159). This terrain, as we shall see, is indeed a spatial locus of subaltern activity in numerous films of the period. The village square is at the heart of Spanish canonical tradition. The *pueblo* (village), unchanging, static and timeless is a much mythologized field of national consolidation, similar to its urban counterpart, the *barrio* (neighborhood), populated by saucy flower girls and rakish costermongers with hearts of gold. In a sense the square represents a contested Spain in miniature. There is, of course, absolutely nothing to sustain the nationalism implicit (and often explicit) in claims of intrinsic Spanishness attributed to these actors but neither should the culturally specific activities, of which they are often protagonists, played out in the village or neighborhood square be labeled escapist trivia. There is a particular tradition in critical theory that dismisses popular culture as exclusively serving the interests of dominant groups; a view perhaps most famously expressed by Theodor Adorno and Max Horkheimer on comedy when they wrote: 'Fun is a medicinal bath. The pleasure industry never fails to prescribe it' (1993: 39). Not infrequently in Spanish cinema the square provides the scenario for the rural celebration of folklore or, alternatively, for urban *sainete* and *zarzuela*. In counterposition to Adorno and Horkheimer, one of Gramsci's many insights lies in his recognition that folklore, like common sense, is a complex phenomenon.

Gramsci draws a parallel between 'common sense' and philosophy by describing it as 'the folklore of philosophy' (1985: 429). However, he also makes the important distinction between 'common sense' and philosophy when, in his political writings, he compares them with religion. This is an observation that will become clearer in the course of this book in discussion of numerous films involving ecclesiastical presence, particularly with regard to the various representations of the *pueblo*:

> Philosophy is intellectual order, which neither religion nor common sense can be. It is to be observed that religion and common sense do not coincide either, but that religion is an element of fragmented common sense. Moreover common sense is a collective noun, like religion: there is not just one common sense, for that too is a product of history and a part of the historical process. (1971: 325–326)

The mobility of López Vázquez and the agelessness of José Isbert or Concha Velasco connect them to other fields of popular expression (carnival, dance, flamenco) that resist reductive categorization. It is precisely the liminality of these actors that proves to be their most 'universalizing' aspect, that which 'coheres'.

And herein lies the paradox of these actors. They not only provoke major decentering within films as clowns (in the way that Bakhtin demonstrates) but also produce a wholesale overlap between genres and across time and space. The paradox lies in the fact that they are typecast as Spaniards yet are universally recognizable as comics who span spatial and temporal boundaries: Julia Lajos is Hattie Jacques, Manolo Morán is Lenny Bruce, Eric Morecambe or Leo Bassi. In 1998 Tony Leblanc was rediscovered for Spanish audiences after an almost thirty-year absence and played a kind of Steptoe in Santiago Segura's first film *Torrente: el brazo tonto de la ley* (*Torrente: The Stupid Arm of the Law*, 1997). Meanwhile, the same year Concha Velasco, the original *chica ye ye*, played Tennessee Williams in a Madrid theater.[15] There is a comic physicality to these actors that ruptures attempts to impose prediscursive discrete identities, precisely through the performing of those very identities.

What occurs with these actors at the level of individual, localized performance forms a pattern that exceeds the geographical parameters of Spain and parallels the experience of other nations. The comic tradition in Spain commencing with the 'quality' productions of Berlanga, Ferreri and Fernán Gómez in the 1950s evolves into the much derided series of tiresome sex romps starring Alfredo Landa in the 1960s and 1970s, which gave rise to the term *Landismo*. This is not so very different to the British tradition which led from Ealing comedies to the *Carry on* films or that which saw the great period of Italian comedy, often featuring Marcello Mastroianni and Sophia Loren, giving way to *Divorce Italian Style* and its various sequels. By the same token, there is considerable cross-fertilization between national cinemas. The 1990s saw 'La Cuadrilla' partnership of Luis Guridi and Santiago Aguilar self-consciously draw upon both Spanish and British post-war comic traditions and by exploiting the interface of global cinema – and its temporality – revealed a rich vein of domestic material.[16] La Cuadrilla's 1996 *Matías un juez de línea* (*Matías, a Linesman*) is Scotland removed to Spain's remote north-western region of Galicia in a remake of Alexander McKendrick's Ealing classic *Whisky Galore* (1948). The reinscription and borrowing of other narratives is frequent and by no means a recent phenomenon. Consistently we see the most Spanish of films such as *Welcome Mister Marshall!* or *The Strange Journey* being influenced by – and influencing – the most cosmopolitan of cinematic terrains. And as we shall, both these films turn on matters of dress and drink. Both Bakhtin and Gramsci prove useful in identifying the politics of the apparently innocuous, amid the multiple discursive and ideological systems that vie with each other, and which in turn may effect a diffusion and displacement of dominant cinematic languages.

The case of Jerónimo Mihura

In the 1940s work of Jerónimo Mihura, high and low cultural domains are blurred in the performance of 'comics'. Leadenly obvious binary oppositions (usually related to the encroachment of modernity, town/ city, innovation/tradition, etc.) are shattered by the apparently centrifugal power of secondary characters who are sucked into protagonism, while usually drawn from the lower classes (peasants or workers), women or the *déclassé*. These characters play for laughs, they mimic and parody their 'betters', they expose their pompous claims, they puncture their solemnity, they indulge in wry incomprehension; they have a freedom of speech and action denied the bulk of the population off-screen.

The fool and the trickster here take various forms (the lunatic, the imperturbable servant, the bullfighting *aficionado* raconteur, the subaltern sidekick). Each one of whom has little life outside of his or her role, neither family, nor personal drama. Bakhtin in his essay, 'Forms of Time and of the Chronotope in the Novel', defines the functions of what he calls rogues, clowns and fools, one of which he says is the unmasking of the conventional, the falsehood that exists within the framework of all human relations. Rogues, Bakhtin says, remain connected to reality while the clown and the fool – as we have seen – are 'not of this world' and for this reason have 'their own special rights and privileges' (1996: 159). Their role is to relativize claims to absolute truth.

In the Bakhtinian sense they are pure performative figures: '[T]heir existence is a reflection of some other's mode of being – and even then, not a direct reflection' (1996: 159). This is not dissimilar to Judith Butler's comments on 'imitative practices which refer laterally' (1990: 138). According to Bakhtin, writing about the novel, clowns and fools hark back to street theater of the public square; clearly in cinema they possess a popular resonance that raises political questions. This is particularly the case when that cinema formed a key part in a state project that sought to forge a unified national identity.

Manolo Morán is one of the great clowns of Spanish cinema whose roles in Mihura's films serve as examples of how the fool relativizes other ideological claims, not by intellectual rebuttal but in performance. In *The Way of Babel* (1945) (Figure 1) he plays the mad Señor Brandole who almost dupes the newly graduated César (Alfredo Mayo) and Marcelino (Fernándo Fernán Gómez) into participating in his scheme to market explosive glass balls with the aim of furthering the glory of the nation. And the glory of the nation and the destiny of its great men is the central theme in the film, spectacularly inverted by Morán's lunatic

Figure 1   The Way of Babel (Courtesy of Video Mercury Films, S.A. and Filmoteca Española)

performance. Brandole is a direct parody of the university rector who in the very first sequence of the film delivers the following graduation speech:

> To all of you [...] who from today onwards commence the organized struggle for a dignified existence, I am under the obligation to remind you, as the final lesson to be received and the most important of them all, that everything you learned here was given to you by the Fatherland and that it is to its greatest splendor and glory that you should devote your learning. Do not ever forget: great men make great nations!

Like Brandole, the university rector is fat and his academic gown and cap exacerbate the solemn absurdity of his words particularly when set against Brandole's later speech, the terminology of which convinces the two young men to throw their lot in with him:

> Didn't you want to do good business? Well I offer you the best. Your names will figure in the nation's golden book and your statues will adorn the public squares with the glorious legend: Benefactors of the Fatherland!

Not only are the sentiments identical to those of the rector, the very cadence is the same to the point of being neatly rounded off in a similar slogan. But the parody does not stop there; the logic of patriotism contains within it its opposite, the enemies of the 'Fatherland'. The rhetoric of Francoism is employed by Brandole to attack first the North American tourist on the balcony adjacent to his hotel room for being a foreign spy, then his own doctor who falls victim to the intoxicated disbelief of the two young men, and eventually the entire hotel community who are subject to Brandole's apoplectic final breakdown as he lambasts them for being 'enemies of the Fatherland'.

While Morán/Brandole is given license to parody Francoist terminology due to his madness, his logic proves infectious. This seems a recurrent feature of the fool; the fool, while being a secondary character, decenters the discourse of the film. By throwing the unity of its central claim off course, the fool casts his influence and allows for the introduction of other elements, which under parodic influence are untraumatically sutured in. This is the purpose of the carnivalesque chronotope. César and Marcelino, gulled into believing Brandole, subsequently celebrate the deal with a dinner that turns into a carnivalesque riot. The singer, also a foreigner (French), sings a song called 'The Dance of Anything Goes', which leads to a cream cake fight and full-scale mayhem. Like fools, foreigners, particularly in Franco's Spain (and after), have a freedom of speech (and social mobility) precisely because they are not taken seriously (or they are otherwise spies, enemies). As in carnival, quite literally, anything goes.

At one stage of the sequence César and Marcelino stage a slapstick brawl in the bathroom and here we see another example of the carnivalesque. A third man enters and drunkenly confuses César for a woman (he addresses him as *señora* while he is standing at the urinal) and moments later tries to intervene when Marcelino punches César ('That's no way to treat a lady' he roars). Gender confusion here is in itself carnivalesque but the subversion is sharpened by the actor. As Manuel Vázquez Montalbán has noted (1986: 75), Alfredo Mayo was the Francoist symbol of manliness *par excellence* during the 1940s, thanks to his heroic military roles in films such as *Raza, Harka and A mí la legión*. Indeed, his lead role in *Raza* (*Race*, 1941) scripted by Franco as a kind of family romance, closely identified him with Franco himself. To confuse him with a woman is deeply subversive.

There is, of course, a lengthy comic tradition of 'nutty professors' and 'mad scientists'. This kind of convention – and we will see further examples throughout this book – often provides cover for indirect and apparently innocuous commentary on current affairs and real historical event. In his biography of the dictator, Paul Preston reveals how in 1940 Franco announced that Spain would shortly be self-sufficient in energy, owing to the discovery by a certain Albert Elder von Filek (an Austrian national who had wheedled his way into the favors of Franco by means of a false tale of having been jailed by Republicans during the war) of an artificial fuel. Such was Franco's enthusiasm for the project that he ceded a portion of the waters of the River Jarama to transport materials and its banks for the construction of the future factory. Indeed a group of enormous underground tanks were built before the fraud was unmasked (Preston, 1993: 348). The figure of Brandole indirectly recalls von Filek. An even more explicit film that closely matched the real events surrounding von Filek is *Destiny Excuses Himself* (*El destino se disculpa*, 1945),[17] made the same year as *The Way of Babel*, again featuring Manolo Morán and directed by José Luis Sáenz de Heredia who also wrote and produced the Mihura film. It is noteworthy that such stories should enter the fictional realm so soon after the real event and even more so when one takes into consideration that their transfer to the screen should be brought about by a cineaste (Sáenz de Heredia) whose direction of *Raza* was indicative of his closeness to the regime.

Morán's other major performance with Mihura is in *Castle of Cards* (*Castillo de naipes*, 1943) (Figure 2), in which he plays a kind of Sancho Panza to Raúl Cancio's Quixote. Rather than being mad, his role is that of the simpleton but he is anything but simple in this film. The binary opposition set up here is that of tradition/modernity. Luis (Cancio) conflicts with Carmen (Blanca de Silos) over his plans to renovate the Piedrasalvas Castle, which he has (mis)inherited due to a gambling debt of Carmen's late grandfather. Paco (Morán) plays the workers' foreman hired by Luis to carry out the work on the castle, while at the same time he is closely allied with Carmen.

In this film mimicry predominates in class relations. On the one hand we have the stuffy bourgeois Luis and on the other the workers, the servants and the aristocrats (Carmen and her grandmother). In each of their encounters, the use and misuse of repetition creates a kind of parody. This mimicry is not limited to servants and workers; the grandmother (who is a kind of crank) does the same under the alibi of senility.

Paco acts as a fluctuating agent who mediates between the parties, moving between them but never being wholeheartedly of them. His every utterance is undercut by another: 'We have to go to work', he tells the workers, 'but with reservations'. As befits a clown he is a kind of

Figure 2 Castle of Cards (Courtesy of Video Mercury Films, S.A. and Filmoteca Española)

'inside outsider', impressed by the rhetoric of speech, not the substance; by the paraphernalia of modernity, not the essence. We can see this when Luis and Paco go to Madrid in search of Carmen and the latter marvels at the showers (and takes seventeen), the telephones, the hotel bell. He is lewd in a way that decorum prevents the other characters from being so. He is an avid consumer and drinker. His entire manner is excessive; his fatness, his baldness, his goofy broken-tooth grin, his gait (he walks with his hands splayed out at the side of his torso like a duck). This physical performance exacerbates his otherness, his relationship with what Bakhtin calls the 'bodily lower stratum' (1984: 396).

The fools and the clowns in Mihura's films not only parody their 'superiors', they parody themselves. This is one of their key features. They play for laughs but their comments are shrewdly calculated. Thus the grandmother, when told that Luis is mad and needs to be seen by a doctor, says, 'But I am also nuts and nobody examines me'. José plays nonplussed yet mimics every word Luis utters. The administrator of the publishing company, who actually looks like Groucho Marx, goes through the ritual of looking for the information Luis and Paco require four times, to find a name, title, address and so on, all of which is contained on the same filing card. The American tourist's one sole phrase in spoof Spanish ('¡Qué *alegría!*') is repeated incessantly, and parodied in turn by the others. These are ritualized mannerisms combined with apparent incomprehension that act as an organizing element in the unmasking of the supposedly seamless unity of the film. Self-parody draws attention to the performance of the characters but it also linguistically reverberates in a space exclusively limited to the parody itself, making parody the real referent. Lies are often exposed by syntactic (mis)appropriation and mistake as when a frantic Luis demands of José: 'Would you mind telling me, how the devil one can go up to the towers?', only to receive the cryptic and unhelpful response from the servant who retorts: 'To the devil of the towers one goes up the stairs'.

Binary oppositions in these films are ostensibly reinforced by the use of uniforms. Yet time and time again these prove interchangeable and variable, they purport to represent specific identities yet they never do. In one of the earliest sequences of *Castle of Cards* we see a gypsy *romería* and a young woman in gypsy clothes singing flamenco just before Luis's car crashes into the rear of the cart. What appears to be a graphic example of modernity clashing headlong with tradition is undone by the fact that shortly afterwards we learn that the singer is not a gypsy at all but Carmen, the lady of the manor. Again we see a representative of 'high' culture performing the role of one of the 'low', just as later we will see Paco in a suit perfectly well adapted to the ways of the modern city.

In *Adventure* (*Aventura*, 1942) (Figure 3) apparent homogeneity, as represented by the Aragonese traditional costumes worn by the villagers, is disrupted by the arrival of a traveling theater company. Clothing, as it affects subaltern groups, stresses a uniform and traditional nature, which is precisely what is questioned in this film. Dress proves to be the means by which the private is linked to the public, the personal to the political. Everybody dresses according to their role and everybody is dissatisfied with their role. Ana, the lavishly attired actress, offers her silk stockings to Flora, Andrés's wife, and Andrés, outraged, orders her not to accept them. Yet Andrés himself hates the village life, dreams of seeing the world (all his life he has dwelt over maps) and, on deciding to abandon his family and go to the city with Ana, dons a suit for the last sequences of the film. That is to say he adopts 'a conception which is not [his] own but is borrowed from another group' (Gramsci, 1971: 327). When Ana's clothes arrive from the city, the young women of the village open her boxes and rummage through them, trying on her various dresses and marveling over her under-wear. This is not prurience, it is genuine excitement that subverts order. The act of dressing up is carnivalesque and transgressive; eventually they are admonished by the older women who intervene to curtail their exuberance.

Figure 3   *Adventure* (Courtesy of Banco Pastor and Filmoteca Española)

Dress here is both a means of enforcing consent and of challenging it. It exposes contradiction across cultural lines.

In this film, all authority is called into question by the intervention of subaltern elements and 'authority' here is implicit in the oppositions, not only that of town/country but also of men/women, young/old, modernity/tradition, art/commerce. Even the belated attempts to reconfirm the order of things have a ring of irony to them. When Flora eventually confronts Ana she outacts the actress, convinces her by force of performance and momentarily becomes a protagonist. Andrés, on finally being rejected by Ana (who acts now in defense of Flora), returns, still wearing his suit, to Flora and their child with the result that the film's penultimate shot of the family reunited in rural circumstances is almost a parody of the nativity scene and a definitive parody of our first view of the village as harmonious and ordered (men hay making, women crocheting, the sequence sutured within the background music of a lullaby).

These various cultural conflicts provoked by the clothing and language of the theater company reach a crescendo of competing voices when Andrés, by now besotted with Ana, bursts onto the stage to defend her honor during the performance of *Peribáñez*.[18] Andrés provides a literal example of Gramsci's challenge to elite concepts of culture: 'There is no human activity from which every form of intellectual participation can be excluded: homo faber cannot be separated from homo sapiens' (Gramsci, 1971: 9). The on-screen audience here is transfixed by and receptive to classical theater, and Andrés's performance demonstrates the fallacy of the traditional division between mind and body, between physical labor and intellectual activity. The Golden Age 'honor tradition' is suddenly made relevant and contemporary. Once more Gramsci is useful in showing how subaltern intervention can turn collusion into contestation. In a film that reflects *Peribáñez* thematically, we see an example of audience participation resulting from the intertextuality that in turn comes to threaten the social order of the village (the mayor pleads with the company to continue for fear that the carnivalesque uproar caused by Andrés will undermine his authority). The collision of the two texts – and a hint of a third, Florian Rey's *Nobleza baturra* (1935) – together with the voices of the villagers as well as the actors in character or out of it, violently dismembers the discrete identities previously established. The use, moreover, of Aragonese popular culture, folklore, dress and customs – also foregrounded in Rey's film – is suggestive of what Landy, paraphrasing Gramsci, terms 'the sediments of earlier dominant cultures that have seeped down into subaltern cultures'

(1994: 88). The town/country dichotomy here is nullified rather than reinforced as both sides of the apparent division implode upon themselves. The figure of authority in the village, the mayor, is not only challenged in the public sphere but is undermined within his own family. The theatrical impresario Rodríguez (José Isbert) bewitches the Mayor's daughter with his poorly executed magic tricks (while, at the same time, he steals her father's *chorizos*) and eventually recruits her as an accomplice to his thefts. Again the trickster here is a performer (at times like Puck, at others like Norman Wisdom) with Bakhtinian concerns of consumption. The mayor at one point challenges him on this:

Mayor: It would seem that the play requires a lot of ham.
Rodríguez: That is right.
Mayor: And a lot of *chorizo*.
Rodríguez: Bear in mind that it is a classical play, and the more classical, the more food.

The trickster (if we take Bakhtin as our guide) is more closely implanted in reality than the fool and the clown, and has a greater need to extricate him/herself from difficulties by ingenuity. Women are often tricksters. César, in *The Way of Babel*, returns to his village with the intention of marrying the richest woman and spurning his girlfriend Laura. But Laura, aided by her clownish friend Encarna, is not to be spurned. In almost every direct encounter between Laura and César, Laura uses the mock heroic language of 'destiny' to echo César's concerns. César, tricked into going to Laura's house on the day of his engagement party, finds himself locked in with her by Encarna and goes into a rage.

César: Tell your friend to open this door or I will kill you like a dog.
Laura: Even if I wanted to I would not be able to. This door has been closed by destiny.
César: Open it!
Laura: You see how it does not open. I do not know what kind of an idea you had of destiny.

It is striking that although Laura and Encarna (and later Elena, Marcelino's wife) play central roles located in reality (they are restricted by the social norms of the village) in the first half of the film, they do not really exist outside of their performance. They too are constructed in pure comedy, making it difficult to view them psychologically or in terms of any other kind of *a priori* 'integrity' outside their appearances on the screen. The fact that their performances are regulated by social norm in a way that other clowns are not requires them to be more circumspect, to be cleverer than their male counterparts. This suggests that their 'tricksterishness' is itself determined by the rules of the society, that the dominant discourse while restrictive on the one level allows for assertion of an empowering alternative on the other. Although they are liminal, the female characters differ from the fools and clowns insofar as incomprehension is rarely the instrument by which they employ parody. They self-consciously appropriate the speech of the men, refracting it to their own ends.

However, if the trickster's alternative discourse emerges and is determined by the rules of society, then something very similar occurs with the clowns and fools. Bakhtin's distinction here seems simply a question of strategy, more a matter of historical specificity providing not only a point of reference but also a cultural alibi. Apparent prediscursive 'authenticity' is decentered by the intervention of liminal, ambiguous characters, of all kinds, whose performative inflections alter the accent of the dominant discourse and produce conflicts. Actual conflict usually occurs between figures of authority who, in turn, seek alliance with subaltern elements, alliances which invariably prove ambivalent and fragile. In *Castle of Cards* Luis buys off the workers (at this point slacking for Carmen) by offering them six times their normal daily pay only for them to decide (logically given the parodic mode of the film) to work only one day a week. The figure of Paco moves freely at all levels of society partly because physically he is identified with the 'bodily lower stratum', but also because, like many characters of this kind, he is *déclassé*, not fully of the workers (he is their foreman) yet clearly not bourgeois. He is often like one of Gramsci's *morto di fame*, a potentially reactionary subversive who will ally himself to anyone to further his self-interest. Dress is one thing that marks him out as distinctive from his workers, a concern with dress rather than any real elegance, a kind of lumpen dandyism. The same can be said of his fascination with the bric-à-brac of modernity. In a similar fashion, the seemingly subversive Juan of *My Adored Juan* (*Mi adorado Juan*, 1949) (Figure 4) is not anything like as adorable as we are told he is. In a film that ostensibly posits materialism against a kind of epicureanism, Juan is in general sympathetic towards his plebeian neighbors, but invariably acts to maintain his own interests. He is more dilettante than saint, one of those petit bourgeois subversives that 'at decisive moments [...] move to the right, and their desperate "courage" always prefers to have the carabinieri on their side' (Gramsci, 1971: 274).

Figure 4 My Adored Juan (Courtesy of Video Mercury Films, S.A. and Filmoteca Española)

Gramsci's conception of hegemony as the 'exercise of indirect power' through the 'mosaic' (Landy, 1994: 24–25) of different civil institutions, each containing internal contradictions and consequently open to the possibilities of counterhegemonic intervention, is particularly germane to *My Adored Juan*. In this film what is presented as of 'universalizing' value breaks down under textual analysis. Behind the Juan who spurns fame and fortune for fishing lies a caricature of Spanish *alegría*. The rejection of materialism carries with it a rejection of modernity as 'foreign', inferior and ridiculous: the goal of the ambitious characters in the film is to travel to the United States to present a paper on how dogs can be trained not to sleep, so as in the future to do the same with human beings, thereby increasing their productive capacities. We can gauge the ideological slippage that occurs in the film by looking at the rivalry between Juan and his apparent foil, the unscrupulous Manrique, inspired by romantic conflict over the female character Eloísa and phrased in terms of ambition and fame. What actually occurs at the end of the film is that Manrique goes to the United States to give Eloísa's father's paper and Juan retains Eloísa whose father (influenced more by Juan than Manrique) renounces his own ambition. That is to say, the romantic rivalry dissolves within a political alliance and the interests of both are served. In the meantime the really transgressive characters, Eloísa and her father Doctor Palacios, while vacillating between the parties, eventually opt for a version of Juan's philosophy but also go well beyond it, exceeding Juan's influence. Eloísa's final act is to steal her father's scientific formulae from Manrique, thus both sabotaging his (Manrique's) plan and obliging Juan to make concessions (with his final words he undertakes to hire a servant, thereby undoing the ethos he has maintained from the start of the film). Indeed, the entire action of the film takes place between the parenthesis of two transgressions committed by Eloísa that are undertaken not only at her own initiative but which also oblige Juan to either intervene or drastically modify his previously rigid (and ruthless) belief system. In this way a major structural inversion occurs: Eloísa becomes a sort of enmasked protagonist, relegating Juan to a secondary role. And here the question of 'becoming' is central. As we have seen, for Gramsci 'change is constantly in the state of becoming' (Landy, 1994: 25; Gramsci, 1971: 355–356). The threat to the order of hegemonic relations here is the product of the unstable coexistence between dominant practices and 'common sense' (in the Gramscian sense). In the dialogue and the performance of the characters, Eloísa is sparkling and vital whereas Juan's performance is, at best, lackluster. His evolution in the film is refracted by his relationship with Eloísa and her father. There is constant discrepancy between what we are told and what we actually see. Juan's reputation is bolstered exclusively by the chorus of minor characters who constantly tell us how marvelous he is. Yet there is nothing particularly marvelous about his decision to adopt a boy whose parents cannot afford to support him and then, on realizing he is actually going to have to feed and clothe the child (that is, work), promptly return him (although, almost inevitably, Juan later rectifies, once more conceding ground to Eloísa).

Juan's internal contradictions always reveal themselves in contact with the subaltern elements of the film. Yet precisely because of its subaltern nature, the chorus itself is not homogenous. The individuals that comprise it act as a conduit between Juan and Eloísa and their perception of the two characters is conditioned by what they come into contact with. Theirs is an uneven development, fluctuating and tenuous, never wholeheartedly unconditional nor particularly submissive. Again the minor characters here, the servants and concierges of the city, to whom we are told Juan is a friend, at times quite literally threaten to drown him out (Juan spends much of the time in bemused silence when surrounded by them) and also make advances within the ideological territory Juan inhabits. The populist nature of Juan is often reduced to mechanical platitude whereas the vivacious Eloísa earns her popularity in a performance independent of the boundaries delineated by her suitors. This is not so much a question of being nice or nasty (being Juan or Manrique) as gaining ideological ground within a space determined by both rivals. Juan's popularity is undone in his own words: 'Humanity is bad and those that sleep are the best'. Clearly the lower-class friends that surround him are in no position to sleep very much, indeed we almost always see them working. His is a populism based on vulnerable premises, highly susceptible to the performances of lesser characters.

Whereas in all these films comic voices undercut the language of 'destiny', 'triumph' and 'fatherland', clearly such voices are not only varied in nature but, as we have seen, they are also ideologically ambivalent. The plurality produces lagoons of ideological contradiction. Gramsci's ideas on subaltern and dominant relations help to contextualize Bakhtin's concept of heteroglossia. Laura employs wit: in the case of José (the servant in *Castle of Cards*) it is the mimicry of incomprehension; in that of Señor Brandole it is madness; with the foreigners it is their accents and idiosyncratic behavior. These different voices (and there are many more) compete and co-habit with those of nationhood, of Lope de Vega, of Madrilenian slang, bullfighting terminology, rural speech, the formal language of decorum and that of adventure stories. Each voice merges with the others, in a cacophony of semantic and ideological systems. We find ourselves witnessing a society riven with linguistic difference (a babble/babel) and what Bakhtin called hybrid constructions: individual characters who adopt different, contesting voices, marked by parody and self-parody. 'Voice' here includes performance, and physical appearance. The rapid and hyperbolic conversion of Paco/Morán to modernity, his imitation of Luis and the way he is so easily impressed combined with his physical appearance, not only stress his ambiguity but make evident his hybrid nature, his carnivalesque function, his construction in performance. This is only one example of what occurs in all these films. The need to enclose difference within a unifying discourse fails, in part because invariably the performative seeps through; it is the performative we see and recognize most readily. More significantly performance, like uniforms and language, is always variable, measured and conditioned by what it comes into contact with, by other performances and other voices.

There is little in the curriculum vitae of those who collaborated in these films that lends credence to the possibility that they were in any way politically oppositional. As we have seen *The Way of Babel* was written and produced by Sáenz de Heredia and stars Alfredo Mayo. Jerónimo Mihura himself began his career as an assistant director on *Raza* and ended it making propaganda for the Francoist newsreel NO-DO. Although it is true that Mihura's brother Miguel, who wrote many of Jerónimo's films including *Castle of Cards* and *My Adored Juan*, ran into trouble during the 1940s with the censors for his editorship of *La Codorniz*. What seems to happen, however, in all these films is that subversion occurs with greater force when the central discourse is mimicked, is undermined in repetition. There is a pattern of appropriation and usurpation. In all the examples above we see this happen. This enables a subversive discourse to emerge and be intelligible within the framework of the central discourse. If, for Bakhtin, the fool's performance is a way of revealing private life within the public domain (1996: 160), then Gramsci's historical analysis helps us to shift that 'revelation' further into the realm of politics. The impossibility of containing the mimicry in the mouths of subaltern characters and the failure to fully assimilate difference produced in performative repetition create a more open space for dissenting reception.

2
Tactics and Thresholds in Edgar Neville's *Life on a Thread* (1945)

Every story is a travel story.

– de Certeau, 1984: 115

The première of Edgar Neville's *The Front of Madrid* (*Carmen fra i rossi*) on 23 March 1940 at the Palacio de Musica cinema on Madrid's Gran Vía provoked a scandal. Neville, probably the most talented nationalist filmmaker of his generation, had directed the film the previous year at Mussolini's Cinecittà studios in Rome as part of his contribution to the war effort. The outrage was caused by the movie's final scenes in which a Nationalist officer and a member of a communist milicia die in an embrace as they are gunned down on the battle front. According to Emilio Sanz de Soto, the film was re-edited, certain dialogue was removed and eventually the negative disappeared altogether and is believed to have been destroyed. The same writer goes on to offer the following analysis:

> Such was the naivete of Edgar Neville that he believed the moment for national reconciliation had arrived as soon as our horrific and incivil war had ended. Neither Edgar, nor anyone at the time, could have imagined that some of us would have to endure Franco's victory throughout the following four decades. (1999: 58)

Neville, in Sanz de Soto's words, was 'neither a communist nor a fascist but something altogether different' (1999: 56). In spite of its slight cuteness, the description captures the ambivalence, symbolized by Neville, of many supporters of the 18 July 1936 military uprising and locates him on the cusp of an ideological and cultural contradiction. Several critics, as we shall see, also identify a similar desire to represent national reconciliation in the film discussed in this chapter, *Life on a Thread* (*La vida en un hilo*, 1945) (Figure 5). Both films encroach upon the shaded zones of the undecidable, the subjunctive, the 'what might have been'.

Neville had learned his filmic trade in the United States where he had been posted as a member of the Spanish diplomatic service in 1927. In Los Angeles, Metro-Goldwyn-Mayer contracted him to write Spanish dialogues and to direct Spanish versions of Hollywood movies. Among his other activities – such as collaborations with Ernst Lubitsch and Harry d'Abbadie d'Arrast – Neville was responsible for making *El presidio* (1929), the Spanish copy of Wallace Beery's *The Big House* (Armero, 1995: 232; Burguera, 1999: 91–92). An inveterate socialite and raconteur, Neville was befriended by Mary Pickford, Douglas Fairbanks junior and Charles Chaplin. Indeed, in 1930, he participated as an assistant in the production of Chaplin's *City Lights*. In 1931, following the proclamation of the Second Republic (of which he approved), he returned to Spain where he continued his cinematic career.

The most striking feature of Neville's cinema, and the one that gave rise to the problems that he would experience with the regime, is the fact that he is a filmmaker of the popular and yet his films, particularly those of the 1940s, are intensely personal. He stands on the interface of the popular/auteurist divide, just as he similarly evokes international influences to make Madrilenian *sainetes*. These are aspects that will be discussed more fully in Chapter 3. For the moment, however, it is noteworthy that ambiguous relations between the localized specificity of the neighborhood and the nation, as well as the national and the international, emerge throughout Neville's work.

In the previous chapter I discussed the comic function of mimicry in creating disturbance within hierarchical relations. The effects of such mimicry are similar to those of carnivalesque reversals and doubling. Inversion is a fundamental component of comedy (what Henri Bergson defines as 'topsyturvydom' [1999: 88]) but it also often involves, as we shall see, what could be termed 'hybrid plays upon identity' that are of significance in the construction of romantic comedy. Such inversion is often expressed through the subjunctive mode. It is with this sense of indeterminacy in mind that in this chapter I will introduce the work of Michel de Certeau on tactics, strategy and *bricolage*.

Dick Hebdige, following Stuart Hall, has punned on the word 'articulation' as being both a synonym for something 'spoken' or 'uttered' and as a linking device, a ligament in the hegemonic vertebrae (Hebdige,

Figure 5 Conchita Montes in *Life on a Thread* (Courtesy of Video Mercury Films, S.A. and Filmoteca Española)

1998: 383). In this inspired piece of wordplay Hebdige (like Hall) captures the dual perspective of Gramscian politics.[1] This, in turn, is an expression of the complex relation – the *combination* of different elements – between different levels 'of force and of consent, authority and hegemony, violence and civilization' (Gramsci, 1971: 170). It is this linkage, the often artful combining of different strands of whatever is available, by means of elements like common sense and folklore, that constitutes – as outlined in the introduction – 'the humus of popular culture'. It is this that distinguishes Gramsci's development of classical Marxist theories of ideology and his insistence upon hegemony as a site of struggle.[2]

de Certeau observes that the apparently powerless employ 'styles of action' – *in between* the articulating structure of hegemony – that 'intervene in a field that regulates them' (1984: 30); 'in-betweenness' enables subaltern groups to turn circumstances 'to their own advantage' (1984: 30). Likewise, de Certeau claims that in the act of reading, the relevance of which will become clear in the course of this chapter, readers manipulate the material of texts 'by insinuating their inventiveness into the cracks in a cultural orthodoxy' (1984: 172).

Perhaps the most obvious orthodoxy or regulatory field of this kind is that imposed by the boundaries of the nation and the obligatory membership it requires of its citizenry. As Alex Callinicos puts it, practically every member of the world's population is 'interpellated' (to use Althusserian terminology) as 'a bearer' of some kind of 'national identity' (1987: 170). The space of the nation and the consequent identificatory process associated with nationality, together with the concomitant complex alignments that constitute national traditions and nationalism itself, provide very obvious examples of the fields within which Gramsci locates the possibility for 'national-popular' engagement. This chapter's analysis of *Life on a Thread* and its use of de Certeau – together with Gramsci and Bakhtin – is designed to suggest how the nuancing of regulatory spaces, such as the nation, might be produced.

Hebdige's and Hall's use of the word 'articulation' recalls the previous chapter's discussion of the way in which the state and 'the people' interact by means of reciprocal 'borrowing' and 'cannibalization' – the appropriation of one another's forms and the piecemeal forging of mixed and often contradictory material – to produce new combinations. As Hebdige says, 'what distinguishes the Gramscian approach is the way in which it requires us to negotiate and engage with the multiple axes of both power and the popular' (1998: 381). If in Chapter 1, I hope to have demonstrated that the Gramscian theory of hegemony provides a politically polysemic framework, similar to the linguistic plurality of Bakhtin's heteroglossia, then it is this articulated 'mosaic' (Landy, 1994: 25) that connects Gramsci with de Certeau's concept of *bricolage*.

Taking his cue from Claude Levi Strauss's definition in *The Savage Mind*, for de Certeau *bricolage* is, 'an arrangement made with "the materials at hand", a production "that has no relationship to a project" and which readjusts "the residues of previous construction and destruction"' (1984: 174). Levi Strauss's wording, as quoted here by de Certeau, is strongly reminiscent of Gramsci's definition of common sense as that which is left behind by previous dominant thought, 'half-way between folklore properly speaking and the philosophy, science, and economics of the specialists' (1971: 326 n5).

Engaging with his contemporaries, Pierre Bourdieu and Michel Foucault, de Certeau traces a distinction between 'strategy' and 'tactic'. A strategy, he says: 'assumes a place that can be circumscribed as *proper* (*propre*) and thus serve as the basis for generating relations with an exterior distinct from it' (1984: xix). A tactic, on the other hand: 'insinuates itself into the other's place, fragmentarily, without taking it over in its entirety, without being able to keep it at a distance'. And, de Certeau adds: 'Many everyday practices (talking, reading, moving about, shopping, cooking, etc.) are tactical in character' (1984: xix). Furthermore, according to de Certeau, tactics 'pin their hopes on a clever *utilization of time*, of the opportunities it presents and also of the play that it introduces into the foundations of power' (1984: 39).

It is in the context of tactics that de Certeau cites *bricolage* as the piecemeal 'artisan-like inventiveness' that constantly eludes and side steps the classificatory impulses of 'statistical investigation' which, in de Certeau's words, reveal 'only the homogenous' (1984: xviii), thus defying the totalizing nature of discourse itself. He remarks, for instance, in terms that help specify the link between Gramsci's hegemonic framework and the Bakhtinian sense of the physical, on the tactics employed by the reader of a text who is 'transported into it, pluralizes himself in it like the internal rumblings of one's body' (de Certeau, 1984: xxi). These elements of *transportation* and the *body* will have direct relevance to this chapter. In observations that are pertinent to the film discussed here, de Certeau comments on games of chance, luck and the problems that popular and unchanneled superstitions pose for power, in terms that stress the mobile and consequently unruly nature of such elements. Powerlessness, according to de Certeau, is distinguished by its 'unmoored' quality, its lack of 'any fixed position' (1984: 86). The two central features of *Life on a Thread* are floating ones: fortune and travel. Both, I will argue, combine to create a field of indeterminacy that destabilizes discrete claims to national affiliation.

Life on a Thread (1945)

Life on a Thread is a film that has frequently been associated with a discourse on Spain pertinent to this chapter's introduction. Both Eduardo Torres-Dulce (1999: 166) and María Luisa Burguera (1999: 168) describe the movie as an allegory on the 'two Spains' and Neville himself was sufficiently moved by the suggestion to disavow it (1977: 37).[3] For the purposes of this chapter it is, nonetheless, useful to relate the figurative territory in which *Life on a Thread* is played out to the nation itself and to Spain's recent history of civil strife. The analogy is perhaps particularly apt in light of the controversy surrounding Neville's earlier attempt to allegedly reconcile the 'two Spains' in the notorious ending of *The Front of Madrid*.[4] In the context of such a discussion concerning national space it is significant that the entire action of *Life on a Thread* should take place in the course of a rail journey that runs from a northern province to the capital; a journey that marks a symbolic trajectory traversing the geographical center of Spain.

The narrative thread (the *thread* of the film's title is fitting) of the movie unravels within the spatial precincts of the nation. *Life on a Thread* centers upon Mercedes (Conchita Montes), a young widow who leaves her recently deceased husband's family home in a northern province to return by train to her native Madrid. From the very beginning of the film her brightness and incongruous laughter suggest a disregard for the conventions of bereavement. Indeed, one of the first phrases uttered by Mercedes on settling down on the train is laden with irony, 'In these places mourning lasts for years'. This is just the first of many examples that we will see of the lengthy comic tradition of laughing at death that Bakhtin explores in depth. It is also one of several self-conscious references to time and duration. Mercedes addresses the person with whom she will share a compartment for the length of the journey, Madame Du Pont (Julia Lajos), a fortune teller who travels with a menagerie of ducks and pigeons that are trained to do circus tricks. Mercedes tells Madame Du Pont of her dreary marriage to Ramón (Guillermo Marín) prior to his death, and the fortune teller responds by explaining what might have happened if only she had agreed to accept the first of two offers of a ride in a car one day in Madrid years before as she sheltered from the rain in the doorway of a flower shop awaiting a taxi. Had Mercedes accepted her first offer, says Madame Du Pont, she could have married the vivacious and artistic Miguel Ángel (Rafael Durán).

In reality, the duality represented by Mercedes's would-be husband and her real husband is more complex than the suggested allegory of the 'two Spains' allows. Miguel Ángel represents the metropolitan Madrilenian Spain: bohemian, liberal, cosmopolitan and witty; while Ramón and his family embody stuffy, provincial and Catholic backwardness. The film plays upon a characteristic of romantic comedy, that of the amorous triangle. These two men (the real one and the imaginary one) mark out both the boundaries that Mercedes traverses and the spaces within which she operates as an 'in-between' character. She is a figure who is associated with *undecidability*. The notion of undecidability links to her condition of 'in-betweenness' and captures the spatial and *national* ambivalence of the movie. This is a film set in the future perfect past tense, rather than an allegory of real historical event; its concern is 'what might have been'.

This is best expressed by the itinerate circumstances within which *Life on a Thread* is played out, its lack 'of any fixed position'. The train journey is suggestive of the fluctuating relationship between movement and stasis that frequently marks the films discussed in this book. Travel is, of course, a conjunction of unstable time and place. The journey in question slices through the geographical space of Spain, from an unnamed province in the north of the country to Madrid, its social and administrative heart. The time of the film compresses and concertinas within the space of the traversed nation.

As if to intensify this sense of unstable time and place, the film further collapses time in its use of flashbacks to tell Mercedes's story. As Susan Hayward has observed the flashback is almost always a representation of subjective truth (1996: 122). It is a trick of time that interrogates the premises of linear chronology and relativizes temporal and spatial claims to certainty. In comparison with her review of her marriage to Ramón, Mercedes's recollection of her life with Miguel Ángel is a subjective projection of what might have happened. The fact is that Mercedes never actually marries Miguel Ángel except in Madame Du Pont's narration. Miguel Ángel represents a possible future and a possible past, a wishful thought. As a foil to the stultifyingly real Ramón, he is constructed entirely in the subjunctive as a fantasy substitute husband. Such indeterminacy, moreover, is expressed through the subjectivity produced of Mercedes's condition as the occupant of an in-between, borderline space marked by the threshold.

This is a film concerned with 'fortune'; that is to say, the film dwells on the long-term, life-altering consequences of the unexpected, of a fortuitous meeting in a flower shop. It also establishes a zone of spatial and temporal unpredictability, populated by circus-like, carnivalesque figures, which functions around questions of chance. Fortune telling is itself inverted and carnivalized in the figure of Madame Du Pont. As opposed to a soothsayer who reads the future, she reads the past. Luck, like other non-discursive elements, makes its own space on the margins of discourse or in-between dominant spaces. de Certeau remarks that superstitions are:

> supererogatory semantic overlays that insert themselves 'over and above' and 'in excess' and annex to a past or poetic realm a part of the land the promoters of technical rationalities had reserved for themselves (1984: 106).

As we shall see, 'luck' or 'destiny' in a context of inversion and reversal are frequent characteristics of comedy. However, the relationship between Mercedes and Madame Du Pont focuses the aura of showmanship and spectacle that enshrouds the film. Madame Du Pont is a circus figure who conforms to the Bakhtinian model of reversal and exposure of convention. Her largeness, indeed her ugliness, are features to which she herself refers: 'Well now I am ready for the night' she announces having removed her make up, 'If anyone comes in now and sees me they will run away terrified'. Her pseudonym with its carnival foreign exoticism stands in contrasting combination with her homespun *castizo* bonhomie.[5] This kind of comic (like Manolo Morán as discussed in the previous chapter) is forever self-referential and self-reflexive. Also introduced here is a comic partnership that, in the case of Lajos and Montes, will re-emerge in another Neville film discussed in the following chapter[6] and which, like many such alliances, is based upon an opposition of physical difference: Lajos and Montes play a kind of female Laurel and Hardy.

What makes the Lajos–Montes partnership subversive is its resemblance to de Certeau's description of superstition, that is to say its liminal nature on the edges of national discourse, its circus-like quality. de Certeau's words are particularly apposite to this when he writes of 'a tightrope walker's talent and a sense of tactics' (1984: 86). We witness two delicately balanced oppositions – life/death, foreign/national – sustained by Lajos's carnivalesque creativity and her apparently straight ally Montes, while in constant motion. One of the keys to this film is that these are marginalized characters who laugh on the threshold, as they proceed through the heart of the nation's geography. In this there is a great deal of *unfinalizedness*. Bakhtin on comic couples writes:

The dialogue of these pairs is of considerable interest since it marks the as yet incomplete disintegration of the dual tone. In reality, it is a dialogue of the face with the buttocks, of birth with death. (Bakhtin, 1984: 434)

The alliance with Madame Du Pont gives a swirling context to the linear narrative provided by the train journey and helps interrogate the centrality of the nation to the film's discourse while nuancing an entire panoply of hierarchical values evident in the critical efforts to secure national seamlessness through a process of containing opposites – in hybridization – and overcoming the divisions inherent in the 'two Spains'.

The Bakhtinian notion of hybridization is problematized in Neville's film in ways that concern concepts of the nation particularly with regard to boundaries. Like all the thinkers that form the theoretical framework of this book, Bakhtin writes extensively about borders, thresholds and territorial demarcations. His exploration of medieval popular culture and carnival involves detailed observation of dialogic parallels symbolized within the body. Likewise his work on linguistics focuses upon dialogic relations in literature and disruption occasioned by in-between characters – fools, rogues or figures from the circus – as we have seen in the previous chapter. Throughout his work Bakhtin is also concerned with both spatial metaphors that define and breach the boundaries of bodily function as well as those of genre, and what he terms 'the ancient link of laughter with time' (Bakhtin, 1984: 143). Bakhtin refers here to the conditioning, regenerative power of laughter which – he emphasizes – concerns 'becoming, change, gay relativity' (Bakhtin, 1984: 142). Hybridization finds expression in his discussion of menippean satire when Bakhtin identifies the latter's distinctive traits in 'dialogues of the threshold', in which propriety was abandoned and the conventions of etiquette violated.[7] Interestingly, he also relates this particular genre to 'an epoch when national legend was already in decay' (Bakhtin, 1997: 192) and introduces a series of elements that recur throughout this book: 'The menippea loves to play with abrupt transitions and shifts, ups and downs, rises and falls, unexpected comings together of distant and disunited things, mésalliances of all sorts' (Bakhtin, 1997: 191).

Although I will return in greater detail to these theoretical points in Chapter 7, in relation to *Life on a Thread* it is worth noting that very real thresholds mark the determinant moments of Mercedes's life. Mercedes meets the two men who will establish the spatial boundaries of her marriage and fantasy in the doorway – that is, on the threshold – of the

Madrid flower shop and decides to share Ramón's car having turned down Miguel Ángel's previous offer. Years later Ramón catches pneumonia and dies and Mercedes is represented – in a Bakhtinian crossing of the threshold – entering and exiting through the doorway that divides the dining room from the rest of the house in a sight gag that marks Ramón's life, abrupt death and the couple's marriage.

Like the use of flashback and the train journey itself, the visual gag – and this instance provides a key example – is one of the most effective techniques of cinematic comedy. Aptly, in the context of this film, the origins of the sight gag are in circus and clowning with their slapstick effects; it is economical, succinct in the extreme and, by its very nature, needs no explanation nor does it require any temporal delay, such as waiting for a punchline (as is often the case with verbal jokes). The sight gag in cinema is a characteristic of silent comedies, particularly those that star Buster Keaton and Harold Lloyd. Once more it is tactical in its quality insofar as it relies on dexterous use of time, of seizing an opportunity at the appropriate moment. As Noël Carroll has observed, it is immediate in every sense of the word but its effect lies in its incongruity (Horton, 1991: 27). The example cited above provides the quite literal turning point of the film. Ramón decides over dinner that it is beneficial for his health, and that it is 'hygenic', to sleep with the windows open and as a consequence becomes ill and dies a week later. In the same sequence we see the family adjourn through the doorway to the other rooms, where it has already been established that the sexes are segregated, only to return through the same curtain-draped doorway lavishly dressed in mourning with no cut in the continuity of the sequence, thus stressing the speed of the death. It is in the spirit of Bakhtin, moreover, that the decision that leads to Ramón's demise should be made at the dining table. As we shall see, death and eating are intimately connected and have a lengthy history in popular comedy.

In light of Ramón's self-induced end, it is worth recalling that Bakhtin contextualizes his concept of the threshold within a relation of life and death. In his discussion of the menippea, Bakhtin refers to the 'gates of Olympus' and the 'threshold of the underworld' (1997: 190). It is something to which he returns in his work on Dostoevsky. Distinguishing the polyphonic quality of Dostoevsky from Tolstoy's more defined narrative, he writes:

> Dostoevsky would have not depicted the deaths of his heroes, but their *crises* and *turning points* in their lives; that is, he would have depicted their lives *on the threshold*. And his heroes would have

remained internally *unfinalized* (for self-consciousness cannot be finalized *from within*). (Bakhtin, 1997: 96)

A significant part of Mercedes's active role as a *bricoleur* – a figure who makes use of the material space available but not belonging to her – is that of living and operating on the threshold. The threshold – and we will see similar instances of this in Chapter 7 in a comparable setting – marks an important fissuring presence in relations of national affiliation. The idea of the nation traversed is once more germane to consideration of the in-between function of the film's protagonist. While the two men are identified with distinct and delimited geographical zones, Mercedes comes to *superimpose* her desires through style and taste upon those territories. Just as her journey in the company of Madame Du Pont involves travelling through the heartlands of Spain, much of Mercedes's maneuvering constituted movement across the thresholds of the areas determined by Ramón and Miguel Ángel.

While the fortune teller is a figure of the fairground, Mercedes is also associated – through one of her premarital friendships – with the circus. The comfortable surroundings of Ramón's family in the household (described by her as 'a nest of profound and absolute boredom') conflict with Mercedes's past. Ramón's fearsomely traditional and Catholic aunts, who disapprove of women – like her – who smoke, forbid Mercedes's friend Isabel from visiting the family house, alleging that she works 'in a circus and rides horseback naked'. In response to this, the transgressive Mercedes retorts with distinctively modern, slick and metropolitan wit: 'Actually no. It was the horse that was naked'. It is noteworthy that circus, with its associations of movement and nomadic groups, proves a contentious issue in a film that takes place in the course of a journey (on the train) and pits the notion of travel against the fossilized quality of provincial life.

Narrating the details of everyday life in Ramón's family home Mercedes says, 'Each day was so similar to those that had previously gone by that one lost all sense of time'. It is out of resistance to this loss that Mercedes's conflicts with the family and with Ramón take place, something that occurs in relation to a particularly ludic Madrid. Mercedes's fury at the refusal of the family to countenance the presence of Isabel in their house frightens Ramón into taking her to the capital to dance. While, as we have seen in the previous chapter, Bakhtin links laughter, games and the circus with time, de Certeau insists that tactics 'pin their hopes on a clever *utilization of time*, of the opportunities it presents and also of the play that it introduces into the foundations of power' (1984: 39).

One of the creative signs of these tactical operations of the margins employed by Mercedes is that of dress. While defined by her own particular 'styles of action', Mercedes is also identifiable by her sartorial style. Throughout the film she is distinguished by the elegance of her dress sense as well as by the panache with which she operates. The fore-grounding of 'mobility' through the nation is thus coupled with an element of 'style' that pervades this film. An ongoing debate prevailing throughout the movie is that concerning taste. Mercedes is a kind of dandy. Dandies, like tricksters and rogues, linger on the threshold, their key features being precisely their *unfinalizedness* and the ease with which they move. As a dandy Mercedes loves dressing up and her taste in clothing proves important. She is forever changing garments, putting on make-up, examining herself in the mirror and has a lavish taste for extravagant hats.

The ambivalent qualities of travel and dress often go hand in hand. Indeed, although not immediately relevant to this movie the Spanish words *travesía* (route) and *travestí* (transvestite) – as in traversing the nation and cross-dressing – link travel to transgression. Introducing her edited collection of essays on dandyism, Susan Fillin-Yeh quotes from Ellen Moers's earlier study of the same subject. The dandy, Moers states, 'had the power to fascinate, to puzzle, to travel, to persist and to figure in an ambiguous social situation' (Fillin-Yeh, 2001: 2).

Outstanding among the examples of conflicting taste that occur in this film is that which takes place over Ramón's family heirloom, a repulsively garish clock. The clock is associated with the oppressive locus of the family. Informed that it has been in the family for genera-tions, the clock haunts Mercedes's married life with its gloomy presence. It is also – when seen with her explicit comments concerning time – symbolic of her loss of a sense of temporality amid the soporific atmos-phere in the household. One of the very first things Mercedes does on departure – and it is an act that confirms and seals her comic alliance with Madame Du Pont – is to despatch the clock out of the train window. This scene constitutes the occasion for a symbolic reclaiming of time by Mercedes and it is significant that it should be carried out while in movement against the spatial landscape through which the train passes.

While the clock is symbolic of time in her marriage to Ramón, Mercedes also clashes with Ramón's aunts over other questions of taste that perhaps have a relevance to space. At one point she orders the portrait of a military ancestor of the family, the 'Brigadier', to be removed and dispatched to the storeroom. In response to the outraged aunts, she justifies the act on aesthetic grounds, 'because he was very ugly,' she says. The issue of taste, exemplified by the dispute over the portrait of the 'Brigadier', highlights Mercedes's subversive function. Military discourse – a discourse of some significance in 1940s Spain – is undermined by the non-discursive questions of elegance, good taste and fine clothing, which are the means by which Mercedes creates her own operational niche, the place that she practices. The military, its officers and its emblems form part of the national discourse of the time as does religion. In spite of its claims to be concerned with questions of fortune, this film does not countenance any kind of divine presence or intervention. Madame Du Pont – allegedly possessing supernatural powers – is in reality a gluttonous Bakhtinian representative of the lower bodily strata and Mercedes is highly materialistic in contrast to the repressive Christianity of her in-laws. de Certeau insists that 'luck' is a matter of temporal factors taking advantage of opportunities within spatial confines and Mercedes insinuates within these small places – the 'fragments, cracks and lucky hits in the framework of the system' (de Certeau, 1984: 38) – just as her situation with Madame Du Pont carnivalizes national space and its associated discourses.

Mercedes's dandyism is given a free reign once free of the provincial Ramón (at least in Madame Du Pont's narration of 'what might have been'). She dons striking hats and yearns for a mink coat. Indeed Miguel Ángel is persuaded to sell his prized El Greco in order to satisfy her craving for fur. Dandyism is something to which I will return in Chapter 7's analysis of Fernando Fernán Gómez's 1964 *The Strange Journey*. Both films, however, confirm Fillin-Yeh's and Moers's insight that dandyism is intimately connected to travelling. Dandies cross thresholds and breach boundaries. Moving about is, of course, one of the 'everyday activities' cited by de Certeau as possessing a tactical character. de Certeau's comparison of the act of reading to travelling could easily apply to dandies: '[they] are travellers; they move across lands belonging to someone else, like nomads poaching their way across fields they did not write' (1984: 174).

For Bakhtin the significance of carnival lies in the death of the old and the birth of the new, which is precisely the starting point of this film. In the very first sequence we witness Mercedes bidding farewell to her in-laws at the station:

> Carnival celebrates the destruction of the old and the birth of the new world – the new year, the new spring, the new kingdom. The old world that has been destroyed is offered together with the new

world and is represented with it as the dying part of the dual body. (Bakhtin, 1984: 410)

Carnival also signifies inversion and replacement of things by their opposites. Bakhtin describes carnival in terms of 'a second life' (1984: 9). This is what provides the dynamic aspect of hybridization in *Life on a Thread*. Inversion, furthermore, very often supplies the raw material of sight gags. And we have already seen that Madame Du Pont is the inversion of a fortune teller who interprets the possibilities of the past. In the same vein, Miguel Ángel is the inverse of Ramón; he is the potential husband who might have been.

Both men are creators: Ramón is an engineer who designs bridges and Miguel Ángel, a sculptor. There is a professionalism to their creativity: neither is known for any other kind of activity and both are commissioned for work considered public. There are nonetheless significant differences between them beyond personality. It is noteworthy that Ramón should build bridges. Bridges are ambivalent communicative links between different spatial points. de Certeau comments that 'the *bridge* is ambiguous everywhere: it alternately welds together and opposes insularities' (1984: 128). In the context of the film Ramón's creations seek to bind 'the space in-between' which is precisely the zone where Mercedes operates. Predictably, Ramón's efforts in his own home prove ineffectual. However Miguel Ángel – Mercedes's projected husband – operates in a field similar to her own, in which improvisation and a sense of opportunity is primary. The dandified *bricoleur* that is Mercedes is mismatched with the codifying, bridge-building Ramón. Miguel Ángel, on the other hand, 'makes do' – like Mercedes – in dominant space, altering, breaching and exceeding its discourses from within.

de Certeau writes of power being 'bound by its very visibility' and that 'the space of a tactic is the space of the other' (1984: 37). Mercedes does not so much inhabit the 'two Spains' as *practice* them. That is to say she operates tactically within a space that is not hers, within which her transgressions mark her *modus operandi*. This is very similar to the role of Eloísa (also played by Montes) in Mihura's *My Adored Juan*. Between the two sides of her life Mercedes negotiates ways to turn things that obey 'other rules', to her own advantage (de Certeau, 1984: 30). She is a consumer and it is as a consumer that she succeeds in imposing or superimposing her tastes on the two men in her life and their respective surroundings. She moves in a field that – to employ de Certeau's terminology – comprises the 'debris' of discourse, an area 'furnished by the leftovers from nominations, taxonomies, heroic or comic predicates and so on, that is, by fragments of scattered semantic places' (de Certeau, 1984: 107).

Bakhtin's physical representation of hybridization as manifested through the juxtaposition of opposite ends of the body, as well as the communicating channels that connect them, is pertinent to the two sequences which introduce Mercedes to the details of married life with Ramón, and which are situated back to back chronologically in the film. Traditionally wedding nights are represented – at least in cinema – by the bridegroom 'crossing the threshold' with his new wife in his arms. Given the film's concern with the traversing of both spatial precincts and marriage, it is of note that this particular tradition is not one that is observed here. Further, the pervasive question of dress returns in Mercedes's recollection of the occasion. The wedding night at the Palace Hotel in Madrid proves a disaster because of a conflictive item of clothing: Ramón's military boots. Ramón, unable to remove the knee-length boots that accompany the officer's uniform which he has donned for the wedding ceremony, is obliged to spend the night in the armchair. As with the aesthetic conflict of taste over the ugliness of the Brigadier in Ramón's home, the sensitive issue of the military is subtly subject to interrogation by the comedy of the film; it is evoked in passing, non-discursively, via an item of clothing.

The sequence immediately following the hotel debacle reinforces the still-born nature of their marriage. Here we see the couple, recently installed in Ramón's family home; while Mercedes tries to sleep, Ramón persists in whistling discordantly while he shaves in the bathroom adjacent to the bedroom. As we saw earlier, Bakhtin on the mennippea observes parallels in the topology of the human body in carnivalesque inversion of hierarchy. These two adjacent sequences involve, first, a striking absence of 'threshold' on the occasion of the wedding night and, secondly, the presence of a real threshold in the archway between bathroom and bedroom – two of the more celebrated spatial arenas where bodily functions are conventionally played out. The depiction of Ramón in the two sequences, moreover, neatly match Bakhtin's representation of bodily schema of *down* (the boots on his feet) and *up* (the face being shaved).

Inversions and thresholds provide a series of articulating links concerning the body that re-emerge throughout the film. Mercedes stops sharing a bed with the desexualized Ramón as part of the brainwave that leads to his death. Ramón suggests to Mercedes that they sleep separately as the couple literally hover on the threshold – that is the doorway – between the dining area and bedroom. While the threshold is normally associated with newly weds, in this instance it marks a kind of divorce. It also marks the Bakhtinian death that heralds the 'birth of the new'.

The threshold also connects to a series of other bedroom scenes. Frank Krutnik discusses romantic comedy in terms precisely of thresholds. 'Validating love as a traversing of borders,' he writes, 'romantic comedy moves each partner from the territory of the known to the sexual and emotional space of the other' (Krutnik, 1998: 26). There are several bedroom scenes in this film that establish a spatial pattern both within the internal topological frontiers of the house that Mercedes shares with Ramón and his extended family, and within the external relationship of metropolis to province. These spatial patterns extend and overlap into Mercedes's relationship with Miguel Ángel. The conflictual barriers in *Life on a Thread* that are created around the spatial arena that constitutes the bed are numerous and comic. The bed, as we have already seen, also connects space with the body, an area that Bakhtin associates with time; that is, with renewal and procreation, with sleep and sex.

Miguel Ángel, recently acquainted with Mercedes, takes her with him to a village to meet the Sánchez family which has commissioned him to construct a statue of a deceased relative. For the sake of respectability, Miguel Ángel invents a marital relationship with Mercedes. In counterpoint to Ramón's apparent reluctance to consummate his marriage, Miguel Ángel is keen to sleep with Mercedes. Instantly a contradiction emerges in the figure of Miguel Ángel between personal desire and a public discourse of respectability. This contradiction is exacerbated by Señora Sánchez, the person who has commissioned Miguel Ángel. An avowed proponent of traditional values, Señora Sánchez presents them with a double bed and addresses the couple in the following terms: 'We assume that you are not like these modern couples who have separate rooms'. The irony of this lies in us, having already witnessed Mercedes's sleeping arrangements in her marriage to Ramón. Mercedes proceeds, moreover – once Señora Sánchez has absented herself – to 'make use' of the space opening within traditional discourse, precisely that of the 'village' she finds herself in, to hold Miguel Ángel at bay. She cites the proverbial advice of her grandmother to fend off his attentions. It is in the carnivalesque vein of the film that roles are inverted, made more so given that the conflict revolves around a bed: while Señora Sánchez defends Catholic morality to incite the unmarried couple to sleep together, the modern and metropolitan Mercedes resorts to rural traditionalism to avoid sharing the bed with Miguel Ángel.

The explicitly temporal quality of Mercedes's tactical operations in Ramón's household becomes clear in her use of traditional discourse in this incident. This ambivalence is the product of being poised on the indeterminate edge of two modes of living; an indeterminacy reinforced by the fact that one of them is purely imaginary. Mercedes is a quick-witted character, whose gaiety is infectious. Bakhtin's insistence upon the connection between laughter and time that we have seen in the comic partnership between Madame Du Pont and Mercedes becomes relevant once more. Bakhtin quotes the Russian critic L.E. Pinsky on an 'indestructible *joie de vivre*, capable of rising above the incidental, to conceive it as something transient' (Pinsky cited in Bakhtin, 1984: 142). In relation to this, Pinsky finds Rabelais's comic sources within an indeterminate field that both denies and affirms:

> there is the feeling of the general relativity of great and small, exalted and lowly, of the fantastic and the real, the physical and the spiritual; the feeling of rising, growing, flowering and fading, of the transformation of nature eternally alive. (Pinsky cited in Bakhtin, 1984: 142)

Mercedes is a borrower and a *bricoleur* who stands mid-way not only between two men but also between a set of discourses that coincide in the unevenly developed nation. These are expressed in her person in a gamut of non-discursive elements that intersect and traverse the conflictive and contradictory fields of the rural and the urban, the traditional and the modern.

Exemplary of Mercedes's pivotal function is the bedroom conflict with Miguel Ángel in the village. This sequence is a parody of Mercedes's real wedding night with Ramón in Madrid. In both instances, the men are condemned to spend the respective nights in armchairs. The irony lies in the reversal of their national-spatial (that is, geographical) locations at the time: the bumbling and provincial Ramón spends his wedding night in Madrid's Palace Hotel while his urban and urbane foil is consigned to the country.

The motif of the village arises in *Life on a Thread*, and it is something to which I will return in greater detail later in the discussions of *Welcome Mister Marshall!* in Chapter 4 and of *The Strange Journey* in Chapter 7. For the moment, however, it suffices to note its importance with regard to the nation. The idea of the *pueblo* or village is significant in the configuration of Spanish 'tradition' and to the way such tradition is *articulated*. It is also indicative of the ambivalent relationship of the

Spanish nation-state with modernity. The portrayal of the village in this film suggests a parody of the nation's imaginary in counterpoint to the metropolitan yearnings of Mercedes. Mercedes highlights the fracture at the center of the national consciousness. She reinforces the incompatibility between the *pueblo* and the metropolis rather than overcoming it. In this way the film does indeed refer to an idea of the 'two Spains' but not so as to reconcile them as to provoke disturbance of the national imaginary via Mercedes's undecidability. As we have seen, much of Mercedes's transgression stems from her urban origins. The attraction of Miguel Ángel has much to do with the fact that he is a resident of Madrid. The myth-like quality of the *pueblo* in the national imagination is the inverse of travel and movement, the distinctive elements that mark Mercedes literally and figuratively throughout the film. Mercedes's city-dwelling dandyism and her association with circus nomadism conflict with the static parochialism of Ramón's family in the provinces.

In Mercedes's and Miguel Ángel's visit to the village where the Sánchez family live, the *pueblo* is explicitly referred to as the nation in miniature. The Sánchez spokeswoman speaks of the patriarch, her grandfather, in terms that depict the village as a kind of *patria chica*, juxtaposed against the outside world. The static nature of village order, moreover, is bound together by means of the dynastic family. Patriarch and *patria* are intimately connected. Señora Sánchez says of her grandfather that he, 'lived and died without ever leaving his village' and adds pointedly that of his three sons:

> Two went to America where they died of want. The third, my father, stayed in the village where with persevance he managed to make a fortune ... he won the lottery.

Once more luck and the nation – in the form of the lottery – function parodically in this sequence. In fact what we see in this is a curious mixture of patriarchs and populism. The lottery is specifically connected with Spain and playing it is an everyday popular practice.[8] The lottery is a focus of Spanish national-popular activity orchestrated by the state. Significantly, winning it is determined by arbitrary events. That is to say, the lottery is another undecidable occasion. The terms upon which the legitimacy of the patriarch is established, financed and phrased are suggestively similar to the process that – beginning with the fortuitous meeting at the entrance to the flower shop – led to Mercedes's marriage to Ramón and are equally questionable.

'A man ahead of his time' is the term used and repeated incessantly by the contracting Sánchez family to describe the village patriarch. It is a phrase taken up and played upon parodically by the mimicking Miguel Ángel throughout the negotiations over the statue. This kind of mimicry recalls the subaltern lampooning of 'great men' of destiny discussed in Chapter 1, with reference to Mihura's *The Way of Babel*. Imitation – Mercedes's clearest 'style of action' – is also employed by Miguel Ángel. Accustomed to such commissions, Miguel Ángel makes use of a standard mold in his possession which can be customized ad hoc. It is, as he explains, simply a matter of changing the head each time he is required to produce such a monument. Although a professional creator, Miguel Ángel is also a *bricoleur* who 'makes use' of officialdom for his own non-official purposes. His sculpture, like the nation itself, is an apparently immobile space that can be altered and transformed with a scarcely perceptible touch or movement. In this context, it is apt that de Certeau should pose the question, 'how does time articulate itself on an organized space?' It is a question he answers in ways that are pertinent to both Miguel Ángel's and Mercedes's means of operating:

> The occasion is taken advantage of, not created. It is furnished by the conjuncture, that is, by *external* circumstances in which a sharp eye can see the new and favorable ensemble they will constitute, given *one more detail*. A supplementary stroke, and it will be 'right'. (de Certeau, 1984: 86)

The space in which Miguel Ángel works is merely a mold at the service of those who contract him, which allows him to earn his living and manipulate possibilities. This is not dissimilar to the kind of activity that, as we shall see in Chapter 6, de Certeau terms the *perruque*, 'the worker's own work disguised as work for his employer' (1984: 25).

Conclusion

Consumers, according to de Certeau, 'trace "indeterminate trajectories" that are apparently meaningless, since they do not cohere with the constructed, written, and prefabricated space through which they move' (1984: 34). In contrast to Mercedes's and Madame Du Pont's creatively temporal trajectory, the railtrack marks an inescapable line connecting two 'points [...] on a space' (de Certeau, 1984: 35) that crosses Spain.

In the introductory passage to this chapter, I quoted Callinicos's use of Althusser's notion of interpellation in the context of national identity. de Certeau provides a more succinct definition of the phenomenon and draws similar conclusions: 'The credibility of a discourse is what first makes believers act in accord with it. It produces practitioners' (1984: 148). The observations of these two writers suggest that hegemonic articulation relates both to the construction of instruments of cultural power – such as tradition – and to the unanticipated uses to which these are put by consumers.

Although phrased in terms of urban space, de Certeau's concept of 'strategy' is primarily concerned with making discursive what was previously non-discursive. The earlier quote on 'strategy', in the introduction to this chapter, is an echo of de Certeau's earlier writings. In *The Writing of History* (1975), he uses similar terms to make explicit the discursive nature of strategy and its function in re-channeling transgression. 'The task of doctors or exorcists' he writes, 'is one of nomination, which aims at categorizing the interlocutors, confining them in a place circumscribed by these doctors' or exorcists' knowledge' (1975: 247).

de Certeau argues that attempts to ensnare everyday practice in totalizing and nominative discourse break down owing to the subtle and insinuating operations of 'resistance' employed by the apparently weak within the very boundaries of power.

The mobile space in which Madam Du Pont and Mercedes operate tactically enables them (and characters like them) to articulate on the edge of discourse. The threshold marks a point of indeterminacy, a liminal area, from which what Bakhtin calls 'gay relativity' emerges (1984: 142). The space of characters like Mercedes and Madame Du Pont – at the margin, related to the circus and the carnivalesque – signifies a juncture grafted within the articulating structure of hegemony. Apparently innocuous, these characters by virtue of the barriers that constrain them often prove lynchpins in the process of transformation that is the mainstay of fictionalizing and story-telling. As Fillin-Yeh says, '[B]oundaries make creativity possible' (2001: 5). Creativity here also lies in the construction of an alternative past.

For a film whose time is funneled into a single overnight train ride across the geography of Spain, it is interesting that such a configuration of time and space should provide it with a transnational dimension. In spite of its resounding failure at the box office, *Life on a Thread* marks a high point in Spain's cinematic history.[9] It is a film whose plot has exceeded national boundaries and those of chronological history. Fourteen years after its cinematic release, Neville achieved success with the stage version which ran at a Madrid theater through 1959. It is also one of the rare Spanish films of the period to be subject to a post-dictatorship remake in Gerardo Vera's 1992, *Una mujer bajo la lluvia* (*A Woman in the Rain*). Aptly, given her starring role in the original, Conchita Montes's final film appearance was a small part in this remake. Its plot is remarkably similar to those of the British film *Sliding Doors* (Peter Howitt, 1998) or the Australian *Me, Myself, I* (Pip Karmel, 1999). All three films play on a narrative trick particularly well suited to cinema which allows for the representation of simultaneity. The distinguishing feature of them all lies in the play of time which perforates borders and depicts alternative lifestyles.

Life on a Thread conforms to the conventions – and constraints – of romantic comedy. Like many films of its ilk, it proposes alternative life styles. As previously noted, rather than being a second husband, Miguel Ángel is an alternative possibility. Peter Evans and Celestino Deleyto, in the introduction to their important anthology of essays concerning 1980s and 1990s Hollywood romantic comedy, observe that the concept of romantic love as derived from 11th-century Provençal poetry, while undergoing multiple transformations, has retained certain distinctive attributes.

To this end Deleyto, following Steve Neale, comments that one of the qualities of romantic comedy is its experiential aspect or 'learning process'. There is often a pattern of choosing the wrong partner before rectifying, overturning all that had gone before and bringing about a more appropriate ending (Deleyto, 1998: 134). As I will argue in Chapter 5, the conventional 'happy ending' of comedy resulting in marriage, while subverted in *Life on a Thread* by virtue of the film's undecided finale, will be discarded wholesale in the mature work of the person who holds most claims to being Neville's cinematic heir, Luis García Berlanga.

In *Life on a Thread* there is an imaginary wedding scene in which Mercedes walks up a church aisle on the arm of Miguel Ángel who, at the edge of the altar, steps aside to give way to Ramón. This makes explicit the alternative nature of Miguel Ángel and the optimistic but uncertain possibilities of her undecided future with him. It is a subjunctive moment. Moreover, it connects to the kind of inversion that we have seen throughout the film; an inversion that has much to do not only with the sight gag but also the mimicry and the doubling to which I have already referred. Mercedes's wedding and its fantasy reversal provide a set piece of comic effect. While Bakhtin associates parody with inversion in the context of the human body, a markedly different writer like Bergson – whose interest lies more in social satire – remarks specifically upon the comicity of inversion in his famous essay of 1911 on laughter when he writes of incongruity in the following terms: 'Picture to yourself certain characters in a certain situation: if you reverse the situation and invert the *roles* you obtain a comic scene' (Bergson, 1999: 88).

In his interrogation of the term 'popular culture' and its relation to 'tradition' Stuart Hall returns to the word articulation: 'Tradition is a vital element in culture; but it has little to do with the mere persistence of old forms. It has much more to do with the way elements have been linked together or articulated' (Hall, 1998: 450). One of the key features of romantic comedy is the apparent contradiction that lies in the combination of its conventional aura and its inexorable necessity to reinvent itself according to the times. It is at one and the same time old fashioned and modern. Its capacity to articulate breaches frontiers between high and low culture and makes it relevant – albeit laterally – to the historical specificity of 1945 Spain, which, as we have seen, critics (such as Sanz de Soto, Burguera and Torres-Dulce) have referred.

de Certeau provides us with the coda to this chapter. In *The Practice of Everyday Life* he sketches out a very short chapter entitled 'Railway Navigation and Incarceration' (1984: 111–114) whose subject matter not only coincides with the real action of *Life on a Thread*, but whose images also recall many of those that feature in my own discussion. de Certeau remarks on how a the traveler trapped in a moving train is 'pigeonholed, numbered, and regulated'. It is, he says, 'a perfect actualization of the rational utopia' (1984: 111). He describes the view from the train compartment's window in similar terms as being beyond the control of the passive, dispossessed and incarcerated passenger. Nonetheless the partitioning glass window through which the outside world is viewed, de Certeau maintains, is at once a jail, that confines the passenger and prevents escape, and a conduit through which thought and speculation take flight. de Certeau extends upon this notion of a metaphorical freedom of contemplation (non-discursive practice) while imprisoned in the cell-like compartment, ensnared in the inexorable railtrack (of discourse). For him the entire journey is a series of frontiers to be considered. The purchase of the train ticket is described, by wry use of a religious simile: 'The historical threshold of beatitude: history exists where there is a price to be paid' (de Certeau, 1984: 113). Arrival at the final destination ('the terminal') involves 'another threshold, composed of momentary bewilderments in the airlock constituted by the train station. History begins again' (1984: 114).

3
Metropolitan Masquerades: The Destabilization of Madrid in the Neville Trilogy

> The recesses of the domestic space become sites for history's most intricate invasions.
>
> – Bhabha, 1994: 9

While stereotyping is central to cinematic comedy in terms of the representation of gender, race or class, it has frequently been treated in Hispanic film studies as an uncomplicated field (Kinder, 1993: 398; D'Lugo, 1991: 34). And just as it is indeed the case that the purpose of the stereotype is to simplify social relations, in what Homi K. Bhabha has termed an 'arrested, fixated form of representation' (1994: 75), in this chapter I would like to build on the work of previous commentators and to problematize the concept.

As we have seen, 'hybridity' is a term employed by Bakhtin to denote the dialogic nature of all communication, of utterances that split, splinter, influence and refract one another. As already noted, in Bakhtin it is something not limited to formal linguistics. From his work on carnival to that of the chronotope and his later work on speech genres, hybridity consistently re-emerges both linguistically and in characters who are marked by multiple, often contradictory, voices.

Bhabha relates hybridity to metonymy and suggests that the latter is fundamentally a 'partializing process', a strategic instrument in displacement that disturbs authority's claims to seamlessness. If the metaphor is the 'substitute', the metonym is the 'shadow' – a mimicking, miming (and mocking) 'appurtenance of authority' (Bhabha: 114–115). In light of this configuration my aim is to analyze hybridity through the prism of history as it is represented by Neville's focus upon the city of Madrid in a trilogy of films made during the mid-1940s and to counterpose such historical representation with the dominant historiography of the regime.

In 1944, the influential Falangist film magazine *Primer Plano* published an editorial, written by the pseudonymous Luciano de Madrid, that singled out Neville's sympathetic depictions of 'stereotypical' daily life in working class Madrid for ideological critique:

> One was under the impression that the honorable 'type', so representative of the *sainete* complete with his militia overalls, had been dealt with on 18 July when History rose up in arms. For this reason, when Mr Neville sides with the fairground masses and sets his face against such a verdict, it has given us sudden start. It is as if Mr Neville had convoked all the honorable 'types' of the *sainete* in plebiscite with the express idea of disappointing us. (de Madrid, 1944: 3)

Such vitriol highlights the sensitivity with which Neville's Republican heritage was regarded and the mistrust of the kind of cinema (and theater) that he was trained in which was, of course, also North American. Nonetheless, Neville's cinematic realism points up several contradictions. Having supported the military uprising, ironically Neville came under attack for his recourse to a national tradition, the *sainete*. A disjunction – or a haunting – reveals itself at the heart of the construction process of tradition and cracks emerge in the ideological amalgam that constituted Francoist cultural thinking precisely because of the regime's need to secure popular consent by investing in populist projects. While the *sainete* was popular during the Second Republic its origins date back to the 18th century; it represents the unspoken (and unspeakable) popular underbelly of the Enlightenment's liberal and secular project, the real enemy of both the Falange and National Catholicism; and Neville was nothing if not a liberal.[1]

The *Primer Plano* editorial makes clear that the signifier of *Madrid*, with which *sainete* is closely associated, is not neutral but subject to the contingencies of time and ideology, particularly in the aftermath of the siege of Madrid. The regime's inheritance of the Second Republic's popular-cultural project produces – and this is suggested by the unease expressed in the tone of Luciano de Madrid's article – a 'doubling' that threatens authority in much the same way as Bhabha suggests is the shadowy function of metonymy. The 'double' to which I refer here is that anxiety that de Certeau has characterized – in a wry gesture to his own Freudian legacy – as the 'stranger [...] already there in residence' (1998: 134). Cities are palimpsestic entities, layered sites of previous experiences whose smooth, untroubled surface in the present is constantly disturbed by the 'heterogeneous references, ancient scars' (de Certeau,

1998: 133) of previous occupants. Bakhtin's observation on the proximity of life to death is not only metaphorically present in all comedy, but is pertinent to the reality of all cultural representation in 1940s Spain, given the taboos surrounding the recently terminated Civil War. As the poet Dámaso Alonso put it at the time, Madrid was 'a city of a million corpses' (1946: 81). As has been well documented, such an intimate closeness relates directly to the rise of the modern city.[2]

Perhaps aptly to Bhabha's postcolonial theory early post-war Spain contains certain features similar to those of the consolidation of an invading force. The fact that the Military was officially referred to as the 'Army of Occupation', the revival of imperial iconography, the resuscitation of the Inquisition, and the obsessive employment of nominative discourse in the changing of the names of city streets locates the ideological project of early Francoism within that of territorial conquest. In spite of Francoist historiography's exaltation of Catholic fundamentalism, the persistence in popular memory – in customs, practices marked in the city neighborhoods – of Spain's Jewish and Arab heritage is suggestive of a subterranean historical reality lurking beneath the surface of official chronicles. Spatial representation of history is particularly appropriate to the cinema screen and Fritz Lang's futuristic essay on class struggle in city society, *Metropolis* (1926), provides an aesthetic model that Neville would, in at least one of the films discussed here, make much of for his own particular historical vision.

Intimately connected to historiography is the fact that the stereotypes of Madrid provide a template of popular activity that enables Neville to approach the complexity of everyday life in the city. The films discussed in this chapter are all set in the most 'typical' and traditional districts of old and central Madrid, Lavapiés and La Latina, areas known for their tenements, their taverns, the settings for popular operettas, and the city fairgrounds, gastronomically complemented by the rudimentary local cuisine. It is in these areas, around which national and popular converge – key fields in stereotyping – that the cityscape of Madrid unmasks its own fragility to reveal an administrative capital of nation and empire built upon the bustle of an unruly and unpredictable population, its present and its past.

The Tower of the Seven Hunchbacks (1944)

Lang's *Metropolis* is paradigmatic in its mapping of social organization with the community depicted in the film divided quite literally in layers according to class: the wealthy masters live on the surface of the

Earth surrounded by verdant gardens, the furnaces of the factories are located in a middle zone and the workers are consigned to subterranean dwellings. More *castizo* and less expressionistic, Neville's Madrid nonetheless remains faithful to the spatial stratification of Lang's dystopia in its representation of urban social relations at ground level and below, but it also makes use of such schema to dovetail indirectly into the specificity of national history.[3]

The Tower of the Seven Hunchbacks, the film adaptation of Emilio Carrere's 1924 novel,[4] tells the story of Basilio Beltrán (Antonio Casal) who is chosen by the ghost of murdered archaeologist Robinson de Mantua (Felix de Pomés) to investigate his death at the hands of a community of hunchbacks who manufacture counterfeit money in an underground synagogue – a clandestine remnant of the Inquisition – built in secret beneath the city. In the course of his investigation Basilio falls in love with Robinson's daughter Inés (Isabel de Pomés, Félix's real-life daughter) and distances himself from the previous object of his affections, the music-hall singer, La Bella Medusa.

This film, like the original novel, is defined by its 'popular' and potboiling nature; it both purports to be historical drama and a comic horror film that disrupts generic, temporal and locational boundaries and does so at the intersection of the popular and the historical. 'History' in *The Tower of the Seven Hunchbacks* is stereotyped as costume drama, a vibrant, recognizable Madrid whose caricatured ways of speaking and behavior recall those of the 19th-century novels of Benito Pérez Galdós. 'Period' in this film, though, is vaguely defined and almost always identified by anecdote. There are no dates mentioned in this film but, as we will see, the film's historical and national specificity emerges in a manner not dissimilar to the synecdochic relation to real event of *The Way of Babel* or *Destiny Excuses Himself* that we have seen in Chapter 1.[5]

Similarly, with regards to the history of cinema, Neville's work, particularly in *The Tower of the Seven Hunchbacks*, displays the influence of German expressionism that goes well beyond *Metropolis*. The cinematography frequently echoes Robert Wiene's *The Cabinet of Doctor Caligari* (1920) and this is reflected thematically in the abundance of hypnotism, mad scientists and archeologists (as well as Italian pseudonyms), which helps to complicate the staple material of the typical Madrid of flower girls and barrel organs.

Susan Hayward observes that many early cinematic stereotypes were inherited from popular theater and particularly vaudeville (1996: 348). Indeed, it is in popular fields such as music hall, gambling, popular religion and superstition where we often see instances of indirect engagement with the historical realities of the time. Early in the film Basilio, desperately in need of money to pay for dinner with the film's vaudeville figure, La Bella Medusa and her mother, ventures into the casino to risk his last peseta on roulette. This is a moment in which contemporaneous Spain intrudes in the form of censorship and converges with the irreality of ghosts and superstition. As far as I am aware, there is no historical period other than the 1940s when utterance of the word 'red' was banned in cinema,[6] yet when the ball falls onto Basilio's red number the croupier calls out: 'the flesh-colored three' (Gubern, 1997: 33). The prohibition of the literal term extends to the ideological synecdoche, and draws attention – by incongruity – to the absence of the original word.

This example suggests that comedy can make present what had hitherto been absent, like the ghost of Robinson de Mantua who appears before Basilio to indicate the number on which he should place his bet. The comic mode enshrouds historical discourse but also permits commentary upon things that would otherwise remain concealed by censorship. When the ghost of Napoleon appears by mistake in Basilio's bedroom he is cordial and comical, quite unnapoleonic in his extreme courtesy; a cardboard cut-out in distinctive headwear. The contrast with Napoleon's real role in Madrid is striking;[7] a kind of non-discursive historical text is produced by using stereotypes and reinscribing them in popular and often urban terms.

In the same way the hunchbacks in this film, although never referred to as Jews, are, nonetheless, associated with Jewishness and particularly with the anti-Semitic caricature of Jewishness as insinuating, sinister, grotesque and grasping. Yet the stereotype is unstable; the hunchbacks are *not* Jews, the 'Jewishness' that surrounds them is metynomic, 'shadowy' (represented by synecdoches of the synagogue and money). However, they are also metaphors for Jews, 'substitutes'. The head hunchback, Doctor Sabatini (Guillermo Marín), is a physician and medicine was one of the traditional Jewish professions in Spain previous to the Inquisition. He also possesses a surname that is explicitly linked to Jewishness in the novel as a derivation of the word Sabbath (Carrere, 1998: 135–136). At the same time it is also emblematically Madrilenian, the surname of one of the city's most renown architects, the Italian Francesco Sabatini – the 18th-century favorite of Carlos III, one of the Austrian monarchs – from whom the Sabatini Gardens in front of the Royal Palace take their name. Moreover, the square of which the Sabatini Gardens forms part is called the Plaza de Oriente and was originally created on the orders of Napoleon's brother Joseph.[8] The Barrio de los Austrias, the district where the action of the film takes place, is built upon the foundations of what was once the city's Arab area and is adjacent to the historical Jewish quarter.

As the case of Sabatini indicates (and this is true of other characters), names form metynomic chains of association that extend to urban history. The ambivalence produced of the alterity that pertains to these people and the places in which they operate is palpable. It refutes the denial of the 'play of difference' that Bhabha associates with stereotyping (1994: 75) and reveals Madrid as a splintering composite that proves to be an agent in the unmasking of those who investigate the activities of the hunchbacks. There is both a hostility towards Jewishness – as manifest in the stereotype – and a fascinated nationalistic archeology desirous to uncover Spain's buried heritage. Such ambiguities run throughout the film. The superstitious Basilio rubs his chips on the humps of the hunchbacks for luck in the casino. The hunchbacks, while being derogatory metaphors for Jews, are also enigmatically attractive, apparent harbingers of good fortune.

Indeed, Basilio's pathological superstitiousness is a symptom of the historical anxiety mentioned in the introduction to this chapter, what de Certeau terms the 'uncanniness of the already there'. It is also a field where subaltern and dominant groups meet. Just as Gramsci defines folklore as a kind of popular philosophy, uneven and contradictory, superstition in this film functions as a structural plank mid-way between historiography and hysteria. We have already seen in the previous chapter how de Certeau remarks upon the potentially subversive quality of 'superstition' and its functioning within 'spatial' boundaries. In the very first scene of *The Tower of the Seven Hunchbacks*, La Bella Medusa interrupts her routine to interrogate the men in the audience as to whether they are superstitious and on receiving an affirmative reply from Basilio points out the presence of a black cat beneath his chair. This both disrupts his pretensions to seduction (by making him jump clumsily), increases his desire, and links him to the urban narrative of the city of Madrid (*cats* are traditional identificatory synonyms for Madrilenians). Superstition, together with Jewishness (the synagogue) and Spain's Arab legacy, comes to constitute a disputed metynomic space that emerges from the margins in the absence of Christian presence, in the form of either church or priest, and casts an influence similar to that of the stereotyped characters.

Superstition, moreover, forms part of a ludic field in which games are often the instruments for its employment. Games, according to Bakhtin, 'are closely related to time and to the future' (1984: 235). For Bakhtin the importance of games of chance and fortune telling lies not in being taken seriously but in their 'related meaning'. Bakhtin explains that games of chance and soothsaying represent a parody of the 'timeless', unchanging hierarchy of things. In Spanish cinema of the 1940s there are a remarkable number of examples of card games, fortune tellers (as we have seen in *Life on a Thread*) and dice players. While often imitating North American *noir* type situations, these examples also emphasize a dynamic element of pleasure in relation to legal stricture. In this film (and this is particularly true of *Carnival Sunday* [Figure 6] discussed below) there is an almost choral linking between games for fun and economic need.

Throughout the first half of the film superstition, gambling and play constantly punctuate the action. Each time Basilio visits Inés at her home in the Plaza de la Paja he has to sidestep the throng of children playing bullfighting in the square or watching the Punch and Judy show in an almost clichèd Madrilenian set-piece.

Meanwhile there is a constant overlap or translation between the Gothic mystery of the *mise-en-scène* and the humdrum needs of material living. Significantly, it is within both fields that the ghosts move. Just as the historically mediated (and spatial) divisions between the temporal

Figure 6　Carnival Sunday (Courtesy of Video Mercury Films, S.A. and Filmoteca Española)

and the supernatural – presence and absence – dissolve in the depiction of the ghosts of Robinson de Mantua and Napoleon, so the frontiers between the high-minded qualities of intellectual endeavor or the noble pursuit of romantic goals also collapse amid the dire straits of economics. The notion of hybridity as a univocity – the subsuming of difference or alterity in a whole – comes apart through the enactment of these practices.

Once more such non-discursive activity is almost always the domain of minor or secondary characters. Basilio's girlfriend's mother (played again by Julia Lajos and stereotyped as both comic mother-in-law and stock Madrilenian), the peculiar codebreaker, the assorted hunchbacks and Robinson de Mantua's lunatic archeological aide, Zacarías, thus have more in common than might at first appear. The grotesque and the ludic are closely related concepts in Bakhtin, for whom the former has none of the sinister associations that are often attached to it. The fool's chronotope emerges in this film in the same way as history does. In fact the two, as the appearance of Napoleon suggests, are closely aligned. What is carnivalized here is history itself. According to Bakhtin, the masks of the clown and the fool 'are rooted deep in the folk' (1996: 161). In the same passage he links the fool's mask to his or her spatial arena of operations which he locates in 'the public square and with the trappings of the theatre' (1996: 161). And it is of some significance, as we shall observe, that much of the action of *The Tower of the Seven Hunchbacks* takes place in, around and beneath La Plaza de la Paja. Pertinent to this chapter, the fool is important for Bakhtin in 'the laying-bare of any sort of conventionality, the exposure of all that is vulgar and falsely stereotyped in human relationships' (1996: 162).

The figure of Robinson de Mantua is often (like many of the other characters) reduced to a cipher 'El Tuerto' ('The One-Eyed Man'). He is one-eyed yet all-seeing, and unseen by everyone but Basilio. His physical characteristics mark him out as self-reflexive in similar ways to the hunchbacks (Jews that are not Jews). These metonymic ciphers (and there are others) instead of diminishing the elements they are associated with form part of the manufacturing process of a form of piecemeal history that runs beneath the surface of dominant historiography. Robinson de Mantua's name is laden with literary associations: Defoe, Dante, Cervantes, Shakespeare. Furthermore, it is pertinent to the self-conscious ficticiousness produced of the reinscription of urban history in this film. According to legend, the original Roman name for Madrid is 'Mantua Carpentanorum', though Hugh Thomas maintains there is no evidence that such a location ever existed and suggests that the name has been invented by Christians to conceal the city's Arab origins (1988: 26).

The story of Robinson is tragic – murdered just when he is about to achieve the pinnacle of his lifetime's work – and yet he is a kind of comic trickster who revels in roulette, appears at unwanted moments and ends the film by stealing Inés's statue of the Venus de Milo. His physicality, his wounds, his ragged clothes, his filthy appearance combined with his general mischievousness and cupid-like functions help to bolster an image which strays a long way from the monkish ideal of the dedicated scholar. Zacarías, meanwhile, has indeed devoted himself to learned investigation trapped in the bowels of the earth as captive of the hunchbacks. This supposed intellectual is an idiot who allows himself to be gulled by ludicrous conjecture. Like Brandole of Mihura's *The Way of Babel*, he stands in the popular tradition (and another well-worked filmic stereotype) of 'the nutty professor'.

Robinson is not the only character whose name reverberates within and without the film. La Bella Medusa is an oxymoron, a hybrid image of beauty and serpent coils. Her name is also a typecast music-hall pseudonym that parodically recalls La Bella Dorita of the pre-war Barcelona cabaret scene. The name of the virtuous Inés is taken from an early Christian martyr and means 'pure' in Greek. The purity of Inés in association with the seven hunchbacks of the film's title conjures up an incongruous echo of Snow White and the Seven Dwarves.

Incongruity is a comic technique of estrangement and Madrid in this film, once the protagonists are beneath ground, is always described in distanced terms as being 'elsewhere'. Repeatedly it is articulated in terms of uncanniness: 'I've come from Madrid,' says Basilio to Zacarías. Inés warns Basilio, 'It is you who should return to the city'. Madrid, like the ghosts of Robinson de Mantua and Napoleon or Jewishness, is simultaneously absent and present, both there and not there. It is apt then that at the end of the film Madrid should implode, should quite literally collapse in upon its own void. Almost all the action of the movie above ground takes place in the historical center of the city and this, in turn, points to an interesting paradox; while Madrid ceases to be present (like the treatment of Christianity or of 'period' as contemporary history) its metropolitan importance persists; the archeological site of the synagogue is described by Zacarías as 'the most interesting place in Spain'.

In this vein, the subterranean chamber is accorded dramatically impressive treatment with, as we have seen, the use of a cinematography influenced by German expressionism. However the looming shadows, spiral staircases, whitewashed tunnels and Gothic structures alternate with traditional – and often stereotyped – local features such as the children's games ongoing in the square where Inés lives. The typecast Madrid that attracted the earlier disdain of Luciano de Madrid is revealed to be (quite literally) an unstable entity, one in which the metropolitan center of National Catholicism is diffused.

Such symbolic diffusion of the capitality of Madrid is reproduced in terms of spatial distortion in a very real, visual sense. As we have observed, Madrid in *The Tower of the Seven Hunchbacks* is built upon a hollow space that collapses in upon itself at the end. Moreover, this is a film structured around a tower that extends downwards in carnivalesque fashion (and I shall discuss the significance of Bakhtin's analysis of downward movement in more detail in *Carnival Sunday* later in this chapter). Importantly, mirrors pervade the film. Robinson de Mantua materializes through mirrors. Doctor Sabatini has a distorting mirror in his office which corrects his hump in an echo of Ramón del Valle-Inclán's mirrors in the Calle de los Gatos (cats again) in another emblematic Madrid text, *Bohemian Lights*, a play that appeared the very same year as Carrere's novel: 'The classical heroes reflected in the concave mirrors give the sense of *esperpento*. The tragic sense of Spanish life can only be represented by a systematically deformed aesthetic' (Valle-Inclán, 1991: 168).

While mirrors help reinforce the sense of place (Madrid) they also connect to the psychological element of the double that so interested Freud, from whom de Certeau derives his terminology. In his famous 1919 essay, Freud defines the uncanny as that indeterminant sense of anxiety related to the apprehension of death and frequently articulated symbolically by ghosts and mirrors. Here, moreover, spatial distortion as represented by the mirror disturbs the classificatory function of discourse within the very 'space' of discursiveness. The concept of *esperpento* has often been used as a blanket term of convenience particularly when describing the peculiarities of Spanish cinema of the 1950s.[9] Both Kinder and Zunzunegui have sought to emphasize its distinctive exclusivity to Spanish cultural production. For the purposes of this chapter, however, in this celebrated instance Valle-Inclán links the nation and national sentiment with deformation, this is reproduced as an ironic mirror image in *The Tower of the Seven Hunchbacks*, that is, a reverse form: Sabatini's back is straightened in the mirror, like the tower that extends downwards, it is the notion of *deformation* that is inverted.

The film's constant merging of the terrestrial and the supernatural, the real and the unreal, marked by the generic confusion between comedy and mystery, Madrilenian *sainete* and German expressionism – multiple doublings – is exemplified by the function of the hieroglyph that leads to the discovery of the tower. Mary Ann Doane's analysis of the hieroglyphic, although written in the context of the representation of women, might be applicable here:

> the hieroglyphic is summoned [...] to connote an indecipherable language, a signifying system which denies its own function by failing to signify anything to the uninitiated, to those who do not hold the key. In this sense, the hieroglyphic [...] harbours a mystery, an inaccessible, though desirable otherness. (Doane, 1992: 759)

In this film the mystery of the hieroglyph – and it is explicitly referred to as a cabalistic text – is very much mediated by the comedy. It parodically plays on 'popular' exclusion; that is, those traditionally excluded from the formation of knowledge – the 'uninitiated' – and it is indicative of different strata of meaning, a subterranean layer associated with Spain's Jewish history. Fantasy, thus, plays a part in revealing the contested nature of the nation's cultural memory.

This in turn opens up possibilities of interpreting the importance of the everyday economy (which plays a major role in all the films discussed in this chapter) in creative ways. From the ambitions of La Bella Medusa's mother to the counterfeit forgers beneath the surface of the street, the symbolic system that Marx outlines by which commodities are fetishizised is shaped by a process that Roach neatly describes as, 'the vesture of material objects in an aura of mystery' (1996: 124). The enigmatic 'otherness', of the hieroglyphic messages of the hunchbacks merges with the mundane notes passed between aspiring lovers and comes to undermine the rules of genre in a kind of mimicry that adopts the mystique of the form and the form of mystique but the substance of which is quotidian. The hidden message, once the hieroglyph is descyphered ('Tonight in the tower of the seven hunchbacks') is acutely reminiscent of La Bella Medusa's earlier note to Basilio: 'As far as I am concerned, I can dine tonight after the show but mother has to come too'.

Once more this kind of overlap, in which the chaperoning mother (suggestive of Christian morality) blends with apparently contrary values of venality, is reproduced throughout the film. The evil Doctor Sabatini is a quack whose medical science involves circus-style hypnosis. The original hieroglyph is effortlessly decoded by the 'expert' police codebreaker whose alacrity reinforces, rather than obscures, the bright-eyed chirpiness of yet another fool, another 'mad professor' type. Just as spatial distortion disturbs a unitary concept of Madrid, these appeals to popular taste – to stereotyping in many instances – help undermine the meaning of mystery itself. Even the absence of dating – and with it the parodying of historiography – fulfills the function of 'mysteriously' placing the film out of the discourse of history – the same parodic field of the 'timeless' to which games pertain – while simultaneously ensuring, in its prosaic representation of everyday Madrilenian life, speech and customs, recognition for 1940s audiences, a period habitually referred to as 'the years of hunger'.

Throughout the film we see multiple examples of the transmission of private messages; from hieroglyphs, to notes passed between lovers, to the employment of musical passwords such as La Bella Medusa's saucy number whose innuendo is an invitation to Basilio or the blind violinist's street-corner solo which facilitates entrance to the 'tower'. Music here seems translatable between people from different social classes and across history and geography but it is particularly interesting to note the moments when music is used diegetically and intra-diegetically. In both instances there is a mixture of music claimed as 'autochthonous' and that from elsewhere.

Above ground we see live music in the *cuplé* sung at the beginning of the film and in the central European (and Jewish) style violin a password to gain access to the tower. The background soundtrack, meanwhile, alternates the pianola playing *chotis* in the sunny square with resounding orchestral melodrama borrowed, once more, from German cinema of the silent era. Music, like the other elements discussed in the film, transcends established boundaries between the local and the foreign.

Such disturbance, whether it be the use of the hieroglyph, musical touchstones or the system of clues within a stereotypical detective narrative, acts to reveal the ambivalence of generic authority. The linear detective story (and all three films discussed here are comic detective stories) is disrupted by spatial distortion and popular, carnivalesque reinscription. The reclaiming of Jewish history for Spain suggests a way by which the loci of history – history (and histories) as a set of temporal hybrids – can be prised open and re-articulated in the mouths of the subaltern groups for their own use. The collapse of the artifact of 'Madrid' upon the subterranean hollow below it and the mirrors link spatial transformation to urban history. Names of streets, locations, historical figures and fictional constructs (Napoleon, Inés, Robinson de Mantua, La Morería, Madrid de los Austrias) make the Madrid of *The Tower of the Seven Hunchbacks* a distorting prism, packed tense with hermeneutic implications. de Certeau, discussing how 'narrative or cinematic techniques' have made the representation of history more flexible, remarks that 'every historiography puts forward a *time of things* as the counterpoint and condition of a *discursive* time' and, in the same passage, goes on to describe such 'discursive time' as 'diegetic' (1988: 88). The varying combinations that we have seen in this film are the result of an urban and spatial history of *bricolage* that vies with a discursive narrative of temporality (that de Certeau claims 'authorizes' 'historiography to be synthesized from contraries' [1988: 89]) to produce an alternative narrative from the subterranean flotsam of 'national' history.

The Bordadores Street Murder (1946)

The Bordadores Street Murder concerns the murder of a moneyed widow Mariana (Julia Lajos) of which first her maid Petra (Antonia Plana) is accused and then so too is the widow's lover Miguel (Manuel Luna), while Lola *la Billetera*[10] (Mary Delgado) stands accused of being an accomplice. However, this is a film in which the 'event' of the murder is subjugated to an exploration of the popular reaction it provokes. As with *The Tower of the Seven Hunchbacks*, it violates classificatory conventions and hangs on a generic line that traverses melodrama and popular comedy, between 'a comedy of manners' and a murder-mystery; it is a courtroom drama resolved in the taverns and cafés of central Madrid. It is in these arenas where we witness a shift in power relations that disturbs Madrid's celebrated function as salon society, an element that is intimately connected to the city's historical role as the nation's political center.

Like the stereotype, the success of the populist project depends not so much on enclosure or on the stasis and inert passivity of the public, as on the capacity of dominant groups and their allies to limit the problematic of subaltern representation that Bhabha discusses. The news editor of the Madrid daily, *El Liberal*, puts it very well ten minutes into the film, a matter of moments after news of the murder and Petra's arrest has broken, interrupting an ongoing discussion amongst the journalists around another 'national' stereotype, bullfighting. He begins dictating the 'story', inventing it without the benefit of witnesses, without indeed even moving from his comfortable seat at the newsdesk:

News editor: Petra, a woman with a ferocious glare and murderous instincts...

Journalist (*enters the news room interrupting the news editor's dictation*): Petra is innocent. The victim's lover has been accused of committing the murder.

News editor: Forget those last sentences. She is just an unhappy wench
from the country incapable of killing so much as a fly. Who is the
lover?
Journalist: Nobody knows. A gentleman...
News editor: That is what I wanted to know: a gentleman on one side,
the maid on the other and the victim in the middle. That is journalistic. We are going to dress it up, give it air, work it so that the
people suspect that the murderer is precisely who it is not and we
will take the side of the most popular. From today onwards, for all
of you, the maid is innocent.

Petra is thus reduced to a couple of contradictory stereotypes ('a woman
with a ferocious glare and murderous instincts' and 'unhappy wench
from the country incapable of killing so much as a fly') laden with
gender and class prejudice, and the entire murder scenario is neatly
defined as hinging on a split triad (Miguel-Mariana-Petra). However, it
points up the function of the press as being that of keeping abreast of
developments among the public and adapting accordingly rather than
simply acting as an opinion shaper, a fact of which the news editor
seems well aware. Social relations are thus, from the very beginning of
this film, seen to be operating within a fluid, two-way process.

In a very brief note in the *Cultural Notebooks*, Gramsci glosses Alberto
Consiglio's 'Populismo e nuove tendenze della letteratura francese' and
its critics in the following terms:

faced with the growth of the social and political power of the proletariat and of its ideology, some sections of the French intelligentsia
are reacting by moving 'towards the people'. This going towards the
people is thus interpreted as a renewal of bourgeois thought which
does not want to lose its hegemony over the popular classes and
which, to exercise this hegemony better, accommodates part of
proletarian ideology. (1985: 363)

But Gramsci goes on to make his own comment and suggests that this
'phenomenon' may:

represent a necessary phase of transition and an episode in the indirect
'education of the people'. A list of 'populist' tendencies and an
analysis of each of them would be interesting: one might discover
one of Vico's 'ruses of nature' – how a social impulse, tending
towards one end, brings about its opposite. (1985: 364)

The press in *The Bordadores Street Murder* plays an ambivalent role, it is nominally attached to dominant thought but it is also particularly susceptible to popular pressures; not for nothing is it denoted as belonging to the *mass* media. This is a highly precarious field. As Gramsci continually reminds us, populism is an instrument employed by dominant groups dependent on the consent of the subaltern but such consent is never granted unconditionally. The function of these floating agents (in this case the press) is to act as a conduit in a tacit negotiating process, which can lead to an alteration in the balance of hegemonic forces, ideological cross-fertilization and hybridity produced of the confusion of overlapping allegiances.

From the very first shot of *The Bordadores Street Murder*, our attention is drawn to two key features in the film. First, the role of time as the camera in this shot shows the clock tower in the central Madrid square, La Puerta del Sol, at 11.30 p.m., half-an-hour after the murder has been committed. And secondly the factor of the transmission of information or the telling of stories as we witness the lurid picture story of a previous murder (committed in Calatrava Street also in the city centre) being declaimed in the same square. This is a film structured around a series of flashbacks. As we have seen in Chapter 2, flashbacks are 'marked as *subjective* moments within [the] narrative' (Hayward, 1996: 122). They are thus themselves ways of recounting and are not always – indeed they frequently are *not* – reliable accounts. The first flashback of this film concerns the reconstruction of the events leading up to the murder and is instigated by the press. If the press is, as suggested above, intersubjective (that is, positioned between the public and authority), then it is vulnerably poised; its concerns lie as much if not more in the tavern as in the courtroom. By means of flashback the spectator learns the antecedents of the case, the motives of each of the parties. But what moves sympathies are the performances of the characters. Later in the film, following the restoration of chronological time, inroads into the domain of power are made by the two courtroom interventions of Petra and of Lola in different ways. The first by a recuperation of time and the second in a performance that challenges the dominant group's manufacturing of time.

These subaltern characters in this film, I will argue, take charge of time and shape it in ways that the populist agents (the press) are incapable of doing, and at the same time undermine attempts to manufacture a kind of 'despotic time' demanded by courtroom procedure and policial investigation. The whole notion of time in this film, fundamental to establishing courtroom knowledge but also crucial to the audience's privileged knowledge, is disrupted by an alliance between Petra and Lola. Lola's courtroom speech (discussed fully later in this section) first helps to undermine the moral authority of the court and clears the way for Petra's dramatically brief intervention: 'At eleven at night I murdered my mistress'. Her subsequent refusal to elaborate upon her reasons for committing the murder, or to plead mitigating circumstances – that is to say those deemed acceptable by the state machinery – such as a familial relationship, sets her apart from the thrust of dominant discourse which strives to incorporate the 'unpopular' reasons for the killing within its own parameters of acceptability. Petra's flashback, framed in the form of confession, flies in the face of authority's time by denying it full knowledge. 'Time' is appropriated by Petra and authority itself is partialized.

Bhabha approvingly quotes Althusser's description of 'despotic time' as 'space without places, time without duration' (Bhabha, 1994: 246; Althusser, 1972: 78). This seems apposite to Petra's recovery of time within authority's space and reminiscent – recall the previous chapter's location of 'the proper' as a synonym for discourse itself – of de Certeau, who writes of the relation between time and space:

> The 'proper' is a victory of space over time. On the contrary, because it does not have a place, a tactic depends on time – it is always on the watch for opportunities that must be 'seized on the wing'. (de Certeau, 1984: xix)

Petra's intervention marginalizes the press's capacity for manufacture and it is apt in terms of explaining her subsequent refusal to tell anyone, including Lola, of her motives. Petra's secret – her coveting of a filial relationship with Lola – is more than mere motherly abnegation. It flies in the face of the moral code of authority while being enunciated in the very space of that authority. Even the court prosecutor (following her confession) offers her a way of avoiding the death penalty: 'If you had been related to Lola it would be an attenuating factor,' he says.

There are three sequences in the film where the use of time – 'in which the opportunity is "seized"' (de Certeau, 1984: xix) – within dominant space finds a form of representation in the movement of the camera. In all three examples the temporal structure of the film slows down, with the camera dwelling on the action from a distance, not pruriently but possessed of the performer and revelatory of power. In light of the neatness, the appearance of progressive forward movement of flashbacks, newspapers, testimony and the detective-like narrative (paradoxical because all these features look backwards; they are put into play *after* the event), this marks a recovery, a victory of time over space – over the discursive 'proper' in de Certeau's terms. In each of these cases, subaltern characters act as agents of their own destiny and do so by working out to the full the stereotypical roles in which they have been cast. It is as if they had upturned the construction process of stereotypes itself. Moreover, two of these three occasions involve the protagonism of Lola, a key stereotype in *zarzuela* (as flower girl and lottery ticket seller), and the third takes place in that most stereotypical of scenarios: the flamenco café. This suggests not only a reworking of the stereotype but also an interrogation of the national discourse as a cultural manifestation expressed through the popular function of music.

The flamenco concert at the Café Imparcial – the very historically specific late 19th-century *café-cantante* of the type where the celebrated Silverio Franconetti established his reputation (Grande, 1987: 339–370) – where Lola earns her living selling lottery tickets is an appropriate scenario for the playing out of the national discourse. As the singer – the *cantaor* – performs on stage, the rapt attention of the public is remarked upon by one of the more illustrious clients, the Duke de Sesto, in *populist* 'national-popular' fashion. 'What might this song have', he comments to an aide, 'that makes all Spaniards equal and brothers upon hearing it?' In a manner of speaking he is right. All oppositions collapse as the camera pans the audience, holding and freezing it in all its melting pot multiplicity; young and old, men and women, rich and poor, *gitano* (gypsy) and *payo* (non-gypsy). That this should be remarked upon by the Duke de Sesto – friend and teacher of King Alfonso XII – and should be placed in the context of Spain is significant. In the mouth of the Duke de Sesto and in this context, 'people' and 'nation' coincide. It is this 'strategic conjuncture' of interests (Gramsci, 1971: 217) – upon which the popular is *articulated*, that is to say linked together, radiating across classes – that is fundamental to an understanding of the notion of securing consent in the Gramscian concept of hegemony. As Landy observes, 'Gramsci complicates the notion of the popular, [...] in an attempt to differentiate populist from popular conceptions of resistance and counterhegemony' (Landy, 1994: 92). Much of Gramsci's critical work on culture and politics revolves around a critique of the 'caste-like' nature of his own country's traditional intellectuals that had inhibited them from engaging with 'the people'.

In Italy the term 'national' has an ideologically very restricted meaning, and does not in any case coincide with 'popular' because in Italy the intellectuals are distanced from the people, i.e. from the 'nation'. (Gramsci, 1985: 208)

A further example of this particular use of the panning camera occurs near the end of the film during the trial and provides a counterpoint to the *café-cantante* scene. In this sequence people and nation, previously synonymous, are divorced by the intervention of the state. The bones of the state are laid bare. The state, in the form of the police officer in charge of the case, has quite literally lessened Lola by expressing irritation at her lack of surnames (she is, as far as she knows, an orphan). However, Lola *la Billetera*, this metonymically partialized person – civically reduced by her lack of surnames – fills in all she is lacking with a series of performances that challenges the authority of dominant groups. Lola *la Billetera* is, of course, also a synecdoche for Madrid. She is the movie's stock *zarzuela* character, the figure of which is critically represented and analyzed throughout the film: from the chorus girls in the staged *zarzuela* who dance *chotis* for the benefit of the well-to-do, to Lola herself at the emblematically Madrilenian fairground at the Bombilla Park who entrances her audience – which includes Mariana's lover, Miguel – with her rendition of a *copla* and is both admired and feared for her looks and her voice: 'She is pretty' concedes Mariana, 'too much so for someone who sells lottery tickets,' says her friend Rosario.

At the very moment, nonetheless, when she is quite literally performing for her life, having been accused of being Miguel's accomplice in Mariana's murder, Lola opts for a remarkably suggestive verbal striptease before the court. In doing so she subverts authority's claims to aloof impartiality precisely at the moment when 'state' and 'people' appear most estranged. Her performance lowers the status, the moral purchasing power, of the court mandarins. Lola makes them look tawdry and lecherous, bereft of the solemn and dispassionate tone by which authority justifies itself, and reduced to a level of equality with the bar-room louts who flirt and harass her in the interestingly named Café Imparcial.[11] In response to the prosecutor's question as to her whereabouts at the precise moment of the murder, her detailed, sardonic explanation exploits 'time' via syntax and slows its tempo:

> I entered my room, turned on the light and began to undress. I took off my suit, then my underwear and then I turned off the light because the neighbours opposite were watching me. I got into bed after putting on a lovely nightshirt that I have, georgeous, with lace trimmings around here and here [she touches her breasts]. And then

I lay my head upon the pillow and set about dreaming, dreaming, dreaming that everyone had conspired to hassle me.

The reaction of the audience (comprised of the assembled lawyers, magistrates and court officials) is striking. Their faces are frozen in the panning frame. These faces of stern authority, masks of age and wisdom, are sullied by Lola's performance. Here contested power relations, as de Certeau observes, are marked by a particular *visibility* that reveals itself in the performance. Lola's presence throughout the film is physical yet fragmentary, a hybrid split across the topography of the city: a warm-hearted standard of *zarzuela*, the Madrilenian *chulapa* yet also a *churrona, socia, mujerzuela*.[12] That is to say, she is both the stereotypical *castiza* figure and whore who, while routinely marginalized because of her class, is also granted cross-class freedom of movement. The jealous Mariana says of her: 'I don't speak to women of her class', and in doing so undermines the Duke de Sesto's rosy-hued view of national-popular unity. As with the news editor's caricature of Petra, she is simultaneously admired and despised, reliably pitiable and dangerous.

Her partialization owing to her lack of a surname – its replacement by a cipher – leads in turn to Lola reinventing herself within the interstices of the stereotypical construct. Her 'lack' becomes the source of her weaponry. Genuinely innocent of the charges against her, she plays out the stereotype to its full and undoes the power structures at play against her in the doing of it. Her ignorance that her mother lives and is her ally seems perfectly apt in the context of an all-knowing court; knowledge and a lack of knowledge play off one another. In a film that is structured around ways of telling (flashbacks, newspapers, courtroom testimony) there emerge 'other' ways of telling, of transferring information by subterfuge, things overheard, passed on and repeated. Petra's sources of information rely on her apparent harmlessness, yet she is the only murderer. Her subaltern position grants her the privilege of being privy to information without fear that she will actually make use of that information. This in turn leads to a subaltern narrative that, on making inroads into the dominant narrative, comes to upturn the narrative of the film itself.

The final example of dominant space being disrupted by the subaltern stilling of time, to which I want to draw attention, occurs in a remarkable sequence involving a fight between Lola and Teresa (Monique Thibaut). Teresa is the French procuress hired by Mariana in a frenzy of jealousy (on Miguel's recommendation) to whisk Lola off to America and away from Miguel. Lola is alerted to Teresa and Mariana's intentions by Petra who has recently discovered that Lola is her lost daughter. As the flamenco singer in the Café Imparcial wails, Lola invites Teresa to accompany her to the storeroom to discuss the proposal. Once there Lola proceeds to take off her earrings before launching herself at Teresa, dragging her to the floor and in a series of short shots tears her dress open, deposits handfuls of Teresa's hair onto the floor, scattering her hairpins. In the struggle, the clock, the hands of which swing brokenly, is knocked to the ground and chimes cacaphonically out of tune before Lola, finally sitting, grins triumphantly astride her rival and spanks her backside while Teresa howls and beats an irregular tattoo with her fists on the floor.

The Juan Gris *mise-en-scène* of the storeroom in this sequence is suggestive of spatial disorder. It is an area contiguous and thus metonymic to the arena where national and popular are momentarily joined in the words of the Duke de Sesto and where Lola's presence is liminal. Temporarily the storeroom is converted into Lola's own space, both real and symbolic. It is she who determines the movements and sounds of the clock and breaks it. Moreover, her actions reach their crescendo in the spanking scene with the slowed down camera and a freezing of the frame.

This temporal conquest over space is reinforced in the sequence immediately following the fight when Lola bursts into Mariana's apartment and, brushing past Petra almost without seeing her, tosses a lock of Teresa's hair (like a war trophy) at Mariana with the words: 'Ah, and there you have the victim's scalp'. Mariana responds with self-conscious recourse to her own space: 'What an outrage! How dare you! In my own home!' Here, one of the many touchstones (the lock of hair) – so typical of the detective genre and necessary in evidential legal terms – connects with an encroachment into dominant space in terms that reduce Mariana's power. Petra's apparent *invisibility* to Lola, meanwhile, helps emphasize her powerlessness and accords well with de Certeau's observation that power is made vulnerable by its own *visibility*.

The articulation or linking together through different fields of popular culture, whether it be via music or the conventions of detective fiction in *The Bordadores Street Murder* and in the other two films discussed in this chapter, is helped along the way by use of a series of clues and touch-stones of which the lock of Teresa's hair is but one example. In each of these films the process of investigation calls into question the method-ology of accruing knowledge. It does so precisely by opening such clues up to varied interpretation and denying unitary conclusions. In the case of *The Bordadores Street Murder* this proves almost anecdotal – similarly to the lateral view of historical reality depicted in *The Tower of the Seven Hunchbacks* – yet leads, as we shall see below, to a dovetailing into historical specificity and Spain's colonial role by means of the subplot of mother/daughter relations.

These touchstones, like the variety of ways of telling, give the film a feel of cubist bricolage as suggested by the *mise-en-scène* of Lola and Teresa's fight sequence. If in *The Tower of the Seven Hunchbacks* touchstones played on notions of mystery and the supernatural, in this film the clues are almost entirely mundane, the bric-à-brac of everyday life. Everyday objects become imbued with an importance that acknowledges their complexity, similar, in fact, to a visual realization of de Certeau's concept by which the piecing together of non-discursive elements in fragmentary form produces a tactical area of operations within dominant space. These 'ordinary' artifacts (Mariana's eye glasses, Teresa's lock of hair, Lola's scarf, the medallion of Virgin of Guadalupe) are contested items throughout the film. Mariana, intent on impressing Miguel, denies that the spectacles in her home belong to her (they are symbolic of age) and tells Miguel that they belong to Petra, yet moments later she uses binoculars to spy on the Governess of Havana's pearls from her box at the *zarzuela*. Lola's scarf (an intrinsic part of the *chulapa* uniform) is purloined by Miguel as a kind of trophy of conquest (a false one) in a peculiar twist that hints at cross-dressing. By leaving the same scarf at the murder scene, Miguel – in the mind of the court – implicates Lola in the crime. Lola's presentation of Teresa's lock of hair at Mariana's house is a much truer trophy of conquest; as we have already seen, she at least won her particular contest while Miguel failed to seduce Lola. In this vein, it is appropriate that the murder weapon should be that most mundane utensil of housebound drudgery, an iron wielded by Petra. There is a tacit alliance between Petra and Lola in the act of murder (as becomes explicit during the trial) precisely where the tangents of contested space and time converge in Mariana's own home. Apparently innocuous articles of domesticity are shown not to be neutral and Bhabha's suggestive comment that serves as the epigraph to this chapter is clearly pertinent at this juncture. It is a relevance, however, that has even greater force when we look at the sub-plot that allows a reinscription of the film's narrative.

Petra's motive in murdering her mistress is formed at the confluence of this series of touchstones which only the spectator is allowed to follow. Petra acts because Lola is her daughter, a fact she discovers only by accident on going to the police station and 'overhearing' Lola's testimony to the presiding police officer following the brawl at the fairground. The fact alone that Petra *overhears* is significant in a film in which hearsay is crucial and flows around a notion of dominant knowledge (upon which verdicts are based and death sentences handed down). Also significant is the fact that she isolates a feature in a testimony that proves of no significance to the authorities investigating the specific event – the brawl – for which they have been convened but that, as far as Petra is concerned, is of primary importance and becomes, in time, the single most important feature of the film, that which motivates the murder. Lola reveals that she has no parents and thus no surnames. She herself is a victim of a disingenuous piece of rumor (that her parents died in the shipwreck of the passenger liner, the *Reina Isabel*, during an Atlantic crossing) that she has been told in the course of her upbringing during Petra's period of twenty years of enforced service in Cuba. It is for this reason that, to the annoyance of the officiously bureaucratic police inspector, she *lacks* surnames. Her only connection with her mother is an inherited medallion of the Virgin of Guadalupe that she carries with her, the revelation of which at the police station alerts Petra to her existence. The clue here provides a secret and very personalized means by which Petra identifies Lola. This is an example of a well-worked convention concerning loss and recognition by means of accidental rediscovery via a sign (scar, birthmark, religious medallions) within the domestic arena. This convention, of course, stretches back to book nineteen of the *Odyssey*, in which Odysseus finally returns home and is recognized by his old nurse Euryclea by the scar on his thigh (Auerbach, 1971: 3–23).

This identification is also connective in a metonymic way. Just as the Governess of Havana is identified by the size of her pearls when Mariana and her friend ogle through their binoculars from their box at the *zarzuela*, Lola is identified in court by her scarf and to her mother by the medallion of the Virgin of Guadalupe. Both Lola and the Governess of Havana are linked – across classes – within the associative field of *zarzuela*: Lola with respect to the scarf and her function as flower girl and *copla* singer; the Governess as spectator at the public performance. Furthermore, in the connection with Cuba, Lola's lost mother Petra and the Governess of Havana represent the two sides of the pre-1898 coin *articulated* – linked together – by metonyms: pearls, scarf, medal and *zarzuela* that connect Madrid with Cuba in a disjunctive historical moment. This in turn leads to Petra's later courtroom confession designed to save Lola when the judges implicate the latter in Mariana's murder on the basis of the fact that her scarf was found at the scene. Confession here marks an alliance that is quite distinct from remorse, the culmination of an articulatory process within which counter-hegemonic consciousness is forged. Petra's motivation, like her secret, subverts both the redemptive mores of authority and disrupts the stability of the discourse surrounding Spain's colonial history. Interestingly, by shunning the possibility of absolution inherent in the Christian notion of confession, Petra eludes the discursive matrix in which Michel Foucault locates the objectives of confession:

> The confession is a ritual of discourse in which the speaking subject is also the subject of the statement; it is also a ritual that unfolds within a power relationship, for one does not confess with the presence (or virtual presence) of a partner who is not simply the interlocutor but the authority who requires the confession, prescribes and appreciates it, and intervenes in order to judge, punish, forgive, console and reconcile. (Foucault, 1990: 61–62)

The disjunctive moment in temporal and spatial relations, with regard to historical event and the city of Madrid, manifests itself through the suture of music and of narrative itself. The two issues are connected. Both are potent populist elements in hegemony, insofar as they help secure consent around the specificity of the nation. They are, though, also unpredictable areas precisely because they are fields in which dominant and subaltern groups meet.

Music plays an important role in many of Neville's films but rarely more so than in *The Bordadores Street Murder*. There are two 'concerts' in this film, the *zarzuela* and the *café-cantante*. What is apparently juxtaposition – and the two sequences are placed side by side – produces, by means of contiguity, the kind of doubling that we have already seen in *The Tower of the Seven Hunchbacks*. Such musical doubling fits neatly in with the reinscription of the narrative touchstones that I have already discussed and which, employed out of their natural context, are 'made use' of as hegemonic instruments of temporality that subvert the space of dominant groups.

Music comes to destabilize seamless notions of Madrid. *Zarzuela* is stereotypically Madrilenian music and Lola is associated with *zarzuela*; as the *chulapa* identified by her scarf, she is to Madrid what Carmen is to Seville. She is also, precisely because of her partialized presence, associated with the 'typical' arenas of central Madrid. The mobility of Lola, together with the accumulation of everyday artifacts, their placing in the film across classes and across the city's geography, makes her and them pulsating points criss-crossing the topography of the city.

Petra's personal narrative of the loss of her daughter is strongly reminiscent of the kind of twisted, subaltern narrative that another emblematically Madrilenian filmmaker, Pedro Almodóvar, has subsequently specialized in more than fifty years after Neville. Coincidentally or not, there are a number of echoes of *The Bordadores Street Murder* in Almodóvar's work: first mother and daughter relationships (*The Flower of My Secret* [1995] and *High Heels* [1990]); the *mise en scène* surrounding the actual killing and the murder weapon (Petra's use of the iron recalls the oppressed housewife who despatches her brutal husband by wielding a leg of ham in *What Have I Done to Deserve This?* [1984]). Indeed the very location where Victoria Abril is held captive in *Tie Me Up, Tie me Down* (1989) is an address on Bordadores Street. However, the connection with Almodóvar is particularly germane if we recall one of the central features of this film which concerns ways of telling. Both Almodóvar (who tends to foreground this aspect) and Neville give voice to subaltern characters, enabling them to fictionalize within the hegemonic framework; what matters is not so much their ability to tell their own story as their ability to tell it in their own way. In the case of *The Bordadores Street Murder* this fictionalization becomes an element of empowerment within the very space of dominant groups. This is particularly the case when we consider that these ways of telling vie with other modes of transmitting information such as the press, courtroom testimony and gossip.

Petra's unlikely and elaborately crafted narration is made more convincing both by the manner in which she maintains her personal secret to the very end and by the equally unlikely and very clearly manufactured nature of dominant narrative production (as evidenced by the news editor's early intervention). Her hitherto marginalized and coveted threshold fiction, once thrust into the centrality of the dominant space of the courtroom, helps expose the crude realities of hegemonic relations.

The complexity of these relations and the spatial working out of them is perhaps made clearer by the function played by don Matías (José Franco), Mariana's neighbor from the floor below her in the same building on Bordadores Street. Don Matías represents the doltish butt of popular comedy, the urban subaltern who is sufficiently self-parodic to be set apart from the social group to which he formally belongs. He is ubiquitously secondary (appearing in the very first sequence of the film, turning up at the police station following the fight at the Bombilla Park, crossing paths with Lola in the stairwell of Mariana's house days before the murder and appearing as a witness in the final trial). He is the perennial unreliable witness, a partial and a partializing presence endlessly striving for protagonism. His utterances are foolish and absurdly inconsequential. Uncommitted to all but himself he is the demonstrable denial of essential representation. The public see right through him. It is the judges who accept his testimony as reliable. He is very much an 'appurtenance of authority' (Bhabha, 1994: 115); a witness upon whose testimony people are convicted or not, yet also a living example of arbitrary and self-interested unreliability. The Bakhtinian aura that surrounds him also marginalizes him. He is fat, waddling, lewd and concerned with food. He cuts a ridiculous figure. Yet he is allied with authority. He is a firm defender of Mariana's values (he too regards Lola as a whore to whom he is attracted) and those of the court. However, he is also a public embarrassment of authority, strangely unmasking his own allies and frequently being told to be quiet (in the police station and in the courtroom) while subject to ridicule from the public gallery. In his unreliability there is something of the intersubjective; he both exists within and without the domain of the dominant, and within and without the domain of the subaltern. He is an arrested presence whose very fixity disrupts and throws into relief the hegemonic struggle ongoing around him. That he should ally himself with authority paradoxically helps hamstring the attempts of authority to reach a discursive solution (that is to say, a verdict) and proves dangerous. Just as the press is intersubjective, don Matías as a subaltern representative is the lowest common denominator to which populism appeals: both its target audience and its extreme edge. It is in his dubious testimony that don Matías proves to be the liminal lynchpin of the film's discourse concerning the telling of stories. The press invents a story based in part on gossip and hearsay in order to stimulate further gossip. Gossip itself proves a cross-class source of conflict; working men brawl in bars, neighbours squabble between housing blocks, bourgeois families begin to question and doubt the good nature of their servants and, in turn, are rewarded with contempt. Any stable notion of 'truth' is subject to a stratified and splitting set of opinions or versions. Hearsay becomes as valid a form of verification as eye-witness accounts, certainly no less nor more reliable. It is in the telling of stories where the popular and the populist meet. The initial comments of the news editor are revealing: the press cannibalizes popular opinion and then seeks to shape it, rather than stimulating it in any *a priori* sense. In a certain Foucauldian sense this is the making discursive of what was previously non-discursive and yet this is imperfectly realized. The metonymic relation of don Matías to dominant groups signals both a destabilization of that discourse and marks one of the main differences between ideology and discourse itself: something that we will see in later chapters.

Carnival Sunday (1945)

Carnival Sunday is a play upon the contingency of time and the contiguity of space: the temporal tensions of the three days of carnival located within the slenderly suggestible confines of a central district of Madrid. The district in question is the Rastro in Lavapiés, which hosts the Sunday morning open-air flea-market that sprawls across its streets and marks the city's heartland with popular connotations as a hubbub of humanity, recycling, trade, transaction and exchange. In its discursive locus this Madrid constitutes something akin to what Terry Eagleton has called – in terms strongly reminiscent of Gramsci – 'a network of overlapping features rather than some constant "essence"' (Eagleton, 1991: 193).

Once more Neville's plot is quirky: a community money lender is murdered, there is an obscure (and rapidly abandoned) tale of cocaine dealing, and a prolonged flirtation between a slow-witted policeman and the bright daughter of a modern day costermonger.[13] Within this *mélange* of narrative material, the central features boil down to the romance between Matías (Fernando Fernán-Gómez) and Nieves (Conchita Montes) and Nieves's quest to free her father Nemesio who has been wrongly accused of the crime. Unlike *The Tower of the Seven Hunchbacks* and *The Bordadores Street Murder*, the action of *Carnival Sunday* is specifically dated. The fact, however, that the film is set in 1917 is, like historical event in the other movies discussed here, a mere detail that is easy to overlook. It is very much a side-on view of current affairs, one picked up in occasional gossipy references by night-watchmen to the crisis befalling the Dato government.[14] Nonetheless, this helps locate and clarify the way in which history and everyday life are manufactured in the earlier films.

Tzvetan Todorov's pathbreaking essay on detective fiction draws attention to the double function of the genre when he comments on the way in which the 'classic' whodunit generally depicts two stories; that of the crime itself as well as the following investigation. According to Todorov – and this is relevant to all three films discussed in this chapter – of these two stories 'one is absent but real, the other present but insignificant' (Todorov, 1977: 46). These observations provide an explanation of how a formula-type narrative structure can be turned into something very different. Although I will return to this point later, it is worth considering that all three of these films end in 'classic' comic style with a family or romantic reconciliation while also being detective stories. The generic formula and its doubles not only provide necessary recipes for popular success but also the grounds for their own subversion. The fluidity of this text is perhaps symbolized in the Spanish word *narices* (noses). 'Narices' are the carnival noses sold by Nieves's friend Mariana (Mariana Larrabeiti) in the market place but it is a word with many different usages. When Matías, a temporary replacement for the real police superintendent who is on holiday, begins to doubt Nemesio's guilt he says: 'There was a well-founded suspicion', Nieves retorts, 'There were *narices*' (nonsense). When the rake of the movie, Gonzalo (Guillermo Marín), asks Matías about Nieves's role in the investigation, he says rhetorically: 'Is she my assistant?' Nieves leaps in ahead of him tartly to say: 'I am his *narices*'. There are two richly contradictory interpretations of this latter use of the word. *Narices* has a dual function, consisting of Nieves's disavowal of any association with the policeman while insisting that she is his 'nose', the one who will do the investigating, the snooping. Like Bhabha's metonym, Nieves plays a shadow to Matías's substitute. Linked to this are the carnivalesque noses in the bustling street and the romantic possibilities of carnival. Bakhtin notes that – as is the case in Spanish – the nose is a traditional bye-word for the male genitals: '*Ad formam nasi cognoscitur ad te levavi*, by the shape of my nose you will know [how] I lift up' (Bakhtin, 1984: 86). This, rather than explicit eroticism, carnivalizes Nieves's position in the film. Nieves goes from being Matías's 'narices' (not only his nose but also his balls) to a resolution at the end of the film which involves carnivalesque mask and cross-dressing. Significantly, the final scenes of the film see Nieves disguised as Spain's most archetypal erotic male myth, don Juan Tenorio.

Matías's introduction to the crowd and the street is Rabelaisian when he spies on Nemesio in the Rastro. Indeed, Nemesio's sales pitch could be lifted directly from Bakhtin's book on Rabelais. Bakhtin writes:

> The man who is speaking is one with the crowd; he does not present himself as its opponent, nor does he teach, accuse, or intimidate it. He *laughs* with it. There is not the slightest tone of morose seriousness in his oration, no fear, piety, or humility. This is an absolutely gay and fearless talk, free and frank, which echoes in the festive square beyond all verbal prohibitions, limitations, and conventions. (1984: 167)

Bakhtin links the cries of the sales pitch to the regeneration of the body, often connected to halting physical decline and particularly with the sale of magical remedies to cure impotence and tooth ache. Nemesio sells some quack unction for tooth ache, which he markets with the prop of a jaw bone that he cajoles and barks at as if it were alive. This too links to 'narices' as Nemesio, jokingly chides a small boy who comes too close and who is actually picking his nose at the time. The market stall performance also depends on hyperbole, on over-the-top tumbling banter that – as in Bakhtin's description – involves close physical inter- action with the crowd in a way that connects the body and its fluids to the meager economy which governs the lives of the traders and their on-screen public.

In the very first sequence of the film, performance as production of the urban economy sets the tone for the rest of the film when two nightwatchmen meet in the street and exchange comments with the young newspaper seller. The newspaper boy is wearing a mask so, once work is over, he can 'play jokes on people. Uh! Who am I? Who am I?' Here the urban economy is linked – as it is throughout the film – to carnivalesque plays on identity. As was the case in *The Bordadores Street Murder* fictional strategy and economic hardship coexist, the one emerging from the other in a similar kind of articulation to that previously discussed.

This is captured in terms of the language spoken by the characters. While the nightwatchmen talk in Galician accents,[15] the local residents speak in the rhythmic and rhyming dialect of Lavapiés; they combine slick sales talk with the adoption of slightly pompous 'literary' rhetoric that undoes their real pretensions and almost always works against them. This is something that occurs particularly with the male characters such as Requena, the neighborhood gossip. Requena, a fan of detective literature – Nick Carter is one of his favorites – lands Nemesio in trouble in his overzealous desire to assist the policeman and is consequently banished from the community collective. Nemesio erroneously implicates himself in the murder with a slip of the tongue and unconvincingly excuses himself by drawing attention to the artificial nature of his own language: 'It was a literary phrase, a piece of rhetoric as they say'. Their labored efforts with language contrasts with the women's dexterity. As in the earlier discussion of Mihura's *The Way of Babel*, there is greater tactical employment of language by the women; they are better at verbal manipulation, in the use of *double entendre* (as in the word *narices*) for example, or the self-reflexive awareness of carnival insignia in the stallholders' sales patter. What we see is the same kind of doubling that we have seen in the other two films, in which the different uses of language undermine rigorous opposition between formal and informal utterance. The rational tone of the policeman's official speech is modified by his romantic pursuit of Nieves and her flirtatious plainspeaking: 'Well, you are an idiot,' she mocks each time Matías's solemnity results in even greater absurdity. The performative artifice of language is no less nor more artificial in the efforts of authority figures to shape formal and rational structures around everyday language than it is in the abundance of sales patter and linguistic playfulness that emerges in the street market.

The use of language in the film is symptomatic of what constitutes a wholesale collapse of the opposition between masquerade and authenticity, aptly in the context of carnival. The entire cast is drawn into the confusion of identities. A large number of the characters are in fact professional performers (the market salesfolk) but even among those who are not identities are blurred amid the play acting and the adoption of fictional strategies.

As we have already seen, the prosaic Matías quite literally performs the role of the police superintendent as a stand-in substitute. Early on in the film, at the very moment the murder is reported at the police station, we see an instance of quite literal play acting when the real superintendent, moments prior to his departure on holiday, talks Matías through a rehearsal of an interrogation as if he were a film or stage director.

Nieves's friend and accomplice Julia (Julia Lajos) sells clothes and costumes in the market. Her clothes serve a real purpose (that is to say, carnival) and a metaphorical one. When Matías and his new-found side kick, Requena, wander through the Rastro, Julia declaims loudly, 'Guises for a grass!'. Requena is an actor in search of a role, a blank signifier subject to a referent. Such is his lack of identity that he does not even possess a fictional name. He is played by the actor Manuel Requena. For a film concerned with carnivalesque transformation, it is noticeable that several of the characters retain their real names as actors (Julia, Julia Lajos; Mariana, Mariana Larrabeiti; Requena, Manuel Requena) while others are known by their associative, metynomic aliases or nicknames as in *The Tower of the Seven Hunchbacks*. This use of types or ciphers undermines the individualization of agency; agency becomes collectivized, emerges as communal identification with the neighborhood – in the speech modes, the curses, the market banter – and is closely connected to the blossoming play of identities.

Some of the central features of the film are those played out at the Masked Dance.[16] These sequences are bolstered by the structure of bodily laughter that billows around – and is often contrary to – the linear plot marked out by the police investigation. Laughter, in Bakhtinian terms, is one of the principle aspects of the film. The events that take place at the Masked Dance condense this idea. The drunkenness of Julia in these scenes is a vindication of 'the right to laughter and gay parody' which according to Bakhtin is 'opposed [...] to the gloomy calumniators, to the enemies of free humour' (1984: 178). Julia's ribaldry and raucousness is directly connected to that of identity, the unmasking of identity and laughter. While the masked Julia teases the outraged and unmasked local authorities present at the dance, Nieves is unmasked by Matías who is dressed – in the style of painter José Gutiérrez Solana – as Death, as the Grim Reaper. Carnival, as we have already seen, has much to do with laughing at death.

Likewise, it is apt that Matías's identity should be revealed by the ring he is wearing. His detective-like obsession with clues, which undoes him at every turn, in this instance unmasks him in the eyes of Nieves. The flow of action from Julia to her well-to-do victims and from them to Nieves and Matías suggests that laughter itself can become a site of contestation, a mask adopted in order to unmask. The mask, of course, is also a form of double, a representation of something else beneath the surface. And in the same vein, as we have seen in the previous chapter, carnival is a kind of 'second life' (Bakhtin, 1984: 9).

Julia is, moreover, yet another personification of the lower bodily stratum; there are abundant references to her fatness. 'I like thin women,' says one of the victims of her jokes. She takes immense pleasure in drinking and laughter and implicitly connects the two activities with the confusión of gender. She plays a female Falstaff to Nieves's parodic Prince Hal. 'What shall we do?' asks Nieves, to which Julia responds, 'Laugh and have as good a time as is posible, and drink a lot. If they see that we are tipsy they will loosen their tongues'. At the end of the film, in San Isidro's Meadow where the carnival finale takes place, Julia takes to wearing a false moustache 'to trick them, so that they think I am a man'. As in *Life on a Thread*, Julia and Nieves together form a comic alliance, feigning aunt and niece, fat and thin, Sancho and Quixote as part of the lengthy tradition of comic couples in international popular culture. As with all comic couples, what is presented as dichotomy, due to physical or performative difference, breaks down into alliance.

The Masked Dance is one of the highpoints of the carnivalesque scenes in this film. It is the crescendo of what has hitherto been gradually building up. The jokes, the games, the playful quality of the reiterative chorus of children that dance through the streets of the Rastro recall Bakhtin's comment on the relation of these elements 'to time and to the future' (1984: 235) as mentioned earlier in the discussion of *The Tower of the Seven Hunchbacks*. Carnival disturbs the generation gap. The neighborhood children prove valuable allies of the adult protagonists of the film. In Julia's first appearance in the film we see her scolding a masked child for having stolen a jacket from her market stall. Later though she arrives at the masked ball thanks to the information provided for her by the same boy, to whom she has promised to reward with a devil's suit 'to wear all year round'.[17] There are shades of Bakhtinian utopianism in this. For Bakhtin, just as death is a serious laughing matter, in popular culture the devil 'is the gay ambivalent figure expressing the unofficial point of view, the material bodily stratum. There is nothing terrifying or alien in him' (1984: 41).

Requena and Gonzalo are the two people in the film who do not don costume at any moment. These two characters are apparent opposites – the most honest and the most mendacious – whose opposition is collapsed by the flux around them. Although neither wear costume they are just as parodic as those who do; both are types who draw attention to their typology. Gonzalo is a libertine and a womanizer. In an autobiographical twist that further blurs the fiction/reality dichotomy, Gonzalo lives at Calle Trujillos no 7, Edgar Neville's real-life address (Lozano, 1997: 139). Requena, meanwhile, plays the fat, nonplussed Bakhtinian fool, a representative of the lower bodily strata: all stomach and brillcream. In these two characters what we see is not the fact that they do not wear costume but that they do: they live their costumes outside the temporal boundaries of carnival. Just as Julia and Nieves's child-spy desires a devil's costume 'for all year round', these two characters breach the artificial structure of the three days of carnival, offering a taste of the utopian ambivalence of carnival of which Bakhtin speaks. Their carnivalesque roles are more subversive for being permanent. They are types carnivalized for the whole year, their marginalization is their most recognizable aspect. Here the collapse between carnival and the other 362 days of the year reaches its most acute point. But this can be taken further if carnival collapses the distinctions between verisimilitude and artificiality, between 'truth' and 'masquerade', then it also undermines the division between the two strains of narrative, the detective tale and the apparently shapeless text of everyday life in the marketplace.

The final sequences of the film, the action of which takes place in the course of the 'Burial of the Sardine' on San Isidro's Meadow – the traditional symbolic ending of the Madrid carnival celebrations – are strikingly similar to Bakhtin's descriptions. For Bakhtin 'downward movement' is connected to the celebration of bodily functions, the belly and transformation. Descent is both earthy and bodily. The burial of the sardine is symbolic of the victory of Lady Lent over Lord Carnival.[18] In this sequence all the carnivalesque emblems come together. As if to recall the function of 'noses' throughout the film, the musicians of the band wear snouts, the identity of the murderers is revealed, there is a burlesque brawl, which involves a drum being pushed 'downwards' over the head of one of the assassins and Nieves – who has been captured, dressed up as the sardine and is on the point of being buried alive – is rescued and 'resuscitated'. Bakhtin writes:

> We see the downward movement in fights, beatings, and blows; they throw the adversary to the ground, trample him into the earth. They bury their victim. But at the same time they are creative; they sow and harvest. (1984: 370)

This final sequence is connected directly to a series of earlier incidents at the Masked Ball. Gonzalo leaps 'downwards' from the box onto the dancefloor in his eagerness to seduce the masked Nieves; Matías dressed as death symbolizes descent; Julia moves downstairs in pursuit of the stuffy members of the bourgeoisie. Bakhtin talks of 'the grotesque swing, which brings together heaven and earth' (1984: 371) and in these two moments – the Masked Ball and the Burial of the Sardine – we see interplay between those in the elevated boxes and the dancefloor, movement *up* the hill on San Isidro's Meadow and *downward* action on the part of the characters (this is of course reminiscent of *The Tower of the Seven Hunchbacks* with its tower that extends *downwards*). Here, just as nothing is absolute ever, metaphor is not absolute; downward movement is often quite literal. Again Bakhtin identifies this succinctly in Rabelais and writes,

> Down, inside out, vice-versa, upside down, such is the direction of all these movements. All of them thrust down, turn over, push head first, transfer top to bottom, and bottom to top, both in the literal sense of space, and in the metaphorical meaning of the image. (1984: 370)

This blurring of the division between the metaphoric and the literal is connected to what I described earlier as the collapse between 'masquerade' and 'authenticity'. But it is also relevant to the confusion of genre between plot and performance, between detective story and popular comedy. Once more this concerns configurations of space and time.

Nieves works at a clock stall in the Rastro where none of the clocks work; real time disperses in the utopian spirit of carnival. The two nights between Sunday and Tuesday are faithfully represented in the film. Yet the effect of time passing goes practically unperceived owing to the fact that the night time sequences are almost always shot indoors. Outside, the daylight scenes are densely populated by dancers, seething crowds, the throbbing, rhythmic sounds of the marketplace, indifferent to the passage of time. Almost all the touchstones/clues that Matías focuses upon prove to be false leads that serve to expose him rather than assisting in the investigation. Just as there is social disruption, there is also narrative disruption. The neatness of the plot construction becomes ragged amid the confusion of identity, time and space. The detective's clues do not have the least bearing on the development of the narrative, but they do influence its complexion. These clues are incidental, anecdotal; they serve as pointers within an ambivalent space.

Many of the street scenes and the activities within *Carnival Sunday* capture this sense of ambivalence. Invariably, as we have seen on many occasions, the raw combinatory material of popular articulation involves music, dressing up or eating. If any dish symbolizes communal eating it is *cocido madrileño*, the emblematic Madrid stew referred to on several occasions in the course of the film, which comes to possess a very particular feel within the context of the neighborhood collectivity. Its symbolism is to be found in the hotchpotch of different ingredients, apparently thrown in at random, of which it consists. It is also a metonymic dish; its name indelibly associates it with the city of Madrid. And yet it is in this association that its ambivalence lies. If a composite product like *cocido madrileño* has been employed with iconic force as a populist symbol of 'typical' Madrid, it remains nonetheless a real dish, eaten and enjoyed by real people, that exceeds the aura of construction that surrounds it.

This can be extended from *cocido* to historical and pictorial representation. The function of painting in *Carnival Sunday* is illustrative. The influence of José Gutiérrez Solana, Francisco de Goya and the black pictorial tradition on the film has attracted the attention of the critics. Neville made use of both painters' work and Solana actually visited the film set, before his death shortly prior to its release. Solana's carnival series provides the template for almost all the costumes and masked characters that populate the streets and cluster around the two major carnivalesque sequences.[19] And Neville drew upon two Goya paintings: *San Isidro's Meadow* (1788) and *The Burial of the Sardine* (1812–1819), both of which are reproduced as *mise en scène* within the film.

Marsha Kinder has dwelt in detail upon the Spanish 'Black Legend' in the context of the influence of Goya upon Spanish cinema, together with the 'black' pictorial tradition to which it is commonly linked. Solana is particularly associated with this tradition, owing to his book *Black Spain* (1920), and many of his paintings conform to the murky, sinister and primitive Spain that has exercised so many hispanists. It is interesting then that the Goya painting that supplies the final panoramic take of the film (*San Isidro's Meadow*[20]) belongs to this painter's white period. Neville by situating his movie in the most Spanish of contexts, that of central Madrid, once more both disturbs claims to generic rigidity and disrupts the 'national' pictorial canon by fudging the back and white traditions.

The combination of borrowings helps to rupture the notion of untroubled linear pictorial history in much the same way as the Rastro and *cocido madrileño* provide promiscuous rehashing of previously categorized items. Manufactured tradition is subverted; rigid time-bound enclosure is turned inside-out in all its aspects, whether in terms of traditional historical knowledge, pictorial tradition or literary genre. Between Solana and Goya there is a welter of difference. In purely cinematographic terms Goya provides the long shot of the city on the horizon and Solana the close ups, the grotesque detail and the dress. But they are also very different painters, the differences between whom inflect the very nature of constructed tradition.

Bakhtin has this to say about masks: 'The mask is connected with the joy of change and reincarnation, with gay relativity and with the merry negation of uniformity and similarity' (1984: 39). The interrogation of absolute truths is crucial to Bakhtin. If the sum total of clues in the detective's narrative constitutes the articulating structure of hegemonic relations, then the city of Madrid provides the terrain where manufactured tradition and popular practices converge.

It is when such gaps emerge in the consensus surrounding national discourse that stereotypes, such as 'black legend', 'black Spain' or, as we shall see, 'black comedy' prove vulnerable to subaltern intervention. The locus of factors that cluster around the 'national' stereotype both destabilizes the intended fixity of the stereotype itself and has repercussions that inflect and refract other perspectives. This is something to be engaged with in the following discussion of the filmmaker who has provoked the least critical consensus on precisely this issue, Luis García Berlanga.

4
Populism, the National-Popular and the Politics of Luis García Berlanga: *Welcome Mister Marshall!* (1952)

> Berlanga's cinema reveals a conservative character – José Enrique Monterde.
>
> – Cañique and Grau, 1993: 275

The cinema of Luis García Berlanga presents a problem. Berlanga, who announced his retirement in 1999 after the release of his latest film *Paris-Timbuktu*, is a constant disruptive presence in Spanish culture of the second half of the 20th century. If Buñuel has been an historical and aesthetic benchmark for critics of Spanish cinema and if the marketing of Pedro Almodóvar has provided its international launching pad, the attention paid to Berlanga has faced problems intimately related to the politics of national identity. His lack of success outside of Spain has frequently been attributed to some sort of untranslatable, intrinsic Spanishness. Since the death of Franco he has been the subject of several books in Spanish which have all tended to follow the same format: a lengthy and highly entertaining interview with the director, followed by synopses of all his films. In this vein there has been a successful endeavor to construct a *persona* called Luis García Berlanga that has very little to do with his cinema: Berlanga the eroticist, the professional *valenciano*, the (safely) apolitical anarchist, friend to Falangists and Communists alike; Berlanga the raconteur, the compulsive liar, the mercurial doubter.

While largely ignored outside Spain, there has been a consistent attempt to create an auteur theory around Berlanga within the national pantheon, remarkable in itself as Berlanga, while possessing his own distinctive style, is one of those directors who more than any other resists such classification. It is, however, no coincidence that the revival of interest in Berlanga has occurred since the death of Franco. There is a clear political interest in appropriating Berlanga for the purposes of politics, an attempt to reclaim him as a representative of native tradition in the form of that generation who, while resisting, neither went into exile nor emerged after the end of the dictatorship. A tradition that connects the Second Republic with the post-1975 period.

This confusion surrounding Berlanga is further complicated by foreigners who have written on his work. If the emphasis in Spanish texts has been to identify him as an *auteur*, a lone representative of 'Spanishness' incarnate, the very occasional mentions from outside Spain have tended to see him as an example of Spanish neorealism (Hopewell, 1986: 48–50; Kinder, 1993: 39), located within a dialogue mid-way between Italian and Hollywood cinema of the 1950s. While there is some truth to these claims, this is an approach that seems to me to be highly unsatisfactory, if only because I think that Berlanga is the most important, most influential and the most complex of Spanish filmmakers.

The problem with Berlanga, and the source of his complexity, I believe, revolves around a notion of the popular. What is constant in Berlanga's work – from *Esa pareja feliz* (*That Happy Couple*, 1951) to *Paris-Timbuktu* (1999) – is his drawing upon popular traditions and practices: the fairground, the fiesta, the lottery, the radio, and the crowd. Coupled with this concern for localized custom is an undeniable foreign influence, from Buster Keaton to René Claire, Capra and Pudovkin to de Sica and Fellini. To a certain extent Berlanga mediates elitist concepts of film by its *use* at a popular level. It is precisely this fidelity to a peculiar vision of popular comedy that never ends well that has confused critics of Berlanga. Although a filmmaker of the 'popular', he has never, prior to 1979, been *popular* at the box office (with the exception of *Welcome Mister Marshall!* (Figure 7)). He has been the subject of fierce debate emanating from both the left and the right (attacked and claimed by both) and, in a very similar way to the ambiguous endings of all his films, the political consensus surrounding Berlanga the *persona* produces a disjunction over detailed analysis of his work: there is little consensus on whether his cinema is subversive or not.

To my mind Berlanga is to be located at a slippery juncture somewhere between popular culture and cultural populism. His work – like that of Fellini, the director with whom he has been most closely been identified (and rightly so, both directors have consistently eluded the categorizations to which they have been subject) – both conforms to a caricature of the Mediterranean while creating an ambiguous critique of Mediterranean *alegría*. Berlanga has been inextricably linked to a discourse on Spanishness

Figure 7 Manolo Morán in *Welcome Mister Marshall!* (Courtesy of Video Mercury Films, S.A. and Filmoteca Española)

whilst remaining its most vigorous critic. Much of this critique revolves around Berlanga's (and Fellini's) particular vision of the grotesque and the body. While the attempts to make an auteur theory of Berlanga's work conform to a populist operation, he himself is a sort of populist, one who connects to a very real popular feeling, who perceives the dislocations and departures of everyday living from the constructed sociological model.

Connected to this is the commonplace description of Berlanga as a satirist. Once more Berlanga poses a problem for the formulation. Just what is Berlanga satirizing? Satire tends to assume an object which I believe is difficult to identify in the work of Berlanga. One of the most distinctive features of Berlanga's work is its much remarked upon choral quality that connects national tradition with subaltern practices and tactics. The chorus in Berlanga is always cacophonic, never harmonious. Berlanga might not have objects of attack yet a stream of elements much cherished by authority come off badly amid the discord of the popular ongoing in his films, from the institution and constitution of marriage and the family to the state itself. To this end, the objective of this chapter is to discuss and develop a theory of film comedy within which Berlanga can be located and thenceforth examine how the cinema of Berlanga acts subversively upon the nation-state.

Towards the end of the previous chapter, I briefly mentioned 'black comedy' as a term frequently employed in the 'national' discourse of Spain. Spanish critics have often sought to explain both the unfathomable bleakness of Berlanga and his unfathomable Spanishness precisely by recourse to the stock epithet 'black comedy'. With an easy flourish thus he is located within a tradition of Black Legend, packaged with *esperpento* and connected to Valle Inclán. Santos Zunzunegui is representative of this thinking when he urges North American critics to pay more attention to *esperpento* and states:

> I think that the richest and most creative seam of Spanish cinema concerns [...] the way in which certain cineastes and films inherit, assimilate, transform and revitalize a series of aesthetic forms that have been historically expressed in the Spanish community. (1999: 100)

Although *esperpento* is indeed the narrative component that most keenly loops into Berlanga's finest work, it is also the case, in my view, that what he subjects to interrogation is precisely the 'Spanish community' for which Zunzunegui claims him. This kind of categorization, furthermore, serves mainly to obfuscate real understanding of the films and their director, although it ties in neatly with the idea of the nominative function of discourse (de Certeau 1975: 247) as absorbing and appropriating subversion by a process of naming and labeling.

One of the more interesting commentators on the work of Berlanga is José Enrique Monterde. In a lengthy interview (Cañique and Grau, 1993: 263–293), Monterde adroitly demonstrates Berlanga's relationship with his cinematic and literary antecedents and is acute in his comments on the director's technical innovations, but is unconvincing in his account of the politics of the films. In his discussion of the differences between Berlanga and his earliest collaborator and long-term Communist Party member, Juan Antonio Bardem, Monterde comes very close to identifying several key points concerning the cultural politics of Berlanga's work but is limited by the consensus in which he himself works in which ideology is limited to party political affiliation. One of my objectives here is to challenge this kind of identificatory process. Such a consensus, moreover, goes beyond 'party politics' in Monterde and manifests itself in conventional canonical definitions. His telling dismissal of the possibility of the grotesque in Berlanga depends on a discursive classification whose parameters are clearly defined: 'The grotesque is more superficial than *esperpento* because it has to do much more with an image than a structured situation' (Cañique and Grau, 1993: 280). Bakhtin's theorization of the grotesque suggests that such assertions are tendentious.

Both these critics and Kinder employ terms such as 'black comedy', *esperpento* and 'satire' while ignoring the popular tradition within which Berlanga works. They are defining elements used in relation to a literary canon. The 'popular' is subversive precisely because of its ability to weave its operations within existing power structures. Simply locating Berlanga as the latest in a line that stretches from Francisco de Quevedo to Carlos Arniches avoids having to interrogate the complex relationship with the state that Berlanga himself has maintained in his films and life.

de Certeau has detailed the ways in which 'multiform and fragmentary' popular operations insinuate themselves within the crevices of 'ideologies or institutions' which are not their own by 'making use' of what is available to them:

> From the Greeks to Durkheim, a long tradition has sought to describe with precision the complex (and not at all simple or 'impoverished') rules that could account for these operations. From this point of view 'popular culture', as well as a whole literature called 'popular'

[...] present themselves essentially as 'arts of making' this or that, i.e. as combinatory or utilizing modes of consumption. These practices bring into play a 'popular' ratio, a way of thinking invested in a way of acting, an art of combination which cannot be dissociated from an art of using. (de Certeau, 1984: xv)

Once more, this connects with a contested and fluctuating view of the Spanish stereotype. If Gramsci contextualizes the politics of culture, the pertinence of de Certeau and Bakhtin lies in the detail. My intention, in using these thinkers, is not just to qualify the work of critics such as Monterde but to raise questions about the nature of 'populism' itself – a tradition which persists to this day in Spanish politics – in the context of the nation.

When Gramsci writes about the 'humus of popular culture' (1985: 102) it is with regard to a political project, not a celebration *per se*. In fact he says that 'to refer to common sense as a confirmation of truth is a nonsense' (1971: 423):

Every social stratum has its own 'common sense' and its own 'good sense', which are basically the most widespread conception of life and of man. Every philosophical current leaves behind a sedimentation of 'common sense': this is the document of its historical effectiveness. Common sense is not something rigid and immobile, but is continually transforming itself, enriching itself with scientific ideas and with philosophical opinions which have entered ordinary life. 'Common sense' is the folklore of philosophy, and is always half-way between folklore properly speaking and the philosophy, science, and economics of the specialists. Common sense creates the folklore of the future, that is as a relatively rigid phase of popular knowledge at a given place and time. (Gramsci, 1971: 326 n5)

Welcome Mister Marshall! (1952)

In a timely, albeit purely anecdotal, coincidence, the recently elected President of the United States of America, George W. Bush, commenced his maiden tour of Europe in 2001 with a visit to Spain, arriving on 12th June, Berlanga's 80th birthday. That evening at a public function in Madrid the coincidence was wryly remarked upon by the film director himself. In a further twist that recalls the final sequences of *Welcome Mister Marshall!*, Berlanga added, the presidential cavalcade had sped past his home in the Madrid suburb of Somosaguas on

its way to the King Juan Carlos's residence in the nearby Zarzuela
Palace.

Welcome Mister Marshall! (1952), the first full-length film that Berlanga
directed alone – and probably his most celebrated – is much more than
the dialogue between Hollywood and Italian neorealism that it has
been portrayed as. Its critical reception and its consequent status in the
Spanish filmic canon mark it out as a singular piece of cinema. Fifty
years after it was made, it can be seen today – in terms that suggest
temporal and spatial disturbance – as a movie that really did alter the
cultural map of Spain. While Wendy Rolph observes that it has achieved
the status of 'comedy classic' (1999: 9) such a status is an uncomfortable
one. Although not, by any means, his best movie, it is undoubtedly the
Berlanga film that has attracted most attention both at home and
abroad, one that has insinuated itself into the cinema mainstream.

Originally conceived of as a vehicle for budding teenage flamenco
singer Lola Sevilla, for which Berlanga was commissioned, *Welcome
Mister Marshall!* unravells into a parody of Francoist mythmaking, most
strikingly involving the manufacture of Andalusia in a Castilian village.
John Hopewell suggestively compares this transformation to the
cardboard props of a film set (1986: 49). Monterde, meanwhile, who
acutely locates the film's relationship with the tradition of Andalusian
film musical, seems theoretically ill-equipped to adequately explain
parody. Monterde's view – like Rolph's – is upon the classification and
confirmation of the film as a 'classic'. It is a defence of the literary/filmic
pantheon offered at the expense of any evaluation of its subversive
quality. Augusto M. Torres takes Monterde's and Rolph's positions to
their logical conclusion to deny the film any capacity for parody. In his
dictionary of Spanish cinema he comments: 'This parable about Spain's
relationship to the Marshall Plan hides a clear message which states that
the only way to prosper is to work' (1996: 114). Apart from the fact that
this is exactly what it does not reveal, the interpretation is nonetheless
interesting. Torres attaches greater importance to the words spoken
(and particularly those of its narrator) than to the action of the film. To
my mind the subversive energy of this film is produced and consolidated
precisely in this disjunction.

It is commonly accepted that there are different times, chronological,
cyclical, rural and urban. Likewise, there are different spaces marked by
distance, volume, shape, pattern and direction, as well as rural and
urban spaces. Although all narrative is constituted by this relation
between time and space, cinema is the medium that enables its greatest
manipulation. '[D]iscourse' writes de Certeau, referring specifically to

cinematic diegesis, ' "advances" at different speeds, slowing down or rushing ahead. By means of this referential time, it can condense or stretch its own time, produce effects of meaning, redistribute and codify the uniformity of flying time' (1988: 88).

Bakhtin's much earlier writings on the relationship of space and time – the chronotope – in narrative also provide a useful instrument for cultural criticism:

> In the literary artistic chronotope, spatial and temporal indicators are fused into one carefully thought-out, concrete whole. Time, as it were, thickens takes on flesh, becomes artistically visible; likewise space becomes charged and responsive to the movements of time, plot and history. This intersection of axes and fusion of indicators characterizes the artistic chronotope. (1996: 84)

One of the interesting features of *Welcome Mister Marshall!* is the relationship between its formal structure and the operations acted out by its characters within the very same structure. At the beginning of the film, its location, the Castilian Villar del Río, possesses a 'timeless' quality. It is noteworthy that Villar del Río is self-consciously bound in by space and is constantly mistaken, as we will see, for its rival Villar del Campo. Given that much of *Welcome Mister Marshall!* arguably concerns the fabrication and the fetishization of an exotic Andalusian other, it is perhaps apt in this context that Edward Said in his book *Orientalism* should suggest that while the western view of the Orient depends upon a 'static system of "synchronic essentialism" ', such a view is disrupted by narrative (1995: 240). In this vein, and connected to the film's parody of nation-building myths, the Roland Barthes of 1957 observes that 'myth is constituted by the loss of the historical quality of things: in it, things lose the memory that they once were made' (Barthes, 1973: 142).

Villar del Río's myth-like aura is established by the film's narrator, played by the well-known actor Fernando Rey, who describes the village in terms of a place where nothing happens, nobody visits, nobody goes away and that is how things have been since time immemorial.[1] According to Rey's voice-over, Villar del Río is a place of temporal stasis; immobile and permanent space. The two centripetal structural features of *Welcome Mister Marshall!* are the narration and the location of the village square in Villar del Río. It is also a film very clearly divided into formal episodes. In the introduction we hear Rey's voice as the village bus arrives in the square of Villar del Río. This despotic narrator intervenes in the sequence of events by calling a halt to the on-screen action, removing or freezing characters within the frame so as to have more *space* to explain the topology of the village to the viewer. Notions of time and space are, thus, already being distorted in the stopping, starting and screen alterations. The square, we are told, is the center of village life. Rey's travelogue-style delivery draws attention to the symbols of time and of space. The clock tower in the town hall possesses a clock that has not worked for as long as anyone can remember. The village schoolroom is adorned with a map so old that it still represents 'The Austro-Hungarian Empire'.[2] Even the indeterminate age of the church is stressed along with the dubious nature of its historical value: 'It dates back exactly to the year three hundred and ... Well, the fact is it is very, very old and the experts say that it has great merit. I suppose they know why,' says Rey. Although this is 'a typical village' populated by stock characters – the barber, the priest, the doctor, the school teacher, the tenant farmer, the mayor, the squire, the gaggle of village gossips – there is also a clear historical charge running through its space. The square becomes the 'place' converted into 'space' by the movement of the population. Just as the village topology is historically marked – with contemptuous imprecision – so too are the characters which populate it. Jenaro the bus driver is introduced in serf-like terms as a commoditiy – a possession of the mayor, don Pablo (José Isbert) – yet only seconds previously we have been informed he learned to drive 'in the war' while serving in a tank division.

These ambiguous lapses in the disembodied narrator's description of the social structure are suggestively wry, especially since the terms he employs most frequently to describe the village and its inhabitants in this prologue is 'typical'. They point up the glibness of the narration's own discourse. The figure of the narrator has proved important to those critics who detect a conservative stance in the film and deny the irony in Rey's delivery.

Undercutting the authority of the presumed all-knowing narrator are the events in the film. The film's prologue comes to an abrupt end when the camera rises above the village and we hear the narrator change tone and say: 'It is morning, almost eleven o'clock. Spring. Everything is going well or, rather, neither well nor badly, like any other typical day. But today ...'. At this point the vertically rising crane shot – establishing, in panorama, the 'space-bound' qualities of the village with its citizens diminished beneath the rooftops – in perfect panoptic harmony with the divine-like narrator, ruptures to a series of quick horizontal inserts. We hear the sound of sirens, women washing by the river bank stop work, we see an official car led by police motorcycles speeding along the road.

It is telling that the disjunction between Rey's sanguine delivery and the space-bound panoramic shot of the village should occur simultaneously in a self-conscious contradiction concerning time. The final shot of this sequence contributes to an apparent powerlessness among the population as the camera rises above the roofs to offer us a bird's-eye view of Villar del Río, isolated and bound in by the surrounding mountains.

The arrival of outsiders in this film is significant partly because they are outsiders but also because of who they are. Having been informed by the narrator in literal terms that the villagers themselves are pawns in the routine of everyday life with no significance beyond that of pure mechanical function we are confronted with functionaries of the state who distinguish themselves by their *uniform* way of behaving. In a visual gag reminiscent of early silent film and Vittorio de Sica's *Miracle in Milan* (1951), they march out of their cars towards the town hall in single file against a background of US Civil War bugle and drum roll. Aside from the filmic antecedents already mentioned, the musical accompaniment here recalls western movies and the circus. The drum roll also signifies a sense of 'temporal' foreboding and imminence, a quite literal 'guillotine' effect. These outsiders mark the beginning of the 'time' of the film in a different way to that of the arrival moments earlier of Carmen Vargas (Lola Sevilla) – 'the greatest star of Andalusian song' – and her manager Manolo (Manolo Morán). Carmen and Manolo step from the village bus at a time when Rey's narrative exists outside of time, in prologue. This both emphasizes an atemporal naturalness to their presence in the village and places them mid-way between officialdom and population. They are – like Manolo Morán's character in Mihura's *Castle of Cards* – figures that belong within an in-between zone of operations.

As discussed in Neville's *Life on a Thread*, de Certeau writes of an art of the 'in-between' as practiced by a subaltern figure (his example is a North African immigrant in France) who 'insinuates *into* the system imposed upon him', while retaining his original customs which 'he super-imposes [...] and, by that combination, creates for himself a space in which he can find *ways of using* the constraining order of the place' (1984: 30).

Just as Manolo and Lola are situated mid-way between officialdom and population – because of their outsider status – so too is don Pablo. The mayor is readily identified not only as the village's most important property owner but also as the representative of the 'people' during the 'official' visits of the state functionaries. These three characters constitute the key elements of the chronotope (to return to Bakhtin's term) that establishes the principal differences between villagers and outsiders and undoes the 'static' view of time proposed by the narrator. As will become apparent, their areas of operations are public spaces: the stage in the cafeteria and the village square. The association of these three figures with space – in light of Rey's defining and despotic *travelogue* – is similar to what Bakhtin calls the 'fool's chronotope', in which 'the entire being of characters such as these is [...] utterly on the surface; everything is brought out on to the square, so to speak' (1996: 160).[3] These people operate across and within a cross-class field that has much to do with popular culture; all three are 'populists' who, characteristically of this kind of chronotope, imitate dominant forms.

Jesús Torrecilla has recently criticised *Welcome Mister Marshall!* For reinforcing the Francoist vision of Spain as Andalusia, and for conceding to foreign stereotypes of Spain (2001). This is his fundamental reason for categorizing the film as 'conservative', echoing Monterde's surprisingly simplistic assessment of the ideological implications of the film: 'In *Welcome Mister Marshall!*, what the peasants hope for is not agrarian reform but the Americans' (Cañique and Grau, 1993: 275).

The construction of an artificial Andalusia in a Castilian village recalls the well-worked metonym in which Andalusia stands for Spain as a totality. In his famous essay 'Walking In the City', de Certeau plays on the terms *synecdoche* and *asyndeton* to describe what he calls a grammar of 'pedestrian activity' in ways that help contextualize the film's three main characters:

> Synecdoche expands a spatial element in order to make it play the role of a 'more' (a totality) and take its place [...] Asyndeton, by elision, creates a 'less', opens gaps in the spatial continuum, and retains only selected parts of it that amount almost to relics. (de Certeau, 1984: 101)

In *Welcome Mister Marshall!* the national stereotype is 'made use of' and debated within the interstices of a dazzling number of constellations: the United States and Spain, administrative officialdom and the populace, Andalusia and Castile, the popular and the populist. The imitation referred to earlier is produced within these interstices. Andalusia is mimicked by the Castilians and an imaginary United States is conjured up among the population.

It is both the imaginary USA and the imaginary Spain that has attracted the attention of, and bemused, the critics. The ambivalent field of Spain and North America – in the popular imaginary – is where the disjunction in critical opinion occurs. Kathleen Vernon has drawn attention to a central sequence in this film in which different sets of statistics are debated between the village school mistress, Señorita Eloísa, and don Cosme, the priest (Vernon, 1997: 41). My aim is to further theorize her insights.

Officialdom and state functionaries in this film are repeatedly parodied, as we have seen. It is appropriate, then, that it should be precisely *statistics* that open a breach in the social order of a village that the narrator has adamantly held to be impermeable to change. de Certeau discusses statistics in relation to those in-between spaces within which popular practices surreptitiously operate and which statistics seek and fail to incorporate in their net: 'Statistical investigation grasps the material of these practices, but not their *form*; it determines the elements used, but not the "phrasing" produced by the *bricolage* [...] and the discursiveness that combine these elements' (1984: xviii). Elsewhere, in a brilliantly argued essay, Andrew Ross focuses on the fetishization of numbers in the arsenal of power and makes the important point – apt in this context – that 'the word "statistics" derives from the German for "state", and the origins of this "science" are inseparable from the rise of nation-states' (1998: 152).

Soon after the announcement of the imminent arrival of the Americans the informational session on the USA, offered by Eloísa, degenerates into a clash of opposing values that Gramsci might call two contradictory world views. In response to Eloísa's breathless litany of the wonders of the American economy presented as a geography class before the whole village, don Cosme intervenes both as a heckler and a mimic:

Señorita Eloísa: In reference to the economy, it is of interest to know that the United States is the greatest producer of iron and steel, with 200 tons a year; the greatest producer of oil, with 300 tons a year; the greatest producer of cotton, with 400 tons a year; the greatest producer of lead, with 800 tons a year, the greatest producer of pigs, with 500,000 head a year; the greatest producer of...

Don Cosme:...of sins with millions of tons a year. There are 49 million protestants, 400,000 Indians, 200,000 Chinese, five million Jews, 13 million blacks, and 10 million...eh...nothing.

Interestingly, Eloísa relates these facts in parodic biblical syntax. This is as much a liturgy as a litany. Just as don Cosme imitates Eloísa's lists of numbers, she in turn mimics his Sunday morning sermons. By the same token, just as priests are aided by altar boys, so too Eloísa delivers her statistical sermon with Pepito, the teacher's pet, on his knees beneath the table with a book acting as prompt. What is being debated here is 'knowledge' as the raw material of authority in the village. In this epistemological discourse hesitation is indicative of weakness – of a lack of authority – compared to the unfaltering delivery practiced by the Francoist newsreel reader in the subsequent sequence or, indeed, exemplified in Fernando Rey's narration. This is a central aspect to this film. If Rey, in the prologue to the film, has previously alluded to the importance or lack of importance of 'knowledge' – and likewise Manolo claims a privileged acquaintance with America where he says he once lived – then the authority conveyed by Eloísa and don Cosme helps dispel and disperse the notion of 'knowledge' as a matter of objective fact.

Both the school teacher and the priest are traditional intellectuals in the Gramscian sense of the term.[4] As traditional intellectuals these characters have a 'populist' function. The role of the crowd in this film, as we shall see in due course, is of some significance. In this sequence it is noteworthy that we see the entire population in the schoolroom. Eloísa and Cosme are not educating children, they are fulfilling their function as 'intellectuals'; that is, as mediating figures – in-between – whose role it is to secure popular consent for the projects of dominant groups.

In the course of this debate the relation between space and time that has been touched upon repeatedly by the narrator becomes symbolically and ideologically explicit as a hegemonic instrument. What is significant here is not specifically Cosme's recourse to a traditional 'spiritual' discourse – he says that 'spiritual peace' will be Villar del Río's offering to the sinful and racially contaminated Americans – in counterpoint to Eloísa's material concerns, but that the same terminology links timelessness to the nation's space. Amid the mass of statistics, Cosme celebrates the static: the *Eternal Spain*.

Similarly, it is noticeable that Eloísa should begin her presentation to the villagers by using the map that Fernando Rey has already discredited in his introduction. Using this prop she draws explicit attention to the borders of the USA with Mexico, to the very regions where moments earlier don Luis – the impoverished nobleman who, uniquely among the villagers, repudiates the impending visit – claims his ancestors were eaten by Indians. Thus it is that within the spatial confines of maps and statistics – the very spaces in which consent for such concepts as nations and states is secured – runs the conflictual and shifting passage of time.

The newsreel broadcast (NO-DO) which follows immediately on from the classroom debate and whose tones emanate from the cinema screen provides a third example of statistical 'evidence' in this film.[5] It is also a form of mimicry: the newsreader smoothly follows on from the classroom debate with even more extraordinary statistics, complemented by images of agricultural bounty and gleaming technological advance. The irony here lies in the employment of the fallaciously pre-modern cultural synecdoche of rural Andalusia designed to seduce the visitors from the United States and thereby gain access to the benefits of economic modernity. It is, nonetheless, *ironic*. Such irony is sharpened if we recall de Certeau's observation – which sits well with Ross's comments cited earlier – on the function, the *mass media*: 'Official historiography,' he writes, 'history books, television news reports etc. – [...] tries to make everyone believe in the existence of a national space' (1984: 125).

The ironic national space of *Welcome Mister Marshall!* is one that, in the vein of the chronotope, involves a very real combination – a *bricolage* – of physical space with plays on chronological time. This is particularly the case when officialdom intrudes into the film. These instances are also important in defining the functions of the two figures primarily responsible for mobilizing the village population, José Isbert and Manolo Morán.

Don Pablo's official role as mayor is described in the very first sequence of the film as 'part-time' but it is also clearly spatial: the village is both his operational 'political' space (as mayor) and, in its practical entirety, his *property*. The narrator sketches him in the following laconic terms: 'In spite of his deafness, he is the owner of the boarding house, the café, the bus, of Jenaro, of half the village and *to keep himself amused* [my emphasis] he is the mayor'. It is noteworthy that on neither of the two occasions when the state officials visit Villar del Río is don Pablo present in his office. In both instances, he is sojourning with his rival and ally Manolo. These are moments when 'time', which has been stressed by the narrator in the film's introduction as insignificant to the humdrum 'natural' life of the village and is indeed irrelevant to don Pablo, transpires to be of utmost importance to the bureaucrats. There is, thus, both a disjunction produced in 'official' mythmaking and a reinscription of time by a character lower down in the social scale. The second government official who visits the village complains that he has had to wait for 45 minutes for the mayor to arrive, a point the character played by Isbert dismisses as unimportant. In this sense don Pablo finds himself poised pivotally between the subaltern peasantry to whom he is supposed to administer and the official bureaucracy upon which his position depends. Static 'time', meanwhile, is exposed as a tool to be employed and distributed tactically between competing conduits in the hypothetical chain of command between the state and its 'people'. At each stage, room becomes available for more and more improvisation.

It is clear from the very structure of *Welcome Mister Marshall!* that real, chronological time has major significance. The 'real' time that lapses between the announcement of the imminent arrival of the Americans and their swift, dusty passage through the village is three days, a fact that impels the villagers to organize their preparations.

Time in relation with space (national space, village space, official space) is connected suggestively to other facets of don Pablo's behavior. Rey emphasizes the mayor's deafness as one of his distinctive character-istics, that which defines him. It is also a subtle weapon of maneuver in his armory. His deafness is selective and tactical. Just as don Pablo makes use of time in his functions as an intermediary between the village population and the state officialdom, it is within the same field that he employs other tactics and deafness provides a clear example. He plays deaf, for instance, as a parody of the Ministerial *director general* – himself an emissary of government – and does so to subversive effect; he mimics his superior. Don Pablo hears everything and feigns deafness when it suits him; it is the *director general* who does not hear, who is oblivious to the obvious, persistently and insensitively confusing Villar del Río with its rival neighbor, Villar del Campo. Deafness links to an earlier pre-modern culture of the ear and mouth (the stammering, oral hesitancy of the villagers contrasts not only with Rey's fluency but also with his – and the camera's – *all-seeing* panopticism), thus undermining 'the visual', a central metaphor for modern bourgeois culture from the 18th century onwards.[6] Indeed, this relates directly to the movie's interrogation of empirical knowledge in the context of nation building and modernity. The statistical debate between Cosme and Eloísa can, thus, be further theorized and approximated to Ross's observations as mentioned earlier.

In a sequence clearly influenced by de Sica's *Miracle in Milan* the inhabitants of Villar del Río queue up before the community leadership to list the gifts they require of the Americans.[7] This is the only moment in the film when the population itself is referred to numerically (there are 1642 inhabitants). The interesting thing here is that the very moment when they are referred to *statistically* as a numerical totality, thereby included in the census and incorporated within the dominant group's classificatory system of surveillance, is precisely the point in the film when they express desire through ellipsis. They doubt, they stutter and, while some solicit goods and tools that are concerned with their work and their farms, many ask for things that have no economic relevance to their daily lives but serve only a ludic purpose. Furthermore, this improvised theater is played out in the communal spatial precinct of the village square.[8] At one moment in the sequence an elderly woman in black shuffles forward and stammers uncomprehendingly, her hand to her ear signifying deafness. Manolo bellows. Rey, god-like, fills in the gaps to inform us that 'Mamá Dolores wants chocolate'. Up to this point in the film, the villagers have constituted a passive audience for the 'intellectuals' or the populist leaders. This is the first moment they are required to act and, like Pablo, Mamá Dolores resorts to a tactic.

This sequence, together with the celebrated dream sequences, – with their multiple references to American (and Soviet) cinema – are those that have attracted most critical comparison with 'other' national cinemas. While many critics tend to leave it at that, my argument is that the interest of this film lies beyond its apparent hybrid mix of neorealism and Hollywood. Statistics, maps, newsreel and the narrator himself have the function of fixing discourse within the film, in much the same way as the classificatory functions of film critics exercise closure off-screen. It is telling, in the action of the movie, that the operations of the village population emerge from the 'traces' or 'relics' of these same discourses. There is a revealing disjunction between Mamá Dolores's adoption of the tactic of silence and the omnipresent, interpretive, allegedly *all-knowing* narrator, mediated by the verbose Manolo Morán. This is a disjunction that marks the *limitations* of dominant notions of space as traversed by subaltern tactical operations.

The dream sequences occur on the eve of the arrival of the Americans in Villar del Río, 'the most important of its history' in Rey's words. All four dreams are densely packed with the piece-meal combinations that litter the film. The idea of swellings and shrinkages (de Certeau, 1984: 101–102) of space and time – chronotope – seems particularly apposite to dreams. Distortion in all dreams is temporal and spatial and, as if to emphasize the point, the characters do not actually move from their beds. In these sequences there is an underlying interplay between movement and stasis that recalls the previous discussion on static time within the space-bound village.

Connected to this is the way each dream functions according to its protagonist's concerns similarly to de Certeau's description of synecdoche as replacing 'totalities by fragments [. . .] Synecdoche makes more dense:

it amplifies the detail and miniaturizes the whole' (1984: 101). Each dream, while making direct reference to the individual's everyday life, condenses their world view. The 'miniaturization of the whole' produces a concentration that gels within the whole film, like the chronotope. The articulations of disparate and syncretic elements – from Hollywood, Italian or Soviet cinema to traditional festive belief (such as Holy Week or The Three Kings) – enables the 'art of being in-between' to take the form of emergent agency.

The occasion for the dreams is also quite literally *in-between*, in the sense that they take place in that space – the night – between the day of the dress rehearsal and the following morning of the Americans' arrival. Hybridity of the dream sequences of *Welcome Mister Marshall!*, moreover, calls into question the basis upon which knowledge is consolidated as authority. Vernon has already demonstrated that there is a direct connection between the dream sequences and the statistical debate discussed earlier between the priest and the schoolteacher (1997: 40–41). I would add that they also reveal an ambiguous, two-way field of appropriation emanating from the colonial influence of North American cinema and interrogate the premises upon which autarchy and national identity are constructed. This process deprives national and international discourse of its 'knowledge', denying essential representation. To illustrate this point, I propose to examine just two of these dreams.[9]

Don Cosme's dream is visually spectacular. Beginning with an Andalusian Holy Week parade, it turns into nightmare as the similarities in dress (robes and pointed hoods) of the Catholic *penitents* and the Ku Klux Klan are explicitly highlighted and we see the letters KKK printed on the backs of the group that leads Cosme in chains. At this point, we hear the single drum beat, distinctive of these occasions, convert into lively jazz. Seville fuses with New Orleans, the Ku Klux Klan with black music. The raw, non-discursive, material of these scenes is clothing and music. In the following scene, we witness a classic *noir* situation when Cosme is interrogated by a group of thugs beneath a single light bulb. This is pure Fritz Lang – both as a Hollywood hard-boiled crime movie maker and in his earlier German Expressionist phase – followed, in turn, by a shot of an inquisitorial-type tribunal with its robed judge, once more heavily influenced by German Expressionism. The further irony of the dream is the analogy between the Catholic Church and the McCarthy period. The high bench which dwarfs the quailing priest carries the inscription: 'COMMITEE OF ANTI-AMERICAN ACTIVITIES'. Overlaying this *visual* 'trial' we *hear* a distorted audio-tape of Cosme's previous statistical onslaught on racial and religious plurality.

By making use of contemporaneous historical event within the context of American and Spanish current affairs – complemented by the use of clothing and musical forms – Berlanga comes to make a searing comment on the role on domestic National Catholicism. Likewise, it is relevant that *Welcome Mister Marshall!* was made a matter of months before the US and Spain signed the agreements which gave American forces access to Spanish military bases.

Significantly, in this final sequence of Cosme's dream, between the seated judge and the inscription there is wrought-iron arrow reminiscent of the seven arrows of the Falangist insignia. This dream plays on the ambivalence of Spanish/US relations. Drawing on parallel ideological histories, it also complicates common histories of Empire. Bhabha neatly describes the ambivalence of mimicry as, 'almost the same *but not quite* [...] at once resemblance and menace' (1994: 86). The Falangist symbol, for example, is distorted but recognizable.

Imitation is often the putting into practice of in-betweenness. The event of the Americans' arrival is far less important than the dress rehearsal that precedes it, in which Manolo, taking his cue from the NO-DO broadcast, plays the role of the visiting American. Indeed he is clearly intended to be imitating George Marshall himself. Manolo is a figure who claims an intimate 'knowledge' both of America and Andalusia. His 'knowledge', though, is as suspect as the narrator's. Between his knowledge and that of the villagers there is only the NO-DO broadcast as a reference. Irrespective of the falsity of real knowledge, it is something that Manolo and the villagers have in common. It is very different to Rey's mixture of despotism and avuncularism.

On the other hand, amid the village populists there are also anti-populists. Don Luis, the misanthropic *hidalgo*, provides the discordant voice in this film, but it is one which helps identify the way mimicry functions. At the height of the contest of speeches between don Pablo and Manolo from the town hall balcony designed to win over the public in the village square – a sequence that serves as a counterpoint to the earlier statistical debate between Eloísa and Cosme – he emerges to denounce the celebrations as a masquerade: 'What do you think you are going to achieve with this *piñata*? Will you play the Indian before these Indians?' He employs imperial references to attack the imperialists and undoes them in the doing of it. *Piñata* is both specifically Mexican and carnivalesque. The official Spanish Academy of Language Dictionary defines *piñata* in terms that recall the carnival mask and the verbal/visual relation: 'Clay vessel, full of sweets, that in the masked dance of the first Sunday of Lent is hung from the ceiling for some of those present, with eyes blindfolded, to try and break with a stick' (1994: 1607).

The NO-DO broadcast provides the model which Manolo Morán appropriates to enact the role of an 'American' (with *cordobés* hat) that is very much *not* Senator Marshall while also clearly intended to be him. Similarly, the NO-DO style of delivery also provides the model for Rey. The newsreader's voice-over, accompanying images of American generosity, is similar to Rey's narrative style. Having first witnessed the powerless ciphers of Villar del Río being inserted and removed at will by the narrator, that is censored, we are now presented with the equally disembodied figure of the NO-DO newsreader doing exactly the same with the representatives of what we have, instants before, been informed is the wealthiest, most powerful nation on Earth. In this way the NO-DO slogan, 'The world at the reach of all Spaniards', takes on a particularly parodic form. This parody becomes clearer when we recall the use of litany employed by Eloísa, which while parodying the priest's sermon is also rhythmically copied in the subsequent news broadcast: 'More things, for more people, more swiftly'.

All this helps locate the problem of how to interpret the narrator within a matrix of mimicry. It is Rey's avuncular narration that has led Monterde, Torres, Torrecilla and others to accuse the film of conservatism, citing the narratorial style as primary evidence for the parable-like nature of the film. Yet this is revealed to be the parodic use of official machinery. The morality implicit in such a parable is rendered ineffectual and comic by Rey's wry delivery. He is ambivalent. There is a self-consciousness to his narration that implies self-parody. He is similar to the NO-DO newsreader *but not quite* and it is this apparent seamlessness that inflects and conditions the entire film, from beginning to end. In this way, the work of Berlanga departs from the easy label of satire with which he is frequently lumbered.[10] Parody has a more intimate and complex relationship with its object of reference. It is a form of mimicry that emerges from within the central discourse, while satire establishes a discourse that parallels its object but exists independently of it.

Rey refers to Villar del Río as 'a *typical* village' both at the beginning of the film and in its epilogue. The small tenant farmer, Juan, is a 'typical' synecdoche of the population of Villar del Río in its entirety. Indeed, Fernando Rey describes him as 'a typical man' in his introduction to the film in almost the same breath as he classifies the village in identical terms. As a representative subaltern member of the community – an everyman figure – Juan's dream is worth comparing with Cosme's. Like the priest, Juan poaches from various traditions to construct his dream. He dreams of Americans dressed as the Three Kings flying over Villar del Río to deliver him a tractor by parachute. If Cosme's dream is conducted in the claustrophobic demi-monde of *noir* cinema, Juan's is engendered with the idealized openness of wheat fields onto which the tractor is dropped. Soviet Socialist Realism blends with the Spanish national tradition of the Three Kings (at a significant moment in the Cold War). These are ideologically flat, uncomplicated representations in their *own* discursive contexts that are made dynamic once borrowed and re-worked. The original cultural products, within Juan's dream, are relocated. These traditions or transmitted images, while originating from previous dominant groups, are inherited and sedimented in the subaltern consciousness. It is telling that the references to Soviet cinema and Italian neorealism occur in *Welcome Mister Marshall!* almost exclusively either with regard to individual subaltern characters (like Juan) or in a popular and communal context. We have already seen the influence of Italian neorealism on the sequence which involved the villagers registering their requests for presents in the village square, and it is germane to my argument that the same square – the communal precinct – should host the film's famous homage to the Soviet filmmaker, V.I. Pudovkin. This shot of the crowd seen only as a sea of traditional *cordobés* hats takes place during the oratory contest waged between Manolo and don Pablo on the balcony of the town hall discussed below. What is international and, in the case of Pudovkin, very much art cinema is here made national and popular. Synecdoche is particularly pronounced here with the 'national' represented by the Andalusian and the 'popular' by apparently bodiless hats.

The relationship between the characters played by Manolo Morán and José Isbert stamps its imprint on the entire film. Between them they cobble together – *bricolage*-like – the words to the movie's signature tune on a quick bus trip around don Pablo's fields; a song whose celebrated chorus goes, 'Americans, we receive you with *alegría*'. We have already seen in the previous chapter's discussion of the press in Neville's *The Bordadores Street Murder* that public opinion is a prized commodity and it is from the rivalry of these two characters – poised between the people and the state – that the entire notion of Spanish *alegría* is lampooned.

In-betweenness in *Welcome Mister Marshall!* helps situate the concepts of hybridity, synecdoche and asyndeton within the scenario of Villar del Río but it also mobilizes the population. The 'relics' here are those left in the wake of dominant discourse, whether it be that concerning the constructed order within the village and the nation or the alleged wealth and generosity of the Americans. While statistics and maps are the instruments employed to shore up dominant discourse they remain representationally inert, like the synchronic and static topology of Villar del Río of which the film's narrator tries to convince us. What de Certeau terms '[T]he trace left behind' (1984: 97) – asyndeton, the 'less' – is reworked by the population. The village population – under the mobilizing orders of Manolo – makes use of the 'relics' or 'traces' of discourse. These operations are carried out within the communal spaces of the village: the cafeteria, the main square and the streets. These are the areas of the village that are transformed into a cardboard Andalusia that stands – in the eyes of the putative Americans – for the whole of Spain. That is, while the villagers' operations constitute the asyndeton that 'opens gaps in the spatial continuum' of discourse, the public zones of the village function as synecdoches of the nation. de Certeau talks of 'a story jerry-built out of elements taken from common sayings, an allusive and fragmentary story whose gaps mesh with the social practices it symbolizes' (1984: 102). That the space within which this story is 'jerry-built' should be the village square is important. In previous chapters we have seen how in comedy public arenas are susceptible to subaltern intervention but never more so than in *Welcome Mister Marshall!* does a square play the Bakhtinian-like role of the belly in the village body-politic. This is not to suggest that it is the cohesive center of village life – although it is that, too – rather that it is the point of entry and exit of the fluid population. This location undergoes constant transformation and renewal. It is in the appropriate context of the village square that the physical presences of Morán and Isbert engage with one another.

Before examining their relationship, I will dwell upon the figure of Isbert himself. Isbert is an expert manipulator but his operations begin and end with an apparent weakness (his age) which he converts into a strength. For de Certeau, 'a tactic is an art of the weak' (1984: 37). Although Isbert first appeared on the screen in 1912, his reputation prior to 1939 was as a stage actor. In cinema he was only cast in major roles after the war when he was well into his fifties. Cinematographically he is always old. His age and his infirmity, his frailness, deafness and his distinctive quavering voice become the tools for a series of tactics that pervade his comic performances.

The relationship and rivalry between Isbert and Morán in *Welcome Mister Marshall!* also relates to the configuration of time and space in this film.[11] Just as Isbert is marked by his age, that is, by time, Morán prominently occupies space, making a physical impact. These actors are signifiers of time and space precisely by virtue of the fact they remain unchanged. Morán, as an outsider in the village, is comparable to the provincial bureaucrat, the *director general* who visits Villar del Río, in two aspects; both are outsiders and both are of similar build. The body of Morán is always of moment. It is worthy of note that the *director general* supplants don Pablo in the mayor's seat on arrival, once it is discovered that he is not present, obliging the mayor to sit in front of his own desk when he finally turns up. Similarly, none of the discussions maintained between Isbert and Morán are conducted in the mayor's office. Pablo usually goes to Manolo's room in the boarding house for advice, very much as a guest (even though, as we have been informed early on in the film, he *owns* the boarding house). Invariably the rivalry between Manolo and Pablo is marked by encroachments into the mayor's 'public' space: the balcony on the Town Hall building which houses his office, the piano in the cafeteria that don Pablo owns. Indeed, it is on the balcony that Manolo literally usurps Pablo's role. In a contest of speeches which reflects the earlier statistical debate between don Cosme and Eloísa, not only is Manolo manifestly the better orator, he physically imposes himself upon the apparently hapless mayor. He maneuvers his body to squeeze Pablo into the background. While it is true that Manolo is a kind of parody of the *director general*, his mimicry is skewed (*not quite*). His physical presence, allied with the diminutive Isbert, throws into relief and emphasizes the *uniformity* – the functionality – of the *director general*. It is this physical similarity that produces the sense of difference.[12] This is produced of a fusion, an alliance of time and space in the comic pact between Isbert and Morán.

Between them, the two actors produce the 'swellings and shrinkages' that mark the rhythm of the film. Theirs is an alliance marked by size and shape. Deafness for Isbert (and not only in this film) is a sort of tactical ellipsis, a means by which he hears only what he wants to hear and edits out what is inconvenient. Morán's creative materialism, on the other hand, is a vindication of expansion. Morán is not one to waste time on doubt in the face of an entrepreneurial challenge (and again not only in this film). Both mimic, in differing ways, the *director general* (recall don Pablo's deafness). Whereas Pablo is circumspect in his ambitions, Manolo is lavish in his. This is physically represented. Isbert is a small, wizened man, Morán is larger than life. Just as Morán is physically imitative of the *director general*, his fatness also connects him, in a very secular way, to the priest. Don Cosme belongs to a long tradition of over-fed clerics of Friar Tuck ilk, one particularly present in Italian cinema of the 1940s and 1950s. As mentioned earlier, the priest-like Morán is the loud intermediary between Mamá Dolores's deafness and the god-like narrator. This places both Rey and Morán within the medieval carnivalesque tradition of parodying the Christian hierarchy. While Morán parodies the priesthood, Rey mimics the omnipotent Christian god. Isbert helps to clarify the subversiveness of this kind of mimicry by reproducing something similar in his relationship with Morán. Theirs is a rivalry expressed first in romantic terms over Carmen Vargas in a parody of the classical triangle of romantic comedy (Deleyto, 1998: 129–147). Later though, this rivalry takes on a political slant with regard to the population of the village square. Don Pablo's deafness is, like that of Mamá Dolores, a tactic of silence; Manolo Morán's tactic is one of noise, of loquaciousness and public performance. Just as the physical similarity that produces the sense of difference between Morán and the *director general*, it is the sense of physical difference that produces the similarity, that fuses the alliance between Isbert and Morán.

As Rey has informed us in the opening sequences of the film, this is spring. By convention spring is symbolic of change and renewal. For Bakhtin, 'travesty' was an indispensable element of medieval folk festival. By 'travesty' Bakhtin explicitly refers to 'the renewal of clothes and of the social image' and in the same passage he refers to reversals of 'hierarchic levels: the jester was proclaimed king, a clownish abbot, bishop or archbishop was elected at the "feast of fools", and in the churches directly under the pope's jurisdiction a mock pontiff was even chosen' (Bakhtin, 1984: 81). This sense of reversal occurs very obviously in *Welcome Mister Marshall!* in the re-dressing of the village with Morán playing the role of both master of ceremonies and the US dignitary. Bakhtin locates these reversals within a discourse of time and space. 'The marketplace feast,' he writes, 'opposed the protective, timeless stability, the unchanging established order and ideology' (Bakhtin, 1984: 81).

The earlier scene in which the villagers queue to ask for presents of the Americans is mirrored towards the end of the film – after the Americans have sped through Villar del Río without stopping – when the villagers queue once more in the village square to give what they can to the village coffers. In the words of Fernando Rey: 'Everyone has to contribute, without blaming anyone, to what has been spent on this carnival'. And the narrator makes explicit the parallel with the earlier sequence when he says: 'He who asked for a tractor only two days ago can barely donate a sack of potatoes today'. It is noteworthy that Pablo's contribution is precisely his hearing aid. He self-consciously refers to the source of his tactics and that apparent physical weakness by which he is identified. In a further Bakhtinian inflection that calls attention to the inversions in the film, Rey adds: 'In reality they are petitions in reverse'. Although the film covers three days, 'calendar' time is condensed into a period that outside the filmic world covers the period from sowing to harvesting. Just as the dream sequences compress time, the village square becomes not only the scenario of the villagers' operational activities but also acts as a stage for the passing of time marked by a cycle of seasons which runs from sun to rain to sun again, in a typical motif of the pastoral.[13] The village square provides a space into which time is funneled.

The first and final sequences of *Welcome Mister Marshall!* neatly echo one another and undo the dictatorial narrator's insistence upon a temporal stasis that denies movement. In the first sequence of the film, we see the village bus arriving from elsewhere (with Carmen and Manolo, who will prove disruptive), and the final sequence is once more the bus moving off to another destination. What Monterde holds to be conservative in this – and he locates the final sequences specifically in a discourse concerning location: 'After the dream they return to the same place' (Cañique and Grau, 1993: 273) – is contradicted by one of the very final shots of the film: the hybrid detritus of a cardboard *cordobés* hat, a US flag and a Spanish flag floating downstream. In spite of the convention that the flow of water symbolizes timeless, eternal, natural flux, the fact is that water does not stand still. Rivers go places, they are connective. This recalls Heraclitus's frequent use of the metaphor of the river to express a sense of the continuity of change in individual things which the following well-known epigram and one particular common in Spanish, exemplifies: 'You cannot step twice into the same river; for fresh waters are ever flowing upon you'. The shot is – in its flowing and fluent combination of disparate cross-cultural artifacts – another representation of the dream sequence. Furthermore, what is shown is not in fact the river, it is an *acequia*, an irrigation channel; that is, an artificial conduit to the river, a space shaped and altered by human beings and introduced historically to Spain by the Arabs. The system of transporting water via *acequias* is particularly connective, both as a system of distributing space and as a human construction. It is both eternal and syncretic, quite literally a 'stream of consciousness' (like a dream) and a man-made chronology of human history. What Monterde maintains is a mark of stasis (the flow of water) bears a similarity to what is generally accepted as being the most dynamic episode of the film (the dreams). Seen in the context of other features on the spatial landscape and the emphasis placed by the narration on Villar del Río being 'space-bound', it is significant that the village possesses a river (as opposed to Villar del Campo, whose name really does conjure up territorial enclosure). The symbol of the flowing water coming at the end of the film adds to the accumulated effect of foreign influence and the impacting succession of visitors to strengthen the connections with other forms of change within space. Communications with the outside world are never innocuous or in any real sense 'space-bound'; they breach boundaries. The villagers' confusion produced by the passage of a cavalcade of workmen trundling along the highway on a steamroller covered in US flags is understandable; it is historically marked, laden with the symbolism of the outside world. Similarly, the promise of a railway station connects – in the imagination of don Pablo – the rivalry between Villar del Río and Villar del Campo, the NO-DO broadcast, American beneficence and the possibility of future visitors and departures. This last sequence brings to mind a certain similarity with de Certeau's idea of 'traces' or 'relics': 'People are put in motion by their waste products, the inverted remainders of great ambitions' (Certeau, 1984: 105). The final shot of *Welcome Mister Marshall!* provides a quite literal representation of that which remains sedimented in the popular imaginary. These people have been 'put in motion' by maps, statistics and newsreel broadcast.

As is evident from Wendy Rolph's insistence that the film has achieved canonical status as a 'comic classic' (1999: 9), temporal and spatial figures also stretch their significance beyond the confines of the screen. My objective in this chapter has been to interrogate what that means and for whom. In an essay concerning *Welcome Mister Marshall!*, Kathleen Vernon draws attention to the fact that, although Spain was never a beneficiary of the Marshall Plan, its outcast status was to be redrawn the year following the making of the film by the 1953 Defence Pacts signed with the United States which would lead to the establishment of US military bases on Spanish territory (Vernon, 1997: 38). It is apposite that the annual demonstrations throughout the late 1970s and 1980s protesting the American presence in the Torrejón air base outside Madrid should have adopted and adapted Lola Sevilla's theme tune for the film, rescripting the chorus from 'Americans, we receive you with *alegría*' to 'Americans, we bade you farewell with *alegría*'.

5
Humor and Hegemony: Berlanga, the State and the Family in *Plácido* (1961) and *The Executioner* (1963)

> Berlanga is not a Communist, he is something much worse: he is a bad Spaniard.
>
> – Francisco Franco (cited in Cobos *et al.*, 1996: 130)[1]

The pivotal function of culture in the relationship between the nation-state and its people has vexed two very different thinkers. José Ortega y Gasset and Antonio Gramsci were both concerned with the consequences of the gulf between 'people' and 'intellectuals' in national culture. As we have seen in Chapter 1, for Ortega, writing in 1921, the reluctance of the masses (or *la plebe*, as he is fond of referring to it with ill-disguised disdain) to fulfill their function – 'to follow the leading minority' – produces a situation of potential national disintegration: 'The nation comes undone, society breaks up, and is followed by social chaos, historical invertebration' (1957: 96). According to Ortega, the public's unruliness in the face of culture is illustrative of this:

> The theater or concert public believes itself superior to any play-write, composer or critic, and makes do with bandying about aimless insults here and there. No matter how lacking in subtlety and wisdom a critic might be, it will always turn out that he possesses more of both qualities than the majority of the public. (1957: 99–100)

For Gramsci, writing in Italy the same decade, the separation between intellectuals and the people that he detected in the absence of a popular literature produced by national writers, was indicative of an historical crisis in the discourse of the nation while condemning subaltern groups to linguistic fragmentation and consequent isolation:

> In Italy the term 'national' has an ideologically very restricted meaning, and does not in any case coincide with 'popular' because in Italy the intellectuals are distant from the people, i.e. from the 'nation'. They are tied instead to a caste tradition that has never been broken by a strong popular or national political movement from below. (1985: 208)

Ortega, commencing with Goya's 'Cartoons' (1774–1792) for the Royal Tapestry Factory in Madrid, identifies a specifically Spanish tradition that complicates Gramsci's theory of the national-popular culture even further. 'During the XVIII century,' he writes, 'a remarkable phenomenon occurs in Spain that fails to appear in any other country. Enthusiasm for the popular, not only in painting, but in all forms of everyday life, seizes the upper classes' (1987: 294).

It is in Ortega's notion of *popularismo casticista* that Santos Zunzunegui finds the basis for his attack on recent North American criticism. 'If', in Spanish cinema he writes, 'classical Hollywood cinema or neorealism [...] overlap with one another, they do so [...] on the foundations of its very own cultural forms ingrained in national tradition and, endowed, in the majority of cases, with deep popular roots' (1999: 100).

Notwithstanding the similar terminology to Gramsci's, it is his debt to Ortega that informs Zunzunegui's theoretical position. Zunzunegui defends a 'native' tradition of Spanish culture which incorporates many of the cineastes discussed in this book. Referring to Fernán Gómez's *The Strange Journey* (1964) – discussed in Chapter 7 – Zunzunegui pronounces it a film that 'affirms that one can only be faithful to one's own traditions by recognizing the porous nature of the frontiers that seem to isolate them [traditions] from other worlds' (1999: 104). The objective of hybridization, in Zunzunegui, is to still the play of alterity. With respect to the *Spirit of the Beehive* (Erice, 1973), he looks to Claude Lévi-Strauss to claim that national cinema, by mobilizing 'a series of *primordial images*', fulfills the function of a *'mythic operator* [...] capable of maintaining in suspense irresolvable oppositions' (Zunzunegui, 1999: 108). An organic national-cultural cohesion is thus woven from the fabric of the social totality, to which end difference is not only subsumed but actively repudiated.

Zunzunegui echoes many other critics by suggesting that black humor is a distinctively Spanish form. In his discussion of Rafael

Azcona – Berlanga's long-term script writer – Zunzunegui maintains that his novels and screenplays 'revitalize [...] with new ferocity, the *black humor* that bathes so very many classical works of Spanish literature and art' (1999: 102). And it is 'black humor' that Monterde cites as the factor that distinguishes Spanish from Italian cinema. Comparing the work of Marco Ferreri – who in 1958 introduced Azcona to cinema writing – to Berlanga's, Monterde says:

> Ferreri brings to an end a defined period because, while maintaining a comic route, his neorealist nature is already relativized by the presence of very different authoctonous elements. In *The Little Apartment* and *The Little Car*, as well as in *Plácido y The Executioner*, one can detect a change towards *a more Spanish sense of humor* [my emphasis]. That component of black humor does not exist in neorealism, at least not as something important. (Cañique and Grau: 265)

Blackness, thus, once more becomes part of the national patrimony.[2] Apart from the fact that it is questionable as to whether black humor is an exclusive trait of Spanishness,[3] it is a notion that sits well with concepts of Black Legend, cited equally by Kinder and Zunzunegui, to bolster an essentialist view of national identity. The mature work of Berlanga, often labelled black comedy and paradigmatic for such approaches, stands at the disputed crux of the Spanish native tradition. I refer to the two films generally accepted as among his finest: *Plácido* (1961) (Figure 8) and *The Executioner* (1963) (Figure 9). My aim in this chapter is to show how Gramsci's theory of hegemony lends itself to a different kind of political analysis of the movies than that previously offered; that is, as the disruptive, reworked product of multiple traditions, many of which are not Spanish at all, appropriated or borrowed from a variety of local traditions and international influences, from both dominant culture and popular practices.

Plácido (1961)

Plácido is a film in which 'organic' notions of society (in Zunzunegui's and Ortega's immobile sense) are exposed, often debunked and realigned. A Christmas film with a direct relationship to Frank Capra's *It's a Wonderful Life* (1946), it follows the day-long odyssey of the eponymous Plácido (Casto Sendra Barufet, *Cassen*) and his family. Pressed for money and time

Figure 8 Plácido (Courtesy of Video Mercury Films, S.A. and Filmoteca Española)

Figure 9 The Executioner (Courtesy of Video Mercury Films, S.A. and Filmoteca Española)

and desperate to pay an instalment on the motorized cart that provides him with a livelihood before sundown, Plácido and his clan to and fro across a provincial town[4] as messengers, gophers and providers of transport for the reluctant bourgeois hosts of a displaced crew of tramps and aspiring cinema starlettes, relocated one Christmas Eve to their dinner tables under the auspices of a charitable campaign whose slogan reads: 'Sit a Poor Person at your Dining Table' (a richly significant echo of similar Francoist events of the period).[5] Plácido's day is marshalled by the man charged with organizing the event, the cajoling and coercive Gabino Quintanilla (José Luis López Vázquez).

Slogans are important to Berlanga. While generally populist instruments, employed by dominant groups with the purpose of forging a cross-class consensus, in Berlanga's cinema they prove to be anything but straight-forward. Invariably they lay themselves open to distortion and misinterpretation; they are represented as half concealed or elliptical, shimmering cinema images, distorted warbling on the radio, banners billowing in the wind with only a few, flapping words of text, flimsy placards shoved across shoulders. The comicity of this film lies not so much in the exposure of Catholic hypocrisy as in the dismemberment of social hierarchy by means of adjacence and closeness; the 'organic' ends proposed by the slogan provoke their own fragmentation.

If *Welcome Mister Marshall!* is a film in which a 'static' place (Villar del Río) is disputed within a formal structure of sequential chapters, then the action of *Plácido* revolves around a series of conflictual places in the mobile topography of dominant space without the formality of chapters. The crowd in Berlanga's films swarms within places, across classes and genders, producing what is often described as the director's characteristic choral effect. This, in turn, has been attributed to *sainete*; that is classified by 'native' literary convention and appropriated for the national discourse.

Early in the film we see Plácido's wife, Emilia, who administers the municipal public toilets, located in the town's main square, which is also the place where the entire family regularly congregate. In a movie elaborated largely around a series of dining tables, it is in the spirit of Bakhtin that the initial terms of the film should be defined within an environment of public bodily expulsion and evacuation. The parameters of the film are determined by its scatological framework. Practically every moment of this brief introductory scene is Bakhtinian and sets off a train of associative links that pervade the entire film. This is a sequence poised around the regenerative duality of the body and its topology. For Bakhtin the key to debasement lies in renewal, in which there is direct correspondence and a confusion between the mouth and the buttocks. This connects to the concepts of *up* and *down* – and carnivalesque inversions – that were previously discussed in the context of Neville's *Carnival Sunday*.

Bakhtin draws particular attention to the application of 'swabs' to the body. The use of the swab, he insists, creates an overlap – a doubling – of bodily functions, to perform 'a transfer of the upper to lower bodily stratum; the body turns a cartwheel' (1984: 373). At one point in this sequence a man enters the toilets, requests a cubicle and is handed a strip of toilet paper. He immediately requests a newspaper. Newspapers, read with one's eyes, and toilet paper constitute two types of paper swabs connecting opposite ends of the body. Moreover, at the moment when Plácido enters the (women's) toilets, his brother Julián (Manuel Alexandre) is standing at a sink soaping his face – a singularly masculine activity – preparing to shave; that is, he applies a swab.

While establishing a direct connection between opposite ends of the body this sequence also pointedly confuses gender oppositions. Plácido marches into the toilets to Quintanilla's cry of 'Watch out! That is the door to the Ladies'. Moments later, though, when Quintanilla himself enters by the same door, Emilia shrieks 'You! Through the door to the Gents, scoundrel!'. At the very end of the sequence an elderly lady confronted by the group of men inquires as to whether it is the women's toilets, to which Julián responds 'Yes, come in, don't mind us, we are just family'. As will become clearer later, the fact that Emilia carries a young baby at this point is of Bakhtinian significance.

One of the clearest Bakhtinian sequences in the film follows shortly after the scene in the municipal toilets. The parade of garlanded vehicles, celebrating the day's event and laden with the minor celebrities, sets off towards the town center from the railway station and meets a funeral cortège mid-way up a hill. If the key to Bakhtin's biocorporal world lies in the proximity of life and death, as symbolized in the duality of bodily functions, the head-on collision of carnivalesque floats and the hearse reinforces it. Moreover, the disputed discourses of the film manifest themselves and seep through the shroud of established order in the production of excess. Quintanilla in a moment of overzealous piety chides the military band for not having removed their caps as a mark of respect for the deceased and is rewarded with a lesson in military etiquette, to which he replies by hysterical resort to *alegría*: 'Ah, you did it in military style. I didn't know that. Very well then, now let's see some *alegría*, more *alegría*! *Alegría*!'[6]

Plácido is a film promiscuously strewn with coy references to the symbols of established order. Moments previous to the commencement of the parade, amid the chaos of the railway station, the Civil Guard escort a line of grim-faced women though the crowd awaiting the arrival of the starlets, amid rumors of the arrival of 1950s sex symbol Carmen Sevilla.[7] The situation of these women as the relatives of prisoners is made clear when somebody remarks: 'Poor men having to spend these days in gaol'. And there is a casual mention that some of the elderly, impoverished beneficiaries of the campaign are war veterans. Just as charity or sloganizing prove vulnerable to plural intervention, the crowd provides camouflage for political comment. The comic mode thrives on this kind of contiguity.

The much commented technique that Berlanga employs to achieve such a cacophonic effect is the long take. The long take, in which an entire sequence is filmed in one shot without cuts, allows for a fluidity between individuals and the crowd; it both sets one off against the other and locates individual agency in a collective context.[8] Technically, it is the absolute opposite of the shot-counter-shot, which Berlanga almost never uses. The shot-counter-shot (very much favored in classical Hollywood) is both a means of generating suspense between two individuals and a convention for representing dialogue. The long take, on the other hand, allows Quintanilla to leap from the motorized cart to berate the band members and Plácido to descend and negotiate with the man to whom he owes money. It permits a flow of different persons across the same 'space' within the same 'time'. This synchronicity expands space while allowing individuals to voice their specific concerns without removing them from the crowd from which they emerge. In turn, this permits the representation of two (or more) completely different contexts to be represented simultaneously, as is the case of the procession and the funeral cortège or of the arrival of the starlets and the line of prisoners' relatives. Furthermore it enables the Bakhtinian schema of *up* and *down* to be complicated. The starlets, who are raised *up* at the train window and on steps, are sneered at by the haughty Señora Galán, who says of one of the actresses, 'She must be a hussy'. Meanwhile, in a shot that echoes the previous lavatory scene, we catch sight of one of the men on the train urinating from the toilet compartment.[9] The reception committee, on the other hand, which consists of a coalition of religious and business representatives are *down* among the crowd adjacent to the prisoners' relatives and the members of the Civil Guard escorting them. There is a certain subversive politics in the proximity, in the physical adjacence, of this depiction within these sequences that is cinematically reinforced by the long take. Moreover, it is precisely analyses of this type of shot that has led other critics to indulge in the rhetoric of national affiliation. In a certain manner this is 'organic' filming. What has been enclosed, however, within an essentialist view of collective Spanishness is, in my view, precisely the means by which the fissures surrounding the discourse of the nation are produced.

Berlanga's oft-proclaimed pessimism – expressed through debasement – with regard to the human condition is frequently associated with his deployment of black comedy. While Monterde and Zunzunegui locate this within a uniquely Spanish tradition, degradation, as we have seen, is ambivalent; Andrew Horton points out that it is distinguished by its 'unfinalizedness' (1991: 13), and Bakhtin writes of degradation: 'The positive aspect is historicity, the awareness of time and of becoming' (1984: 124).[10] This, moreover, dovetails into Gramsci's terminology, for whom the 'organic intellectual' is the bearer of an emergent discourse, who 'becomes' (1971: 355).

Bakhtin's open-endedness connects directly with Berlanga's comedy. Bakhtin writes that 'Grotesque realism knows no other lower level; it is the fruitful earth and the womb. It is always conceiving [...] Degradation digs a bodily grave for a new birth' (1984: 21), and endings in Berlanga have always posed a problem, particularly for those critics who seek classificatory closure. Bakhtin's observations, moreover, prove useful tools with which to analyze the reversals of social relations, discussed above, as expressed through bodily functions.

Gramsci writes that 'the jargons of various professions, of specific societies, innovate in a molecular way' (1985: 178). This linguistic definition of hegemony relates to the evidently molecular composition of *Plácido* and opens it up to political analysis. It is film situated at the convergence of legal, medical, clerical, military and religious discourse that the comedy unmasks. Spain, the nation, and its synecdoche, the dreary provincial town, typical of the pre-war dramas of Carlos Arniches,[11] are subjected to penetrating treatment through the prism of comedy. The porous discourse of civic cohesion established at the beginning of the film through the campaign slogan is delicately sustained by the discourses of medicine and law as is made clear by the central banquet sequences.

Each of the town's well-to-do families bids in auction for one of the starlets and in inverse compensation is alloted a poor person as accompaniment to share the family's Christmas meal. Shot in long takes, the dinners are clustered and claustrophobic miniatures of the parade/funeral cortège. What is envisaged as unchanging in the campaign slogan is, moreover, problematized by the constant references to medicine and law. The radio journalist, engaged as a master of ceremonies to publically convey this impression in the spirit of the season, sees his populist efforts consistently undone in similar terms to Quintanilla's earlier notion of *alegría* that sat ill with military etiquette.

Reporter (pleading): Please say something.
Actress: But you sir, you must be very old.
Old man: Really old, my dear, ancient. Next October I'll be 79.
Reporter (hissing): Alegría, alegría!
Actress: How funny you are Sir, But you look good for a man of your age.
Old man: No don't believe it. They are just appearances. I ache all over this side. The nuns don't say so, but I think it is cancer...
Reporter (interrupting): How marvellous it is to see the serenity of this venerable gentleman who now toasts to his hosts (*this is untrue, the hosts at this point are absent*).

Immediately following this scene, the camera shifts to another residence where another one of the poor guests, Pascual, has been taken genuinely ill. Álvaro (Agustín González), the priggish son-in-law of the Helguera household, takes his pulse. As is apparent in almost all of Álvaro's igno-minious interventions, he knows nothing yet claims to be an expert on everything, but particularly matters concerning law and medicine. His expertise is continually exposed. Solemnly he takes Pascual's wrist and fails to find the pulse. Pascual's moving head, nonetheless, demonstrates that he is patently alive.

The interesting feature of the legal and medical discourses is that, in spite of efforts to bind them together and of the fact that they sit well as accoutrements of respectability, they continually produce disjunctions. Álvaro is a kind of lawyer who is unmasked by the legalistic vocabulary he employs. His qualifications – in law and medicine – rely exclusively upon gesture and rhetoric. He goes through the motions of finding Pascual's pulse and brandishes a thermometer. Hegemonic conflicts thus reveal flaws and contradictions in dominant thought. It is discovered that the moribund Pascual lives with a woman to whom he is not married, offending the Catholic sensibilities of the Helguera family. To a backdrop of the rosaries being chanted by the women – religion here supplies a hegemonically gelling element – Álvaro enters the room accompanied by don Carlos, a friend of the family with military status who is apparently qualified to conduct weddings. It is within this framework that military and religious doctrines are flimsily *articulated* in the form of vacuous jargon:

Don Carlos: But then the patient has been demobilized and thus is beyond my juristdiction. Aside from that, I am on secondment.
Álvaro: It doesn't matter. In certain questions he remains a subordinate. I repeat, according to the law of 12 February, 1871, a superior officer can act in a case like this. Besides, I assume that in a wedding conducted in *artículo mortis*, a military commander can intervene as a legal representive.

This quack legal jargon parallels, as we will shortly see, the false medical verbiage of don Poli, the dentist and neighbor from downstairs who is summoned to administer to Pascual. It also overlaps with the military bluff which indirectly pervades the movie. The doubling at work here concerns both discourse and the consequent *disarticulation* of 'knowledge' from 'power' – exposure of its rhetorical fragility – that is further reinforced by the dentist's own impoverished guest, Rivas (Luis Ciges). The roguish and unscrupulous Rivas makes an accurate diagnosis – and boosts don Poli's medical credibility – when he supplies his friend Pascual's clinical history.[12] Similarly, it is upon the testimony of Rivas that Álvaro makes a legal diagnosis. 'They live in a state of *concubinage*!' exclaims Álvaro when Rivas reveals Pascual's and Concheta's, domestic arrangement. Álvaro's legal definition is mistaken; the Spanish word *concubinaje* was the legal term for male adultery not for unmarried cohabitation. Just as Rivas makes a correct assessment of Pascual's illness – 'angina pectoris' – he is also more legally precise in his description of Pascual and Concheta's circumstances. He transpires to be both a better doctor than don Poli and a more competent lawyer than Álvaro.'Knowledge' is, of course, central to the nominative function of dominant groups and yet here 'definition' consistently eludes the discursive net. Even the name Pascual is ironic, as Peter Evans has pointed out, with its echo of the Paschal lamb of the Christmas dining table (2000: 218).

The language of *appearance* provides the raw material of these formal discourses (legal and medical) but it also proves their undoing. Appearances not only justify authority, they undermine reliable diagnosis. They both sustain the order of discourse and demonstrate its fallaciousness. Don Poli is revealed as an oddity when we are introduced to him dining with his guest, Rivas, and his pampered, overfed dog, who has pride of place at the table. Meanwhile, his devoted and uncomplaining sisters wait on him. The gluttonously opportunistic Rivas is uniquely perceptive to this disjunction:

Rivas: Aren't your sisters going to eat?
Don Poli: I keep them on a strict diet.

When the Helguera family shout down for medical assistance, it is Rivas who makes the observation, 'But aren't you a dentist?' The arch response he receives from one of the sisters is that her brother is an *orthodontist*. She too employs the hollow jargon of science; like her brother, who wearily explains with leaden condescension that orthodontology 'is a medical specialization, a great specialization'. Don Poli's medical knowledge is a matter of performance. As he himself has already confessed, his experience of bodies amounts to little more than his failed attempts to insert a *prosthesis* into his pampered dog's mouth. Armed with the accoutrements of medicine – stethoscope and white coat – and a keen concern for appearance – he barks at his sisters: 'Make sure the white coat is clean' – his actual *appearance* in the Helguera household is very much dependent upon the trappings of the profession. This public image correspondingly carries with it a notable ignorance of the substance at hand. Hence the importance of the privileged information that don Poli receives from Rivas and which enables a public diagnosis. Rivas, unconcerned with the class niceties of appearance and recognition, seizes whatever food he can lay his hands on.

As in the earlier sequence in which Quintanilla chides the military band members for their lack of respect shown towards the dead, the language of authority is not always interpretable to those who do not possess the requisite knowledge. Within this failure to cohere around appearance and gestures the discourses of medicine and law break down. The magnificently stroppy maid in the Helguera household rebels against the prospect of Pascual being placed in her bed by appealing to the same medical discourse: 'No Señora. Who knows what he might have. It could be contagious and one is very apprehensive'. Similarly, moments later, on learning that the rival Galán family are to visit, Señora de Helguera sets about bullying first her husband and then the maid into adopting the correct dress for receiving visitors. On being ordered to wear her servant's headpiece, Antonia once more refuses: 'No Señora, I have just had a perm'. When the doorbell rings Señora de Helguera exclaims, 'And I've still not put on my make up!'. Rivas's shameless greed embellishes and reinforces his subversive function. He and Antonia provide a link between the dining table and death while exposing the fragile authority of the bourgeois family whose status hinges on the delicate discourse of civic respectability, sustained by a combination of appearance and medical, legal, military and religious verbiage.

The characters of Plácido and Quintanilla represent appurtenances of their own respective classes. In part they play foils to one another, but they are also condemned to share the same cramped space for much of the film. Their adjacence to one another also sets them apart from their respective social groups. Quintanilla prides himself on his family connections and those to come (he is engaged to Martita Galán, the daughter of the campaign president). He always introduces himself to establishment figures (the notary and the bank manager) as being of the same class as them. His prospects as a son-in-law place him close to Álvaro in the Helguera household (it is Álvaro's status to which he aspires in the Galán family) and this is an alliance reinforced by the complicity arising out of the discourse on medicine. On learning that Quintanilla has caught a cold, Álvaro lends him the thermometer and produces a contraption for steaming out congested chests.

Meanwhile, Plácido wages a battle to accommodate himself to legal requirement. Just as Álvaro is fond of spouting legal statute, Plácido is the innocent victim of the same discourse. The narrative thread of the film is provided by Plácido's terror of losing his means to a living by failing to pay the installment on his motorized cart before sundown, as the law demands. Falacious interpretation of the law is both an instrument that threatens to deny Plácido his livelihood while swirling around the death of Pascual. In both instances, the discourses are clumsily perpetuated by figures of authority: Álvaro, the bank manager and the notary. They are discourses that Plácido, from the very start of the film, uncritically accepts. The requirement to pay is phrased by him, for most of the film not only as legal obligation but as civic duty. Confounded time and time again by bureaucratic exigence, Plácido goes from his humble explanation to the notary's clerks at an early stage in the film, 'I want to pay. I am a serious person' to outright rebellion – when he is finally able to pay – upon learning that his creditor's name does not figure on the documents and thus he is not legally obliged to honor the agreement:

Notary: If you hadn't wanted to pay it wouldn't have mattered.
Plácido: You what? Are you telling me that if I don't pay nothing will
  happen to me?
Notary: That's right. The documents lack executive power.
Plácido: Gentlemen, Merry Christmas. I am not paying it.
Notary: But where do you think you are going? Morally, you are
  obliged to pay it.

The legal discourse upon which civic cohesion rests is promptly supplanted by morality when it suits the dominant group. The question of 'ethics' only becomes a factor when Plácido finally defies established order. The cleavage between medical and legal discourse that distinguishes the figures of Álvaro and don Poli is further complicated here. Legal discourse is, once more, exposed as a rhetorical nicety, as jargon employed as a means of enforcement. In this sense power works, as both Bakhtin and Gramsci maintain, in the use of technical euphemism (forming the basis for consent) but once that fails coercion comes into play; such material is aptly supplied by Christian charity and Christmas.

Adjacence is a distinctive component of social relations throughout the film. Rivas, who dines with the fake doctor/dentist, is the contiguous link to Concheta and Pascual: he is their neighbor. As we will see, this couple also lives close to the Civil Guard barracks. Señor Helguera lives in comically paranoid fear of his neighbors, like the dentist. More than anything else the proximity of life to death, and of death to eating, helps bind the ambivalence of the word *alegría* that reverberates throughout the film. 'No meal can be sad,' writes Bakhtin:

> Sadness and food are incompatible (while death and food are perfectly compatible). The banquet always celebrates a victory and this is part of its very nature. Further, the triumphal banquet is always universal. It is the triumph of life over death. In this respect it is equivalent to conception and birth. (1984: 283)

For Bakhtin 'the feast was a temporary suspension of the entire official system with all its prohibitions and hierarchic barriers' (1984: 89) and Mari Luz, who plays host to Concheta takes advantage of the charitable event to invite her lover, Ramiro, to dine.[13] In this sequence we see the man washing up – consigned to the threshold of the kitchen – in a reversal of the earlier sequence in which the dentist dines with his dog and Rivas while attended to by his sisters who are confined to the kitchen. The spatial differences in this sequence are the product of panoptic surveillance – Mari Luz and Ramiro live in dread of a visit from the civic committee – but they also generate a kind of adjacence, a marginal space on the threshold of authoritarian discourse which clarifies the boundaries of power, those which are transgressed. Ramiro crosses traditional gender roles (he is restricted to the kitchen) and, like the dentist's sisters, is separated from the banquet participants. The window that communicates between the kitchen and the dining room provides a means of both contact and segregation. The one occasion Ramiro dares abandon the kitchen his worst fears are realized. There is a knock on the door and he dives into the wardrobe to hide, carrying a bottle of champagne. This signals the arrival of Gabino Quintanilla who has come – at the behest of Álvaro and the Helguera family, in a clear policing role – to fetch Concheta to be forcibly married to Pascual. At this moment we hear a loud pop (as the champagne cork detaches itself from the bottle) and then the following conversation that takes a similar turn to the earlier one in which Quintanilla, erringly juxtaposed *alegría* with military discourse. This time though it is Mari Luz's quick thinking that resolves the potential crisis:

> *Quintanilla*: A shot! I heard a shot!
> *Mari Luz*: No, no . . . just the seasonal *alegría*.

Once Quintanilla and Concheta have left, Ramiro staggers out of the wardrobe clutching his eye which has been struck by the flying cork. The panoptic legal discourse concerning *concubinage* (the presence of Concheta, the prying inspection of Quintanilla and the fact that Ramiro and Mari Luz are terrified illicit lovers) connects to the military vocabulary and the discourse of medicine and illness (Pascual's 'angina pectoris', Quintanilla's oncoming cold and Ramiro's self-inflicted injury). It does so, moreover, in a scenario in which death and eating converge. The two unmarried couples – Pascual/Concheta and Ramiro/Mari Luz – are the uncomfortable objectives of Catholic morality as staged around a dining table.

In these circumstances the word *alegría* takes on a degree of joyless desperation. Employment of this word in Berlanga is always droll. If contiguity – exemplified by adjacent relations and juxtapositions that cluster around the contradictions produced within the fields of religion, medicine, law and the military – mark ambivalent hybrid sites, then *alegría* is the fracturing impulse that pervades the 'national' discourse. The Spanish party animal (the *juerguista*) is a stock figure of such a national discourse and one put into play almost simultaneous with the making of *Plácido* by the then Minister of Tourism and Information, Manuel Fraga Iribarne. Fraga's slogan 'Spain is different' was designed to attract foreign tourists to the nation's beaches. The economic benefits of the tourist boom also brought undesired consequences, concerning the liberal sexual mores that accompanied the influx of foreigners.[14] As we will see in the discussion of *The Executioner, alegría* also connects to the breakdown of comic convention.

In both *Plácido* and *The Executioner* the figure of the Civil Guard appears. The state at its most menacing – rifle raised and cocked – and the family merge into a conflictive moment marked by death in both films. Plácido's family and Concheta are challenged in the language of the battlefield ('Halt! Who goes there?') by a uniformed member of the Civil Guard positioned on the roof of the building where Concheta and Pascual live, as they carry the latter's lifeless body back home. This is a critical moment in the film, one that emerges in a sequence that provides a choreographic foil to the earlier episode featuring members of the Civil Guard at the railway station. Plácido is not acting here for money or under duress, his behaviour is the product of genuine charitable concern for Concheta. This 'charity' positions him quite literally in a battlefield; similar, in fact, to a real spatial boundary (the guard challenges him and his family as if he were on the edge a frontier). The metaphorical notion of a leaking border between discourses is given literal representation. Two contiguous points meet in a familiarly Bakhtinian configuration; the Civil Guard is *up* on the roof and Plácido's clan is *down* below making their way up the stairs to the dwelling. By the same token, the Civil Guard has a panoptic function. Just as many Spanish towns and cities were ringed by military quarters, it seems apt that Concheta and Pascual live in contiguous closeness to the barracks. The up/down positioning of the Civil Guard/Plácido and company also has a corresponding side-by-side relation.

Much of this film can be read as a laying-bare of the anatomy of social differences between classes and genders. Yet, as has already been established in the sequence that takes place in the public toilets, the very notion of *dwelling* is ambiguous. A dwelling is a place of refuge, beyond the scope of panoptic power. Plácido's action – conducted as if he were crossing a no-man's land with the wounded of the battlefield – recalls the pattern of his day's movements zig-zagging doggedly between the respective territories of the bourgeois families, the public toilets, the bank and the notary's office. Plácido's ambivalent mobility complicates *place*. Place is an adjunct, a liminal zone (a dwelling) often located at the very center of power. Just as Concheta and Pascual's hovel is both beneath and beside the Civil Guard barracks, so too the public toilets used by Plácido's family as a base are in the town's main square. Adjacence does not always indicate physical marginality in relation to the loci of power; sometimes it places disparate social elements at its heart, insinuating – at times discreetly, at others explicitly – from within. It is within 'place' that the contingent signs of history peep through to caress the contiguous signifiers of location. Such adjacence produces disjunction in the discourse of social cohesiveness but it also disturbs the 'togetherness' with which comedy is traditionally associated.

Berlanga breaks with the tradition of comedy which ends in reconciliation, happy endings and often marriage. Berlanga's endings are rarely happy, indeed his characters usually end up on their own; their failure is palpable. In *Plácido*, between the initial Francoist slogan 'Sit a Poor Person at Your Dining Table' and the final song – whose bitter refrain goes, 'In this world there is no charity, there never has been and never will be' – a considerable voyage has been made though the hierarchical parameters of civil society. It has been the thesis of this analysis that such journeying through overlapping and contradictory discourses within the molecular structure of hegemonic relations generates borderline experiences, adjacent spaces, thresholds where the flanks of dominant thought remain unguarded and vulnerable.

The Executioner (1963)

If *Plácido* is primarily concerned with civic discourse and the family, Berlanga's following movie brings these elements into direct and conflictive relation with the state. *The Executioner* (1963) is Berlanga's bleakest and most sustained film and yet its strength lies in being precisely a comedy.[15] This tragi-comedy tells the story of a man who inherits his father-in-law's position as state executioner when he is browbeaten into marriage. Thus it is that the conflicts of the diegesis are waged along and within the boundaries of the middle echelons of society but they particularly occupy that terrain where the state and civil society meet. The film's organization around this relationship turns on the performance of a representative of the state at its most repressive, the executioner (José Isbert). Isbert plays Amadeo who, in the words of his future son-in-law José Luis (Nino Manfredi), 'seems like a normal person [...] you would never imagine that he was an executioner'. His 'normality', his amiable bonhomie vies with the macabre nature of his trade, symbolized by the ubiquitous briefcase, containing the implements of the garrote, that inspires dread in everyone he meets. Isbert's performance is fundamental to this effect: grandfatherly, archetypically Spanish (complete with beret), concerned with food, commonsensical and pragmatic with a shrewd line in comic observation. Of José Luis's job in the funeral parlor he says: 'It's very reliable, there is never a crisis.' Apparently malleable, Amadeo is also completely manipulative: a representative of the state but by no means fully of the state.

It is from within this combination of pragmatic common sense and superstition that the film unravels into an exploration of Francoist society of the early 1960s. Above all, *The Executioner* details how the uneven and unstable alliance between state and civil society depends, in large degree, upon the mercurial figure of José Isbert's character. Isbert's performance functions at the juncture of a series of non-discursive elements which, as in *Plácido*, form the vertices of this film. If death in Bakhtin is an ambivalent representation, then rarely has a movie expressed this ambivalence better than *The Executioner*.

The music backing the title shots of *The Executioner* captures this pertinently. As the drawings and captions emerge on screen, we hear a cheerful, jazzed-up rendition of the twist that fades into the first sequence and fuses with a *martinete* (a gypsy prison song) murmured against the dialogue, which in turn takes place simultaneously with an execution.[16] The funeral parlor where José Luis works is the inappropriate scenario for a jam session for the band members who play the twist number while Amadeo's daughter, Carmen (Emma Penella), lingers at the doorway to announce her pregnancy to José Luis. As the previous discussion of *Plácido* implied, the coexistence of death and birth is of Bakhtinian significance. At the very end of the film when José Luis has recently carried out his first execution and, while in the midst of the grimmest depression, a group of foreign tourists arrive and the music – the same twist – bursts into life once more. In both these instances death stamps its emblematic imprint on modernity. *The Executioner* appropriates the twist to invoke both the Americanization of Spanish youth culture and the arrival of a 'libidinous' tourism from beyond the frontiers of the nation. The twist played in the funeral parlor, moreover, provides the backdrop for all José Luis's frustrated ambitions to travel to Germany where he had planned to train as a mechanic, an ambition curtailed by Carmen's announcement.

Almost invariably dress and music are the means by which encounters between the state and civil society are expressed. In an extraordinary long take shot when José Luis is finally summoned to Mallorca to perform an execution, a pair of uniformed Civil Guards track him down to the Drach caves (a well-known tourist spot on the island) and tannoy him with a megaphone that sheers against the Offenbach being played for the sightseers. One of the most eloquent and enduring images of Spanish cinema occurs in the penultimate sequence of the film as José Luis is dragged, half-unconscious and vomiting, to perform the execution leaving the straw hat, with which he had been enjoying his holiday, on the floor behind him (a uniformed prison warder returns to fetch it) as the guards oblige him to wear a tie, forcing it upon him as if it were itself the garrotte itself. The two groups of people walking slowly through the long white room to the small door at the far end provide an apt culmination of the previous moments when José Luis had been comforted by the prison governor and the priest. Desperately expectant of an imminent pardon, José Luis is attended to by the priest. From the moment of his arrival on the island José Luis is transformed into the condemned man: from his parodic 'arrest' by the Civil Guard when the family step off the boat to this remarkable sequence he is propelled inexorably towards the scaffold. Strikingly, this shot is filmed without music, against the barely audible murmur of the priest's prayers.

Just as José Luis as state executioner becomes the condemned man, the sequence of events that leads José Luis from Madrid to Mallorca constitutes a parody of the institution of the family. Carmen actually refers to it as kind of honeymoon. When José Luis is summoned to the Mallorcan capital, Palma, she says brightly, 'At the end of the day we never had a honeymoon.' Within this context, the accompanying presence of a new born baby and the father-in-law disturbs the symbolic locus at the heart of traditional discourse and becomes the raw material of a critique of the state at its most repressive.

The wedding as a comic scenario is important. Far from being the point of reconciliation, in both *Plácido* and *The Executioner* the wedding marks the most desperate and disjunctive of solutions. This is more than just a reversal, it is a particular reworking of the discourses of law and family. If in *Plácido* the wedding marks an act of Christian conscription, the press-ganging of a couple into dubious legality and the enforcement of a doctrine in which the totalizing intentions of discourse breakdown, in *The Executioner* this coercion intimately links the family to the state. Outraged, José Luis observes that Amadeo wears his work suit to his daughter's wedding. This departure from conventional comedy of marriage in either the Aristotelian or Shakespearean senses of the word also undermines the discourse of literary tradition (Merchant, 1972: 69–78).

In both *Plácido* and *The Executioner* Berlanga's hapless heroes are the fathers of new born children who live in close proximity to death. Death and birth are molecular symptoms of the proximity of the state and civil society. In *The Executioner* José Luis, upon finding himself in the similarly adjacent position of son-in-law – that is, a character both inside and outside the family unit, someone who is *not quite* a full member – to those characters already discussed in *Plácido*, resorts to his condition as a means of denying his discomforting inheritance. On being introduced by Amadeo to a hack writer whom Amadeo admires for exalting the death penalty who dedicates his book, 'To the future executioner, successor of a family tradition', José Luis retorts 'I am the son-in-law, I am not a member of the dynasty.' José Luis, condemned by his condition as son-in-law, is also able to exploit this marginal status, to use it as an alibi; just as Álvaro and Quintanilla in *Plácido* make use of their positions as sons-in-law to bind discourse, they are also the key figures in its undoing.

Furthermore, José Luis's 'denial' of any direct familial ties to Amadeo provides an eerily poignant echo of the ostentatious denials of their heritage by Jews who faked their conversion to Christianity during the Inquisition. It is apt that José Luis's first execution should be performed in Mallorca, home to one of the longest surviving cripto-Jewish communities, the *Chuetas*.[17] Fernando Sánchez Dragó has pointed out that the descendents of *Chuetas* executed during the Inquisition were also publically held to account for their familial lineage in, 'The famous lists of names or *sambenitos*, placed in the cloisters of the church of Santo Domingo and on which the surnames of those executed were displayed as opprobrium for their descendents' (1997: 180).

In *The Executioner* the consumption of food provides a rhythmic marker throughout the film. The use of pork in the Inquisition has been well documented as either a means of coercion – the obligation of converts to eat ham in public as proof of their non-Jewishness – or as a tactic of subterfuge, as an excacerbated demonstration of Christian willing, undertaken by the converts themselves. The ham-eating tradition continues today on the island of Mallorca in village *fiestas*. As in *Plácido*, it is in the spirit of Bakhtin that each time 'death' arises in this film somebody is eating. During the execution that Amadeo performs early in the film, the prison warder is put off his food by his briefcase; José Luis is plied with food and drink in the prison previous to carrying out his first execution; at the very end of the film when José Luis returns to the departing ship and vows never to perform another execution, the only comment his wife makes is to offer him a sandwich.

Hopewell echoes many other critics when he comments on the 'failure' of Berlanga's characters: 'Chance, mishap, chaos and compromise sweep mild-mannered José Luis [...] from being caught in bed with the executioner's daughter to being dragged to an execution chamber, as the state's official garrote expert. José Luis has joined the system' (Hopewell, 1986: 62). In fact matters are rather more complicated than Hopewell claims. It is true that outrageous misfortune deals José Luis a poor hand but what is questioned here is more the state itself than any individual. While civil society bursts with dissenting voices, fears and misgivings, the representatives of the state, even when they are caricatured, are 'normal' human beings. *The Executioner* is a powerful indictment of the death penalty, not a tale of individual misfortune; it is an investigation of how the state inhabits a paradox and makes victims of its closest allies, of how its objective of consensus proves not only contradictory but lethal. Chance is not what is allowed to count in this film. In almost every instance of apparent misfortune that befalls José Luis lies the manipulative hand of Isbert/Amadeo, yet he is the most attractive character in the film. Amadeo leaves his case in the funeral parlor van (deliberately?) and thereby introduces José Luis to his daughter. On finding José Luis in bed with his daughter, Amadeo employs traditional morality – echoing the rhetoric of a Catholicism he clearly does not practice – to oblige José Luis to propose marriage, and once there is a child and the possibility of state-subsidized housing, Amadeo and Carmen morally blackmail José Luis into taking on the role of executioner. Amadeo is in some ways the personification of the state, sufficiently benign to be acceptable but perfectly capable of ruthlessness. He is a kind of 'son-in-law' to the state: an adjacent figure, socially marginalized by his job but instantly recognizable. He is a figure that moves on the frontier between state and civil society, between the family and the scaffold, a borderline character at the center of the Bakhtinian schema of death and rebirth. His inimical Spanishness (the same kind of Spanishness often cited today to explain Berlanga) is made parodic by his performance, precisely by his pragmatism, his employment of common sense, his handling of the more dedicated state servants and most importantly by his 'timelessness'. As the previous chapter's discussion sought to draw attention to, Isbert is always old. This timelessness is similar to other facets of popular culture; *fiestas*, flamenco and carnival persist in their popularity outside of marketed time. What happens with Isbert is that his Spanishness eludes complete incorporation by the state. Difference not only oozes from the kaleidoscopic set of foreigners, costumes and family conflicts in the film but is also to be found in the otherness of Amadeo/Isbert himself. Isbert's performance, which is as much verbal as physical, is crucially the clearest example of the tacit agreement between state and civil society. Isbert's *inimical* Spanishness becomes a parody of Spanishness. I am reminded of Judith Butler's comment:

> The loss of the sense of 'the normal' [...] can be its own occasion for laughter, especially when 'the normal', 'the original' is revealed to be a copy, and an inevitably failed one, an ideal that no one can embody. In this sense, laughter emerges in the realization that all along the original was derived. (Butler, 1990: 139)

Isbert plays a type Spaniard, he is always referred to as 'normal', and undoes Spanishness in the playing of it. His parody hits at the heart of the appropriative objectives of the Spanish state. The attempts to identify Spain with the state are rendered redundant by Isbert's exposure of the manufactured nature of the Spanish state itself. In this way Isbert transpires to be the most subversive character in the film. Intrinsic Spanishness does not exist and Isbert's performance is crucial to the unmasking of the 'original'. Connected to this is what I originally conceived of as a problem arising out of Nino Manfredi's performance. Manfredi also plays a stock Spaniard, the *calzonazos* – the down-trodden, hen-picked man of much 1950s and 1960s cinema and one of Berlanga's favorite types. Manfredi, however, was Italian, a fact well known to Spanish audiences. His foreignness is very different to that of other actors from abroad who appeared in Spanish films. Manfredi does not play an outsider – the other – he plays the most stereotyped Spanish man. Here, while Isbert's voice is distinctively his, Manfredi's is dubbed into Spanish. At first I attributed this to miscasting (it is an ideal role for Fernando Fernán Gómez), yet in light of Butler's comment Manfredi's performance becomes more interesting. Disturbance is caused over the very question of Spanishness, not only in the parodic performance of Isbert but also in the casting. More than that, the excellence of the typecasting of Isbert helps to define the comedy of Manfredi, helps to establish that *'all along the original was derived'*.

Conclusion

At the very end of his great book on carnival, Bakhtin reflects on how Rabelais has been critically received in the following terms:

> The main failure of contemporary West-European Rabelaisiana consists in the fact that it ignores folk culture and tries to fit François Rabelais' novel into the framework of official culture, to conceive it as following the stream of 'great' French literature. (1984: 473)

In this passage the name Luis García Berlanga could easily replace that of Rabelais. The post-dictatorship period has seen Berlanga subjected to a concerted effort to make him 'officially' Spanish. At the expense of serious analysis of his movies, he has been co-opted within the national Spanish national canon both by domestic and foreign arbiters of the cultural economy. Rarely is the work of Berlanga considered as the engagement of popular culture in a material relationship with the state, the family and local customs. In the discussion of *Plácido*, I briefly mentioned the figure of the *caganer* as alluded to in the railway station sequence. In *The Executioner* there is a second and more explicit reference to the same figure. The *caganer* is a threshold figure who defecates at the margins of another family scenario – the 'holy family' – in the Catalan nativity scene. José Luis, Carmen and Amadeo – under the mistaken belief that, once married and now that José Luis is a state functionary, the family has a right to public housing – visit the building site where they believe their apartment is to be constructed. José Luis shouts abuse at a man squatting suspiciously on the distant fringes of the land below them in what is manifestly a reproduction of the *caganer* image. The sequence becomes further complicated, choral and cacophonic with the sudden arrival of another family which, it transpires, has been assigned the same apartment. The point, though, concerns the ambivalence of the articulating function of apparently innocuous popular tradition in both providing linkage with the state, while disturbing the locus of the model Christian family. This sequence, moreover, reflects the historical reality of massive publicly funded construction projects, undertaken in Spain's cities at the end of the 1950s and 1960s.

The idea of the 'organic' continually splinters in these films and exceeds the discourse of the nation. Ortega's (and Francoism's[18]) sense of the organic is captured by Bhabha's definition of '*the many as one*' (1994: 142). It is interesting that much of Berlanga's critical reception should have focused upon organic claims concerning the chorus. Whereas Ortega's elitist cultural critique posits a select intellectual group whose wisdom and teaching radiates downwards in the expectation of raising the educational capacities of the masses, Gramsci proposes the opposite: the organic production of subaltern intellectuals who actively engage the purveyors of traditional ideology. Hence, in this latter view, hegemony as the site of struggle, in which different cultural perspectives – high and low – meet. The chorus in this sense becomes the cinematic representation of that site. In the work of Pedro Salinas and Juan Ríos Carratalá, the chorus is confined (and enshrined) as a distinctive element of an exclusive national tradition, *sainete*, which also interested Ortega (1987: 301–302). It is undeniable that the nation is an inescapable presence in Berlanga's cinema, whether in terms of the 'typical', the 'topical' or the 'traditional'. Parody necessarily involves a dialogue with the schema of hierarchy and yet this is expressly what critics of Berlanga – concerned with establishing his 'national' status – ignore.

It is pertinent here to recall that Berlanga's own life has involved a peculiar criss-crossing of the borders of the 'two Spains'. His father was a Republican deputy sentenced to death following the Civil War and Berlanga, after serving as an auxiliary in a medical unit of the Republican forces, volunteered for the Spanish unit sent by Franco to fight for Nazi Germany, the so-called 'Blue Division', in an effort to save his father's life. The insistence of contemporary critics to encase Berlanga within an exclusively national discourse invariably omits serious discussion of the politics of this ambivalence.[19]

6
'Making Do' or the Cultural Logic of the *Ersatz* Economy in the Spanish Films of Marco Ferreri

> Those were the times when the merit was in substitutes, in sweets without sugar or honey, coffee without coffee [...] And people told the story about the man in the bar who said to the waiter, 'Coffee please,' 'Yes.' 'But is it coffee?' 'Yes sir.' 'Real coffee?' 'Yes sir.' 'But *really*, real coffee?' 'Oh no sir, not that sir.'
> – Fernando Fernán Gómez (in Galán, 1997: 91–92)

In the synopsis of the script for his final film *My Street* (1960), Edgar Neville wrote the following:

> There are the poor and the rich, workers and slackers, the virtuous and the sinners, the good and the evil. Those who are lucky live in the street, but so do those who are not. Each individual believes himself independent, yet in moments of danger or joy, they find themselves tenderly united by that neighborly relation. (quoted in Ríos Carratalá, 1997: 88)

This idealized view of daily life in central Madrid, which constitutes a central discourse of the *sainete*, aptly serves to exemplify Bhabha's critique of 'the many as one', to which I referred at the end of the last chapter. The holistic theory of the community or the nation as an untroubled social totality is often culturally expressed – especially with regard to comedy – in the nostalgically smug terms that Neville employs here. The *sainete* usually takes the form of brief sketches of life in the crowded and cramped confines of a Madrid tenement building, invariably involves a romantic dalliance between a stereotypical *castiza* couple, bolstered by a chorus of neighbors and complemented by a rousing musical interlude. Neville is, of course, being disingenuous. The above quote is not a fair portrayal of any of his own films (including *My Street*) which, while exploiting localized customs and deriving from *sainete*, are also consistent in disrupting the totalizing harmony of their own caricature.

In contrast to Neville, British comic Robert Newman, recently criticized the widespread ethos in comedy that celebrates 'a world in which everything has been sorted out [...] and we're all working together like a team'. Newman complained of the difficulty of performing effective and informative political comedy in a society in which the entire genre has been appropriated and absorbed within the vehicles of dominant culture:

> Every news and current affairs show has its gonky comedy bit. I like to think that my stand-up shows are one of the few places people can escape this incessant humour, the wall-to-wall comedy of our chuckle-culture. Even as audiences queue up, an expectant grin on their vacant maws, I like to watch them through a crack in the dressing room door and think: I'll wipe that smile off your face. (2000: 9)

Aside from Neville, there are literally dozens of films of the 1940s and 1950s that sought to plumb the possibilities of the *sainete* tradition. To this day, as Zunzunegui and Ríos Carratalá have rightly indicated, the residue of *sainete* emerges in cinema in differing ways but generally within a discourse of the city, to which the Madrilenian comedies of the 1980s, and particularly the films of Pedro Almodóvar, testify. With the evolution of *sainete* in film an additional element, that of transport, joins its central theatrical characteristics of the dwelling and the workplace. Film provides a mobility denied stage production and almost all the films in the period under discussion are densely populated with cars, buses, motorbikes, bicycles, home-made vehicles in the form of carnivalesque floats – as in *Plácido* – and even horses. Tony Leblanc, the favored star of many of them, almost invariably plays roles as either a bus conductor or a car mechanic.

We will see examples of these conventions in both of the films discussed in this chapter but its central concern is to illustrate how such conventions can be broken down through comedy. One means by which the *sainete* is disturbed, in what will prove to be a distinctive trait of the work of Marco Ferreri, is through a discourse that revolves around the body. The body in Ferreri is distinguished by imperfection and functional failure. The partialization of the body, I will argue, is a matter of some subversive moment and is also a consuming entity. The body-politic, moreover, is a much employed metaphor to express a notion of seamless totality not dissimilar to Francoist notions of an organic collectivity.[1]

Joseph Roach has historicized the relationship between 'memory, performance and substitution' by use of the term 'surrogation' as the reproduction of something for which the original is absent, an alternative forged by 'survivors' from 'the cavities created by loss through death or other forms of departure' (1996: 2). Two things can be observed here. First, the attempted erasure of the memory of the Spanish Civil War was disrupted by the obstinate presence of the mutilated war wounded, even in the late 1950s, together with the bombed out buildings of the nation's cities in graphically illustrative demonstrations of the individual and urban consequences of the dismembered national body-politic. Secondly, the surrogate is, by its very substitutive quality as replacement, suggestive of the uncanny double. In both instances the notion finds rich expression and representation through the human body and generates a particularly non-discursive form of dual or parallel consciousness. The term surrogate, while undoubtedly crucial to concept of the performative that Roach attributes to it, also connotes the inauthentic and the second hand.[2]

In this context, it was of some cultural significance when Italian-born Ferreri approached the then virtually unknown novelist and impecunious hack writer on *El Codorniz*, Rafael Azcona, with a view to adapting his novel *The Little Apartment* (*El pisito*). Both men would in the course of their lengthy careers in cinema (which continues in Azcona's case) prove obsessive in their concerns with the body. Indeed their most celebrated collaboration was that spectacularly Bakhtinian depiction of excessive consumption, the 1973 *Blow Out* (*La grande bouffe*). At the stage of their meeting, however, neither Ferreri nor Azcona had made or written a film before, although Ferreri had worked in the early 1950s with many of the leading figures of Italian neorealism – among them Zavattini, Visconti, Fellini, de Sica and Antonioni – on the short-lived newsreel *Documento mensile*.

The Little Apartment (1958) was made in the midst of the Spanish state's attempts to reform the Spanish economy. The 1959 Stabilization Plan was the radical solution adopted to halt inflation and shore up the alarming deficit in Spain's balance of trade. The entrance into government, in 1957, of a group of Opus Dei technocrats had signalled the end of any further efforts at economic self-sufficiency and a definitive abandoning of autarky. Raymond Carr, referring to the changes undertaken during the two-year period from 1957 up to the implementation of the Stabil-ization Plan, interestingly describes them 'piecemeal, with interruptions and hesitations' (1980: 156). Carr's description, while resonating with overtones of bricolage, of Gramsci and de Certeau, could equally well be applied to the composition of this movie.

Rodolfo (José Luis López Vázquez) and Petrita (Mary Carrillo) are desperate for a house in order to be able to marry and thereby relieve the twelve years of enforced celibacy to which they have been condemned. At the flippant suggestion of his boss, Rodolfo marries his elderly and infirm leaseholder, doña Martina, with a view to inheriting the tenancy of the boarding house he lives in when she dies. The film is thus structured within the classical format of *sainete* and firmly located in the home and the workplace. Indeed the *inhabition* of the structure of *sainete* is indicative of the 'making do' that pervades the diegesis that, in turn, suggests a kind of 'squatting' within literary convention in an echo of both de Certeau's notion of 'insinuation' (1984: 30) and Gramsci's idea of mixed or contradictory consciousness (1971: 327–333).

From the very first sequence of *The Little Apartment*, the film's discourse on the body exceeds the plight of the ill-fated couple. Almost all the characters either experience physically the strains of economic scarcity or are stricken by strange bodily ailments. Such discourse entwines itself densely around the two vertices of *sainete* (workplace and home). Rodolfo's fellow residents in the boarding house live off the bodily concerns of others while simultaneously being active and avid consumers themselves.

One of them is Mery, who although never described as such is some kind of prostitute. In the introductory sequence of the film – which takes place outside at dawn – she appears in the company of North American man. Indeed, the very first lines of the film are incongruously in broken English. Seemingly inconsequential, this series of shots and their accompanying soundtrack establish a pattern for the entire film. Mery lives off her body and she does so close to the emblematic central thoroughfare of Madrid, the Gran Vía. It is this street that Rodolfo's authoritarian boss, don Manuel, will later refer to by its 'democratic' name and not by its official post-1939 title of *Avenida de José Antonio* (in commemoration of the founder of the Falange, José Antonio Primo de Rivera).[3] Mery's companion, on this early occasion, also introduces a much-employed and ambivalent comparison in post-war Spanish film – that emerges in various ways throughout the film – with the United States. In this initial sequence the extra-diegetic music we hear is vibrant bebop jazz, while the film is saturated with the same recurring *chotis* played on the organillo so distinctive of Madrid. This combination of musics provides an interesting twist to the presence of indigenous and foreign influence. While it is well known that jazz derives from a mixture of influences, primarily African and Latin, Madrid's very own *chotis* is itself allegedly a mispronunciation of the word 'Scottish', first performed, relatively recently, in 1850, it was variously denominated *schottisch* or 'the German polka' (Montero Alonso *et al.*, 1990: 170). One of the most typical and purportedly traditional manifestations of the nation's capital transpires to be a 'borrowing' from other nations. Jazz, of course, was frowned upon by the regime not only because of its mixture of racial influences but because of its modernity.

The presence of *chotis*, in turn, relates to the function of the city of Madrid as an important scenario for most *sainete*. Mery is both the most 'scandalous' figure in the film, and yet is linked to don Manuel, ostensibly the film's 'respectable' character and the owner of the precarious confectionery business where Rodolfo works. This connection is established in two ways: both in the field of the city by means of their respective associations with the Gran Vía and as a locus of 'consumption' concerning the conflictive body. Furthermore, these two characters are unwitting agents in the identification of Madrid itself as an unevenly developed space. Early on we are approvingly informed by don Manuel of the central location of the boarding house ('Next to the Gran Via,' he comments) and yet in this very first sequence, upon Mery's arrival, we hear a cockerel crowing. Similarly, when Rodolfo and Petrita later travel to the outskirts of the city to view the new housing projects under construction, they are obliged to negotiate their way through a herd of goats and their shepherd. One gets a sense, in these sequences, of the rural encroaching on the urban and vice-versa, a graphic reminder of Spain's historical underdevelopment. This, in turn, helps make Bakhtin's work, on both the persistence of popular festive forms and carnivalesque inversions, relevant to the activities of the community of the film.

While Rodolfo earns his measly pay packet rolling individual cigarettes for the firm's in-house idiot, Sixto, to sell on on a tray in the street, don Manuel devotes himself to ingenious means of keeping the company afloat. One of his schemes is named *higalmendra* (a compression of the Spanish word for fig with that of almond), an apparently – or so it is claimed – autochthonous composite of figs stuffed with almonds. Almonds and figs, of course, are distinctive to the Spain only because of their introduction to the Iberian Peninsula by the Arabs. *Higalmendra*, however, is abandoned when the company obtains the exclusive rights and machinery to produce and to market a new American product: popcorn, which is hawked around movie theaters. The use made of juxtaposition with the United States is neither submissive nor xenophobic but rather critically *mixed* in ways that recall the relationship of social realism to *sainete* – as a form of squatting – and thus make Gramsci relevant. According to the Italian Marxist's theory of ideology, man has

> two theoretical consciousnessnesses (or one contradictory consciousness): one which is implicit in his activity and which in reality unites him with all his fellow-workers in the practical transformation of the real world; and one, superficially explicit or verbal, which he has inherited from the past and uncritically absorbed. (1971: 333)

In previous chapters, I have argued that the limits that demarcate dominant discourse also open spaces that facilitate the articulation of an alternative subaltern discourse. Part of that articulation consists of appropriation. Dominant United States culture provides a case in point to which Gramsci himself drew attention as being potentially productive for counter-hegemonic intervention. 'Contradictory consciousness' is an apt description of what motivates and mobilizes subaltern practices in this film insofar as those operations illustrate the complexity of the everyday detail at street level of the modernizing processes that Spain was undergoing at national and international levels.

In the vein of all these elements, it is noteworthy that *The Little Apartment* revolves around the production and the consumption of 'things' and concepts that are explicitly *not* 'genuine'. One of these is 'romance' itself, a key characteristic of comedy. The names Rodolfo and Petrita are not only resoundingly old fashioned, they constitute a parodically low-life version of Romeo and Juliet. It is precisely in the manufacturing of substitutes and in their usage that the discourses within this film turn. Don Manuel's dominant position ensures that it is he who articulates many of those discourses and reveals their weaknesses. It is he who first flippantly suggests that Rodolfo should marry doña Martina and then, on being taken seriously, he balks and says, 'That is no solution. That... that is unspeakable... we're not in America.' The telling coda points up the tense contradiction at the heart of Francoist relations with the United States in the 1950s: that between economic modernization, of which consumerism was central, and simultaneous rejection of its social or cultural counterpart. This latter factor was of course transmitted and perceived in the popular imagination – as the reference to the popcorn of don Manuel's own production suggests – largely by means of Hollywood cinema.

Don Manuel then is a key figure in the *ersatz* economy that pervades the film and functions to undo him and all he represents. There are, nonetheless, many other examples which clarify how the substitute is put to use by subaltern characters. Don Dimas, another tenant in the apartment and Rodolfo's principal advisor, is a kind of prototype for don Poli in Berlanga's *Plácido* – also an Azcona creation – yet more voluble and more clearly positioned as a rogue. Dimas is a chiropodist whose white coat grants him the authority to attend to all kinds of ailments irrespective of his lack of qualifications. His bedroom doubles as a surgery and is crowded with the paraphernalia of medical accoutrement: false leg, stethoscope, white coat. Although we have seen similar elements in preceding chapters – interrogating clinical discourse is one of Azona's favorites – the function of Dimas helps clarify other quack practitioners of medicine. Dimas is a cheap substitute for what is beyond the economic means of the neighborhood population. Just as he is 'making do' for the time being – and he harbors ambitions to set up business in the upmarket Barrio de Salamanca – his clients also 'make do' with him. Like the character of Paco in Mihura's *Castle of Cards*, he operates in-between the poverty-stricken reality of the community he caters to and the discourse of *faux* respectability represented by don Manuel. In this sense, he provides a revealing and mimicking foil to don Manuel himself – almost a substitute but *not quite* – as is attested to by the fact that, incongruously, he is accorded the respectful treatment of 'don', a title that is never applied to Rodolfo for example. Although they rarely meet – indeed, they coincide on only two occasions and both are, significantly, ceremonial – don Dimas and don Manuel constantly echo one another in vacuously discursive terms. The latter, when his purported contacts in high office prove ineffectual in assisting Rodolfo to gain possession of the leasehold, shrugs and says feebly, 'The law is the law'. Some time later when doña Martina finally dies Dimas, who has been awaiting the occasion with some impatience and is at that precise moment fending off a creditor, assumes a posture of dispassionate professionality (as if he were a real doctor) in the face of the condolences of one of his regular patients and neighbors, and resorts matter-of-factly to natural law: 'It is natural, she was very old. It is the *law* of life'.

Such borrowing works both ways. Dimas mimics Manuel's phony legal discourse and yet previously Manuel has resorted to Dimas's Bakhtinian concern with food in the same context. Don Manuel's 'respectability' – sustained by his military demeanor and apparent strictness for order – is tarnished by the passing revelation that his wartime activity was played out on the black market. Indeed, the fact that it was his underground business that provided him with high-level contacts captures the ambivalence of the discourse of respectability, and undermines it by linking directly – Dimas-like – to consumption. Of his parlamentarian friend, Manuel thunders, 'He ate during the war thanks to me'.

The wartime reference, as we have seen previously in other films discussed in this book, positions the facts of real history – the Spanish Civil War – adjacent to the humdrum activity of everyday life. Historical event although censored into oblivion is, nonetheless, pertinently and poignantly present in surrogate form. Many cinema goers of the time would have had very real and persisting memories of the war when the film appeared in 1958 and would certainly be able to identify the influence-trafficking blackmarketeer of the submerged economies of the war and post-war periods.

Likewise, don Manuel's militarism is often undone by its own ideological flimsiness, so riven with contradictions that it constantly threatens to fall apart. In his treatment of Sixto we see an example of the substitute functioning as a metonym in military discourse, namely though uniform. While the key function of uniforms lies in homogeneity (uniforms after all should be *uniform*) Sixto, the most partialized character in the film, is also the only one in uniform. As a sandwich-board man, he is defined as a walking advertisement who pounds the streets and is quite literally nothing more than a set of synecdoches. Moreover, he is repeatedly reduced to an infantalized adjunct of his own mother by don Manuel who, pressing home the point, says to him:

You, without a uniform, are nothing. The uniform is what gives you personality. And look, look at how you are wearing it; dirty, without buttons. Get that handkerchief away. And tomorrow I want your mother to come and see me. I am going to tell her the sort of son she has.

Sixto's dutifully submissive salute in response to this outburst accords well with the idea that conformity can suggest contestation by mockery which, in turn, links metonymically to a chain of values with which don Manuel is associated. We will return to the implications of uniforms later in this chapter's discussion of *The Litte Car* (*El cochecito*).

Dimas's medical 'knowledge' positions him as an *intermediary*, professionally located between medicine proper and the community he serves. His authoritative tone generates a credibility with his clients and points up the parody. To Rodolfo and Mery he pronounces at one stage, 'The old lady is seriously ill,' adding, 'And this time I concur with the doctors'. His Bakhtinian status is reinforced by the fact that he is not even a fully qualified chiropodist but a lowly callous remover (a job associated, euphemistically, with treatment for venereal disease). His concerns extend beyond feet to other forms of flesh. At the very moment of death – at lunch after Rodolfo and Petrita have secured their inheritance – he lewdly fondles a plucked chicken. This adjacence is important to his function and recalls Bakhtin's comment, referred to earlier in discussion of *The Executioner*, that 'death and food are perfectly compatible' (1984: 283). Indeed, the white coat that bestows medical authority upon him is tellingly similar to a butcher's apron. At the very end of the film, following Martina's death, Rodolfo is accompanied in the funeral cortège by don Dimas and don Manuel while in the background a market worker walks by, a side of beef slung across his shoulders.

This final sequence not only places don Manuel and don Dimas together, but also recalls the only other occasion in which they coincide: Martina and Rodolfo's wedding. The wedding is recorded in a series of photographs, represented on screen as stills. It is also 'celebrated' at the same church from where the funeral cortège will later leave. And it takes place next door to the market, the contents of which are so feverishly sought after by all these characters. These sequences are symptomatic of the way in which Christianity is put to 'use' and placed side by side with consumerism throughout the film. Don Manuel combines Christianity with superstition in the workplace. Behind him, on the raised bench where he sits – and fittingly for a Francoist – looms a prominent cross adjacent to which hangs a horseshoe.

In the context of the body and its relation to power stands the figure of don Luis, the owner of the building in dispute. The allegedly infirm Luis plans to demolish the housing block once Martina is dead and travel to Switzerland for treatment. His body is his alibi when confronted by Rodolfo and Petrita; and he claims a particularly Bakhtinian ailment: 'This, that seems like health, is water. Touch it, touch it,' he encourages Petrita, pointing to his thigh. 'And I have to go to Switzerland for it to be extracted.' He goes on to describe doña Martina's impending death and his own as a race against time: 'This is a contest to see who dies first, whether the leaseholder or I.' Bakhtin, referring to the influence of the 'Hippocratic anthology' on Rabelais, stresses the importance attached by ancient medicine to bodily elimination and fluids:[4]

> In the physician's eyes the body was first of all represented by the elimination of urine, feces, sweat, mucus, and bile. Further, all symptoms were linked with the last moments of the patient's life and with his death and were interpreted as the issue of the struggle within the patient's body. (1984: 357)

This interest in quack medicine links Luis to Dimas and – within the consumerist vein of the film – confirms his illness as a kind of surrogate ploy in the face of economic reality. This conversation takes place at don Luis's home, which is decorated by prominently framed boxes of his butterfly collection. The lifespan of butterflies is, of course, symbolic of the metamorphosis that has been denied Petrita and Rodolfo.[5]

At an early stage in the film, Rodolfo and Petrita return from a day out in the country; it is an occasion for reflection on the passage of time and on age. Depressed and on the verge of separation, they return to the city at nightfall when a one-legged man comes speeding past them on crutches and exclaims: 'Look with only one leg, I move faster than those who have two.' Here we see a literally partialized person who is conceivably a victim of the Civil War and who is reliant on his crutch, a substitute leg. This foreshadows a later sequence when Rodolfo drunkenly fondles a false leg he finds in Dimas's bedroom surgery. The *ersatz* economy either plays on substitution or on the counterfeit. Both Manuel and Dimas are frauds of a kind. The entire marriage between Rodolfo and Martina is based on a falsity, one whose religious ratification is suggestive of corruption at the heart of Christianity. Even Rodolfo's choice of partner is founded upon fragile terms with regard to anything resembling authentic 'love'. It is a debate he has with himself throughout the film and declares himself inexorably condemned to be with Petrita. Even doña Martina observes Rodolfo's lack of willingness when she brightly suggests that he marry Mery once he is widowed. Although firmly located within an economy of need and greed the *ersatz* is also present in the discourses that surround the family and the romantic couple. As Evans and Deleyto have noted, romantic comedy has proved particularly flexible and adept at reinventing itself (1998: 3–6). Earlier, I suggested that the names Rodolfo and Petrita constituted a parodic Romeo and Juliet and in this vein *The Little Apartment* is an anti-romantic comedy framed within the matrix of the original. Rodolfo and Petrita – whose yearning for children is manifest – even become surrogate parents for a day when they accompany her sister's children to the zoo. And of course the film terminates with an ironic ceremony of inversion; that is, not the conventional conclusion of romantic comedy, marriage, but a funeral. This particular funeral – set on the bustling, hectic street – is ironically counterposed to the earlier wedding, a truly lifeless affair, symbolically represented by the static photographs.

Human rituals, such as weddings and funerals, are generally held to be precious moments, whose authenticity is not only preserved for posterity but depends on it. These moments, though, prove to be the most demonstrably false of the film. The consumerist Petrita excuses herself altogether from attending Martina's burial in order to go shopping.

The materialist topography of the body establishes the structure of *The Little Apartment*. While the large issues of existential humanity, in the form of death and birth, physically mark the parameters of the film (Martina's impending – albeit prolonged – death, and Petrita's longing for a child), such a structure is reflected in the bodily detail. At one point Petrita is preparing sandwiches at the dining table of the extraordinarily overcrowded flat she shares with her sister's extensive brood. Sitting on a chamber pot on the same table is a toddler who is being fed by his mother, Rosa. The scene provides a living example of Bakhtin's bodily cosmology which is distinguished by the intimate relation between the mouth and the anus. The child consumes simultaneously to the act of elimination in the kind of image that Andrew Horton, in his Bakhtinian analysis, describes as 'an unfinalized state of *becoming*' (Horton, 1991: 13). Meanwhile, Rosa bemoans Petrita's unwanted presence in her home and indirectly refers to another pending expulsion. Rosa, at this precise moment, is not only feeding the baby but also applying 'swabs' to his various orifices, the significance of which was discussed in Chapter 5. Furthermore, this key sequence that dispells and makes discordant any notion of a unified body-politic is immediately preceded by a shot of Rosa's children racing a wheelchair, in which their own landlord is confined, up and down the outside hallway of the tenement block where the family lives, thus providing an apt link to the second film to be discussed in this chapter.

If the action of *The Little Apartment* revolved around the static loci and locations of dwelling and the workplace, Ferreri's third film *The Little Car* (*El cochecito*, 1960) (Figure 10) – and the last one that he would make in Spanish – is explicitly related to questions of age and mobility and, once more, works within a discourse of consumption. When the protagonists of this second film are not stuffing their faces they are fasting.

The period beginning around the mid-1950s and lasting through to the early 1960s witnessed the rise of two curious genres. On the one

Figure 10 The Little Car (Courtesy of Pere Portabella Films 59 and Filmoteca Española)

hand, there was the child-star vehicle, which commenced with the eight-year old Pablito Calvo's leading role in the celebrated morality tale *Marcelino, Bread and Wine* (*Marcelino, pan y vino*, 1954) and reached its pinnacle of popular success with Joselito who made his debut in 1956 with *The Little Nightingale* (*El pequeño ruiseñor*) and Marisol, whose spectacular career began with *A Ray of Light* (*Un rayo de luz*, 1960). The other side to this coin is what might be termed the 'oldster' comic crime movie (Marsh, 2001b: 8–9). The clutch of films that constitute this latter category bear a distinct resemblance to British Ealing comedies such as *The Lavender Hill Mob* (1951) and include among its most outstanding examples José María Forqué's *Hold Up at Three O' Clock* (*Atraco a las tres*, 1962) and Juan Atienza's *The Dinamiters* (*Los dinamiteros*, 1963). *The Little Car* belongs to this group.

Based on Azcona's story *El paralítico, The Little Car* centers upon don Anselmo (José Isbert), the film's elderly protagonist, and his desire for a motorized wheelchair with which to be able to accompany his friends on their excursions. To obtain the wheelchair he has to persuade his lawyer son – who controls the family purse strings – to make the purchase. The film follows the various misdemeanors he commits and the maneuvers he employs to get his own way before he eventually resorts first to stealing the necessary money from his family and then to poisoning them, although he repents and relents at the very last moment.[6]

As the titles roll across the blacked-out section of the split screen in the opening sequence of *The Little Car*, don Anselmo stumbles through the crowds along a busy Madrid street. He arrives at the entrance to a building just as a line of workmen march out in single file carrying pipes under their arms and with upturned toilets clamped onto their heads. Kinder has observed insightfully that the choreography of the workmen in this shot places them as Quixotic figures, helmeted with lances beneath their arms (1993: 121).[7] Just as in *Plácido* and *The Little Apartment*, the low scatological imagery of the toilets is entwined with high-brow literary reference. As we have already seen in the previous discussions, such references to bodily functions – and particularly those involving elimination – are suggestive of corporeal cycles, of replenishment and renewal. It is significant, for example, that these workmen are clearly engaged in the renovation of an old building.

Like Quixote himself, don Anselmo is surplus to needs. He is cast as a redundant and expendable body put out to graze, a figure in his twilight years nearing the end of his time. This shriveled, consumed being nonetheless proves also the most avid of consumers. It is his apparent tragedy – his age – that provides the source for his rejuvenation and the means by which he manipulates. *The Little Car* is a film stamped throughout with recurring images of resourcefulness, recycling and transferability; and at the intersection of all of these stands don Anselmo.

Once more the family is at the conflictual center of the film's action. Don Anselmo is subordinate to his own son, the 'patriarchal' Carlos, who constantly disauthorizes him and who has a similar role to that of don Manuel in *The Little Apartment*. Just as don Manuel lectures Sixto on the function of uniforms, uniforms themselves come to play an important role in this later film. Uniforms are often worn and manipulated by frauds. They supply the substance of appearance that frequently belies an array of counterfeit professions within a discourse of respectability. If in *The Little Apartment* we saw the white coat and false leg of don Manuel's foil, don Dimas, in *The Little Car* we are introduced to two other parallel figures: Carlos and don Hilario, the white-coated 'expert' on orthopedics who persuades Anselmo to acquire the wheelchair.

A sense of the substitutional purpose of uniforms is gained by the ludicrous figure of Álvarito (José Luis López Vázquez), fiancé of Yolandita, don Anselmo's granddaughter and the family's potential son-in-law.

The ambivalently adjacent positioning of the son-in-law within the family is similar to that already analyzed in the earlier discussion of Berlanga. Moreover, Álvarito always wears some kind of uniform depending on the activity in which he engages. When the family goes fishing he dresses as a caricatured angler; his 'student' status is impressed upon us when he dons the costume of the *Tuna*, a university musical troupe, yet such status is later revealed to be phony given his persistent failure. His connection with Carlos is not only that of budding son-in-law, it is also a material relationship between employer and employee not dissimilar to that of Sixto and don Manuel in *The Little Apartment*. However, even as an employee his condition is suspect. He possesses no contractual leverage to be able to legitimately claim a wage, for example, and depends on hand outs. Significantly, he is seen eating in almost all his appearances.

Don Anselmo sees Álvarito receiving his token remuneration from Carlos's secret hoard of cash and decides to steal the money he needs to buy the wheelchair. On returning home with the vehicle, Álvarito and Carlos are outraged and return it to the shop, resorting to spurious qualifications to threaten don Hilario with legal action for having exploited the old man's gullibility. At this point don Anselmo exposes them as frauds: 'They are not lawyers,' he insists. 'This one has not finished university and the other one is nothing more than a judicial clerk.' Just as don Dimas in *The Little Apartment* or don Hilario in this film are false doctors, it transpires that these two are very much makeshift lawyers.

These various up-ended relationships between father and son and granddaughter and son-in-law form an unstable constellation, the like of which recalls other films discussed previously in this book. The very word 'family' is ambivalently turned about, as if it could come to mean a variety of things; indeed as if it could substitute for other forms of community. Don Anselmo, after all, pursues a kind of 'family' among the group of friends whom he wants join on their trips and refuses to accompany his own blood-related family on theirs. This kind of reversal within the family itself is explicitly referred to in Azcona's novel when don Hilario, says to Anselmo: 'But are you not the *pater familias?*' to which don Anselmo responds, ' I am a mere unfortunate with a family, don Hilario, that is what I am!' (Azcona, 1999: 312).

Within this surrogate framework, in which inversion predominates with Carlos acting as if he were his own father's father, it is of some importance that it is precisely the symbols of future familial legacy that are pressed into use by don Anselmo for his own gain. He steals the family heirlooms and takes them to a used-goods shop. The dealer in second-hand commodities – like the pawnbroker – is a central figure in an economy in which 'making do' is the distinguishing element. That it should be resorted to in connection with the family helps contextualize the very transferability, the slipperiness, the *ersatz* quality of the family itself. Among the items that Anselmo sells is his own dead wife's wedding ring which is destined for his granddaughter: the same person who is courted by Álvarito. The aspirations of the marginalized figure of the son-in-law (Álvarito) – and the person who is the most demonstrably strident defender of familial continuity – are undone by that other sidelined figure (the grandfather) who wilfully disrupts all notions of familial cohesiveness. Once more, what is generally held to be enduring and authentic proves – like the function of ceremonies such as weddings and funerals in *The Little Apartment* – perfectly subject to the whims of transaction and exchange.

To this end such symbols – especially given the manner in which they cluster around the Christian model of the family – are enshrouded in additional insubstantiality by the anecdotal prevalence in this film of religious iconography. While don Manuel, in *The Little Apartment*, combined Christianity with superstition and positioned a cross adjacent to a horse shoe at his desk, Carlos's patriarchal status is reinforced parodically by another huge cross before which don Anselmo quails while being reprimanded by his own son. Christianity, on one level, is used to enforce domination; however, on another, its transferable and *usable* nature is made explicit. The shop window at the second-hand dealership where don Anselmo sells the family jewelry is crammed with an eclectic array of other people's belongings. Among the amassed bric-a-brac there is a very prominent Catholic icon in the form of a large portrait of the Virgin Mary. This is very much a second-hand, transferable Christianity upon which deals can be done.

In this vein, it is interesting that the venal and exploitative don Hilario – the epitome of the purveyor of *ersatz* economics, a salesman disguised as a doctor – makes gestures to a Christianity that articulates the operations of making do. Don Hilario is unique among the characters of the film to cross himself at the dining table (and, as we shall see later, this is a film that involves a very great deal of eating). The notion of Christianity as sales pitch is apt. Hilario himself compares his profession to that of a priest. Previously we have seen Bakhtin's reading of salesmanship in the discussion of Neville's *Carnival Sunday* and carnivalesque inversion here, in which Christianity is parodied, recalls the role of Manolo Morán in *Welcome Mister Marshall!* Morán's character in that film also intercedes on behalf of 'the people' with God; that is to say he is a kind of intermediary figure. Intermediary figures, such as don Hilario while helping locate the partial, mixed and *ersatz* cultural economy of *bricolage* within which the film can be located, are also active agents in the formation of its piecemeal composition. Don Hilario, when demonstrating the wheelchair to don Anselmo, stresses its 'Americanism' – like don Manuel's popcorn machine in *The Little Apartment* – as indicative of its surrogate modernity: 'It is of domestic construction but with an American license,' he says.

In the continuation of the film's first sequence, moments after his encounter with the toilet-helmeted Quixotes, don Anselmo visits his friend Lucas who has just obtained a motorized wheelchair. This sequence is the first to introduce the contentious issue of the family and provides a series of discordant notes that persist throughout the film. In counterpoint to what we will learn to be Anselmo's relation to his own family, Lucas dominates and oppresses his. Lucas's family lives in perpetual fear of him. In this introductory sequence, moreover, there is an echo of the scene in *The Little Apartment* when Rodolfo and Petrita are overtaken by the one-legged man in the street. Lucas celebrates his new acquisition – and provokes Anselmo's envy – by celebrating the substitute over the thing it replaces. The wheelchair, he says, 'is better than real legs'.

As in *The Little Apartment*, in this sequence we see rural incursion into the urban center of Madrid. Lucas and his family own a milk bar and sell dairy products. They also have cows in stables in the back yard. The juxtapositioning of the dairy with the motorized wheelchair immediately conjures up an image of the 'new' combined with the 'traditional' and does so within the *sainete* convention of mobility. This is something that is highlighted by the gaggle of daughters and granddaughters who anxiously surround Lucas, convinced that he is going to have an accident. When one daughter exhorts him to wear a Saint Christopher's medal, he mocks her with the telling phrase, 'What fusspots! Anyone would think I was going to America!'.

Closeness by association – such as that suggested by don Hilario's link between the priesthood and sales – produces a series of interesting mixtures of ideological signifiers that connect modernity with tradition and America with Spain. It is perhaps in this context that the earlier Quixotic workmen should be viewed; just as don Hilario and Manolo Morán play parodic priests, the plumbers destabilize the literary canon, similarly to the way in which Rodolfo and Petrita operate as a parody of literary 'star crossed' lovers. This consideration of the construction workers of the film's initial sequence as parodic low-brow synecdoches to the literary canon maybe appropriate to the context of the thrust of counterfeit production; they are, after all, quite literally *bricoleurs*.

It is via the mediation of don Hilario that Anselmo comes to meet don Vicente and his minder, Álvarez (like Hilario another significantly intermediary character). Don Vicente is the severely disabled heir to a fabulously wealthy marchioness. Confined to a wheelchair, Vicente can do little more than squawk and drool and it rapidly becomes apparent that the purpose of his specially made motorized transportation is to alleviate the weariness of the man who customarily pushes him. 'It is me who needs the car,' says Álvarez, 'my feet cannot take any more of this.' Here the wheelchair is explicitly substitution; it is being manufactured to replace the arduous nature of Álvarez's employment. Such reasoning is reminiscent of de Certeau's discussion of the ruses that employees engage in on 'company time', as we have already seen in Chapter 2; that which he terms the *perruque*, defined as 'the worker's own work disguised as work for his employer' (1984: 25).

It is noteworthy that, in a film that deals with the body and its mobility, don Vicente's mother never physically appears in the film. In her two interventions she is nothing more than a voice that emanates from out of the depths of her Rolls Royce or barks orders to her kitchen staff through an internal megaphone. Heirs such as Vicente, of course, are also substitutes, they eventually supplant their progenitors. While his invisible mother is a disembodied voice at the end of an intercom system – a synecdoche, a voice that is a fragment of her totality – Vicente is her absolute opposite; he is nothing more than a twitching and convulsed body, glaringly present but, to all intents and purposes, speechless.

The marchioness is a figure who is not only never actually seen but also never sees what goes on within the very space that belongs to her. At one point in the film Álvarez invites don Anselmo to eat at his employer's mansion. While the incorporeal marchioness entertains guests in the *upper* chambers, Álvarez, don Anselmo and Vicente stage a mock banquet of their own in what Bakhtin would term the *nether* regions of the same building. Here space – the real constructed space of the mansion – corresponds to the Bakhtinian topology of the consuming human body. Kinder is right to identify the banquet sequence as a key moment in this film (1993: 117–118). It is also important to note the bodily representation involved in the topography of the mansion itself. In this sequence the body and the substitute converge in a locus that is germane to my argument.

Out of the marchioness's line of vision Anselmo, Álvarez and Vicente lunch lavishly on the best selection of cold meats, lobster, fine wines and Montecristo cigars, attended to at all moments by solicitous waiters. Álvarez, mimicking the marchioness herself, adopts all the airs of his employers and complains when the cigars are not served on a tray. The performance, complemented by the servants game acquiescence, recalls de Certeau writing of the worker who 'with the complicity of other workers [...] succeeds in "putting one over" on the established order on its home ground' (1984: 26). Álvarez's imitation of his aristocratic bosses is framed – and its performative quality drawn attention to – within frequent resorts to popular sayings. Once again, the scene is symptomatic of a kind of substitute family with Álvarez patriarchal in the manner that he chides don Vicente for eating *chorizo*. The fact that Álvarez plays substitute father to Vicente (whose real father is never mentioned) also pinpoints the divergences within the film's discourse on the family and clarifies the distance between the substitute and the reality it provisionally replaces. While it is true, as Kinder has observed, that don Vicente is repeatedly infantalized (1993: 118) by Álvarez, there is, however, a permanent element of wariness in the latter's attitude. He has never completely forgotten the vulnerability of his employee status and is capable of informing don Anselmo in almost the same contradictory breath that Vicente is 'like a baby who is still being breastfed', and 'if you do not give him whatever he wants he is capable of telling his mother, because he is absolutely no fool'. A fact which is testified to when the hitherto incoherent Vicente becomes suddenly lucid and very nearly gives the game away as the unseeing marchioness speaks to them though the intercom and Vicente splutters his only complete phrase of the film: 'Mother, I have eaten *chorizo*!'; an outburst that provokes Álvarez into threatening him with his raised hand.

Álvarez's patriarchal role bears certain similarities to don Anselmo's own inverted family. Indeed, the mock banquet is inversely paralleled in don Anselmo's own household soon after when the old man embarks on a fully-fledged campaign which eventually leads to his hunger strike. This campaign exploits, once more, familiar questions of illness and authenticity. Don Anselmo feigns the loss of all feeling in his legs and is exposed when the clownish family doctor, don Julio, is called. This physician is yet another oddball character who brings to mind a Marx brothers character. Don Anselmo's fake malady is pitted against the ailments of his son Carlos – himself a fake lawyer – who throughout the film coughs and splutters into a handkerchief and that of Yolanda, whose health is of particular concern to don Julio. This doctor proves no more authentic and no less of a quack than Azcona's other fraudulent physicians don Poli, don Dimas and don Hilario. The real doctor's remedy is no more clinical in this instance – and considerably less imaginative – than anything prescribed by the *ersatz* figures of the medical profession. 'The old folk are like children,' don Julio pronounces, 'A good purge will sort him out.'

This sense of the unreliability of the *real* practitioners of medicine has already been alluded to by Álvarez – precisely the person who places the most faith in, and vouches for, the fraudulent don Hilario – earlier when he resorts to an inverted view of medicine as punishment to gain leverage over don Vicente: 'You play at motorbikes and do not cause me any trouble,' he growls, 'Otherwise I will take you to the doctor for an injection'.

It is in this context that don Anselmo makes his protest, first by refusing to get out of bed and then by staging a hunger strike. In the face of his son's threat to have him confined in an asylum under the auspices of a medical discourse that has already been exposed as fraudulent and positioned in the service of power, he empties rat poison into the food that the maid is preparing. It is perhaps apposite to this book, in light of the earlier mention of *cocido madrileño* in Neville's *Carnival Sunday* that, as the passage in the novel makes explicit, the food into which don Anselmo pours the poison is *cocido madrileño* (Azcona, 1999: 338). Not only is food, once more a significant element in both the forging and the undoing of social cohesion, but this particular collectively consumed dish resonates within a specific urban environment whose spatial practices discourse seeks to enclose.

Conclusion

At the beginning of this chapter, I quoted from Edgar Neville's portrayal of a harmonious community in his idyllic *sainete* street scene and one very much contradicted by Ferreri's films as they have been discussed here. Nonetheless, early on in *The Little Apartment*, Rodolfo returns home and we are privy to a long take that conforms well to Neville's caricature, but with significant differences. A young girl comes forward to meet Rodolfo and leads him by the hand towards a group of children huddled around a litter of new-born kittens; moments later Rodolfo exchanges pleasantries with an old man who has a rooster in a cage and they amiably discuss what they are going to have for lunch. The entire sequence conforms neatly to Manuel Vázquez Montalbán's wry observation on the regime's post-war sloganizing in which Spaniards were typecast as 'miserably poor but jolly all the same' (1986: 49). It is a sequence shot amid the bombed-out ruins of the street. In *The Little Car* don Anselmo smiles benignly at the one-armed man he crosses paths with at don Hilario's shop and, as we have seen, in both films there are a number of mutilated people. These examples, together with the black marketeering of don Manuel in *The Little Apartment* recall the Spanish Civil War. We are witnesses to a nation's body-politic that has been maimed and finds itself precariously balanced upon mounds of rubble with a population of amputees, infirm and starving.

While the Bakhtinian topography of the human physique is reproduced in the pattern of consumption and elimination, the up versus down schema of both films, in neither does it reinforce the notion of an organic and unified body-politic. This is a society riven with unresolved antagonisms. Not for nothing do we see the transportation of a slab of cold and severed meat in the final sequence of *The Little Apartment*. The concern of both these films lies with the fragmentary body.

The Little Car begins with don Anselmo walking through the bustling streets of central Madrid and pausing to marvel at the line of Quixotic workmen. It ends with his arrest by the shadowy figures of the military police, the Civil Guard, as he traverses the bleak flats of the highway that leads southwards away from Madrid. In both instances we see the old man set against symbols of the 'nation-state' and its sustaining traditions, literary and military, consensual and coercive.

In this final sequence the Civil Guards, significantly mounted on bicycles, escort don Anselmo back in the direction from where he has come in his wheelchair. In the characteristic environment of *sainete* the dwelling, the workplace and transport are elements that suggest a adaptation within a genre – a 'making do' – that, in turn, makes claims to being nationally specific. As we have seen before, 'making do' involves an allusive and an elliptical relation to national tradition in which subaltern characters pick, choose, poach and combine elements of various dominant discourses. The aim of this chapter has been to explore how these combinations might function subversively. The bicycle, for example, is a much employed instrument of mobility but it has also become a motif of Italian neorealism. To this end, I would suggest that there is an ambiguous relation between mobility and repression. The piecemeal re-working of discourse that pervades both films discussed in this chapter is not dissimilar to what de Certeau describes as a 'rhetoric of walking' (1984: 100). In this synecdoche combines with asyndeton, which as noted in Chapter 4, is a figure that 'practices the ellipsis of conjunctive *loci*' (de Certeau, 1984: 101). Aptly, in the context of the examples cited in this chapter, de Certeau defines asyndeton in the following terms:

> in walking [it] selects and fragments the space traversed; it skips over links and whole parts that it omits. From this point of view, every walk constantly leaps, or skips like a child, hopping on one foot. (1984: 101)

Within the framework of Spain – its history and its geography – we see the synecdoches of the Francoist state in the patriarchal family, the paternalistic workplace, the imagery of Catholicism and the Civil Guard. And we see these in combination with the relics – and they are often quite literal 'relics': amputated limbs and bombed-out buildings – of the war. In terms of subaltern practice this manifests itself in the hybrid musical forms, free – albeit aimless – wandering across the city, and the scrounging of edible leftovers. Politically this is also symbolic of that which is absent – 'evacuated' or 'eliminated', the exiles, the executed and the political prisoners who lost the war – from the Spanish body-politic. While the body is often cited in national discourse as the sum of the parts of a territorial whole, in both these films Ferreri and Azcona make much of a Spain that is second-hand, substitutional and tawdry; a nation which has obliged its subaltern population to make do. The *ersatz* economy is both articulated by – and an articulation of – de Certeau's combination of synecdoche and asyndeton. As in *Welcome Mister Marshall!*, consumer desire is something realized and put together from the leftovers, the 'waste products' and 'inverted remainders' (de Certeau, 1984: 105) of dominant discourse.

José Enrique Monterde has commented that Ferreri's cinematic career was marked by what he terms 'the negative utopia of impossible reconciliation' (Riambau, 1990: 114). By contrast, romantic comedy, in the words of Frank Krutnik, 'is founded on the promise that the differences between the man and the woman will ultimately be overcome' (Evans and Deleyto, 1998: 23). Although not romantic comedies in the strict sense of the word, the insistence of both *The Little Apartment* and *The Little Car* upon the substitute or surrogacy serves not only to bring into question the premises upon which 'national' genres, such as the *sainete*, are constructed but also to interrogate those cultural elements that exist beyond purely representational boundaries. It is upon the myth of authenticity that utopian claims of romantic love are sustained. The perfect body, of course, is also a utopian ideal. If the utopian body and the idealized family are debunked in the films of Ferreri discussed here, then in the following chapter we will see how, in the work of Fernando Fernán Gómez, such subversion extends to the construct at the utopian center of the Spanish national discourse: the *pueblo*, the home village.

7

The *Pueblo* Travestied in Fernando Fernán Gómez's *The Strange Journey* (1964)

> [E]very power is toponymical and initiates its order of places by naming them.
>
> – de Certeau, 1984: 130

Fernando Fernán Gómez is arguably Spain's most representative living cultural figure. For more than sixty years his gangling, gingery and unhandsome features have dominated the Spanish screen from his actorial debut in Gonzalo Delgrás's 1943 production of *Cristina Guzmán* to his cameo role in Almodóvar's Oscar winning *All About My Mother* (*Todo sobre mi madre*, 1999). As a novelist, playwright, memorialist and participant on television chat shows, he has conveyed the image of the blunt and forthright Castilian straight speaker. The repeated homages to which he has been subjected of late threaten to make of him a national icon. All of this is maybe surprising for a person who was born, in Lima (Peru), the illegitimate son of an actress in a travelling theater company, held Argentinian nationality until the mid-1980s and professes to be a republican and an anarchist.

Fernán Gómez's career as a film director has been prolific yet uneven. Although he continues to direct cinema, there is a general consensus that his best films were those made during the six-year period that stretched from 1958 to 1964 beginning with his third film, *The Life Ahead* (*La vida por delante*, 1958) and ending with *The Strange Journey* (1964) (Figures 11a and 11b). The first of these and its flawed sequel, *The Surrounding Life* (*La vida alrededor*, 1959), are heavily influenced by Bardem and Berlanga's joint debut film *That Happy Couple* (1951) in which Fernán Gómez played the male lead and by the string of hugely popular Italian comedies that came onto

(a)

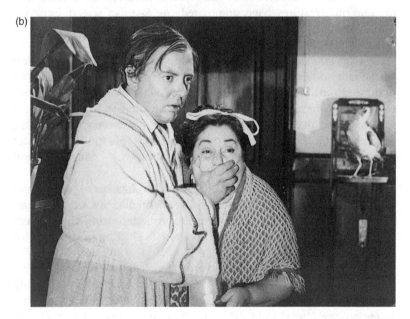

(b)

Figure 11   The Strange Journey (Courtesy of Impala S.A. and Filmoteca Española)

the market towards the end of the 1940s. Indeed, *The Strange Journey*, to be discussed in detail in this chapter is based on an original idea of Berlanga's.

With little evidence, other than the fact that Bardem and Berlanga (together with their classmates from the Madrid film school) attended the Italian film week in Madrid in 1951 and a handful of strident articles in *Objetivo*,[1] Italian neorealism has been proclaimed as a significant influence on Spanish cinema. However, the series of comedies – often starring Sophia Loren, Gina Lollobrigida, Vittorio de Sica and Marcello Mastroianni – that emerged in the aftermath of neorealism has indeed had an impact on the work of Spanish directors. Italian film comedies of the 1950s, nonetheless, have attracted the familiar disdain of critics working in the United States of which Angela Dalle Vacche is representative (and echoes Monterde's on Berlanga, mentioned in Chapter 4), when she attributes a capitulation of neorealism to market forces that commences with Silvana Mangano's celebrated dance in the paddy fields in Guiseppe De Santis's 1948 *Bitter Rice*. 'Mangano,' she writes, 'is a character with a neorealist profession: a day-worker in a northern Italian rice paddy. This class feature, however, is eclipsed by her looks, since she has the sex-appeal of an American pin-up' (1992: 54). Dalle Vacche – in terms that have a direct relevance to this chapter's discussion of *The Strange Journey* – takes her cue from Michael Silverman who sees in Mangano's performance, 'Not only voyeurism and the gaze, not only the Bazinian middle distance, but the documentable trace of American investment is marked by the movement of that skirt' (Silverman, quoted by Dalle Vacche, 1992: 54).

Elsewhere, Mira Liehm dismisses 1950s Italian comedy with the label 'pink neorealism', the ideological implications of which she traces (similarly to Neville's depiction of *sainete* with which the previous chapter began) as follows: 'Everything was nice and rosy in the films of pink neorealism: even poverty, sickness, misfortune. Everyone looked beautiful, everything was glittering, and the establishment was pleased' (1984: 141).

This rosiness – the movement of Silvana Mangano's skirt – raises important theoretical points that go beyond these rather austere reactions. Pam Cook's short work on costume in British cinema, *Fashioning the Nation* (1996) provides an compelling analysis of the relationship between clothing and national identity, whose implications will prove pertinent to this chapter. Throughout this book we have seen that – together with food and music – dress, as a field of non-discursive activity, plays an important role in the disturbance of community and consensus.

Chapter 4 analyzed *Welcome Mister Marshall*'s 'dressing up' of a Castilian village as Andalusia as disruptive of the symbolic nation's claim to be 'timeless and unchanging' (Cook, 1996: 27). The Spanish village (*pueblo*), as a meeting point of national motifs, re-emerges with remarkable frequency throughout the history of cultural representation. The *pueblo* of Lope de Vega's Fuenteovejuna is a key emblem in a tradition of literary and political populism that persists to this day. Several of Almodóvar's films end with their protagonists returning to the family's rural origins. Florián Rey made two versions of *The Accursed Village* (*La aldea maldita*) in 1929 and 1942.[2] In light of the post-war mass exodus towards the country's major cities, the concept of the *pueblo* has a particular poignancy in the Spanish imaginary, most graphically captured in *Furrows* (*Surcos*, 1951), José Antonio Nieves Conde's crude portrayal of a peasant family's arrival in Madrid. Few images produce better evidence of Spain's uneven development than the *pueblo*. It stands at the heart of the 'typical' and the 'traditional' while also forming a locus of tension that comprise its popular and historical composition. Nonetheless, as a concept, it has long been the subject of a 'utopian' idea that captures the essence of nationhood. The Spanish *pueblo* is the unpredictable 'home' at the center of the nation's Arcadian imagination. We have already seen the effects of the encroachment of outsiders upon the Spanish village in terms of conflictive and disruptive knowledge, whether contaminating or educative, in films like Mihura's *Adventure* and Berlanga's *Welcome Mister Marshall!* In *The Strange Journey*, the same questions arise but they do so in ways that go even further in de-legitimizing the 'utopian' and national status of the *pueblo*.

Drawing on James Donald's 1992 book on British national identity *Sentimental Education*, Cook argues that 'collective identity depends on the construction of boundaries which mark the difference between a social group and those it must exclude in order to maintain its unity and coherence' (1996: 37). The boundaries here recall Bakhtin who is also important because of his interest in 'travesty'. Travesty, as we have seen in *Welcome Mister Marshall!*, is directly connected to the function of clothing in subverting hierarchical and spatial order.

From the wearing of clothes turned inside out and trousers slipped over the head to the election of mock kings and popes the same topographical logic is put to work: shifting from top to bottom, casting the high and the old, the finished and completed into the material bodily lower stratum from death and rebirth. (Bakhtin, 1984: 82)

The symbolism of upward and downward movement has emerged at various points in this book and Bakhtin uses dress as a means by which to express the concept. As a conceit it connects the body with both transformation and renewal and links to the ongoing interrogation of claims to authenticity throughout this book. Cook maintains that 'fashion's appropriations are also a resistance to purity,' adding, 'Costume is rarely authentic: [...] even national dress, which is supposed to represent unique cultural values, is a mixed bag of cross-cultural borrowings' (1996: 45).

In similar terms, Susan Fillin-Yeh discussing dandies observes that they are not simply elegant dressers. Like comics they are liminal figures who move in-between discourse. One of the distinguishing features of dandies is that – as we have already seen in the quote from Fillin-Yeh in Chapter 2 – they are travellers who traverse boundaries and, like tricksters and clowns, inhabit the street, the public square and the marketplace. Citing Bakhtin, Fillin-Yeh continues as follows:

Boundaries make creativity possible. Their abutments offer the physical sites for the resonance of many voices, for dialogue. In language that gives immediacy to the performance of aesthetic activity, Bakhtin enacts the visual dialogue of dandies, who, as observed and observers, raise the stakes of both enterprises. (2001: 5)

Santos Zunzunegui (1994) is one of the few people to have written about *The Strange Journey* yet, in contrast to these writers, he does so in terms that stress the 'authentic' national quality of the film. While usefully identifying a series of elements such as the use of music – particularly the format of *zarzuela* in the movie – Zunzunegui insists that this is the very autochthonous material that provides evidence of an essential Spanishness. Serge Salaün, who writes well on Spanish popular song, has demonstrated the composite nature of *zarzuela* itself and its foreign (French and Italian) influences. In the vein of de Certeau, Salaün remarks upon the 'combinable ingredients' (1990: 16) of *zarzuela*. For Zunzunegui, however, *zarzuela* is 'pregnant with "Spanishness"' (1994: 36) in an early demonstration of this writer's cultural nationalism that, as we have seen previously, depends on a particular use of the term 'hybridity'. Herein lies the basis for his later sorry attack on North American transnational critics (1999). In Zunzunegui's perspective, I will argue, textual analysis constitutes little more than the classification of stylistic innovation. Paralleling this, in both the work of Zunzunegui and Marsha Kinder, is the depiction of parody as a kind of depoliticized playfulness among cinematic elites, foregrounded to the detriment of the study of popular cultural forms. That popular culture might be the field that gives rise to parody is of little interest to such critics. Zunzunegui's critical position – and Kinder's – reflects an ideological one that seeks to incorporate such forms into the nominative function of its own discourse. Both critics are concerned, for instance, to protect the exclusivity of the epithet *esperpento* for the Spanish canon. The following discussion of *The Strange Journey* seeks to interrogate Zunzunegui's approach to the film to demonstrate how that most precious of 'national' – and popular – Spanish nucleus, the *pueblo*, might prove a potent destabilizer of its own status. Once more, in the context established by Zunzunegui, Salaün provides an interestingly appropriate – albeit droll – observation on classification:

> The relationship between certain Spanish cultural objects and their *label* has a long tradition of originality. Faced with the generic denomination, what is generally preferred is a metaphorical or metynomical substitute or one that is simply picturesque that distracts and confuses. To call *zarzuela* what is, at the end of the day, lyric theater or comic opera is a taxonomic perversion that never ceases to have consequences with regard to how the object referred to is perceived. (1990: 14)

The Strange Journey (1964)

One of the earliest sequences of *The Strange Journey* recalls Mangano's performance in *Bitter Rice*. Angelines (Sara Lezana) dances the twist and is dressed for the city. Kicking off her shoes she takes to the dancefloor in a performance that is attractive, erotic and modern. Her barefoot imitation of Mangano is set against American music with her foil – and future ally – Beatriz (Lina Canalejas), standing in front of an advertisement that reads: 'Coca Cola refreshes better'. This is contrasted with the rustic appearance of the village men, almost unanimously uniformed in the rural garb of berets and braces. Immediately, the two destabilizing vertices of *The Executioner*, music and dress, emerge once more as significant elements in a text that plays on the nation's uneven development.

Angelines's dance sequence prompts the other villagers, men and women – in what will later prove an important factor in the collectivization of agency – to join her on the dance floor. In this way the initial rupturing dichotomy between modernity and tradition is healed as is that between urban society and the country. Indeed the figure of Angelines – subject to both the lurid gaze of the lecherous elderly men and the stern disapproval of the women and is clearly being 'set up' as a figure of sexual desire – is given contestatory force. At this stage in the film such empowerment, although significant, amounts to little more than the granting of a degree of ambivalence. The apparent opposition created between Angelines, whose boyfriend Pepe forms part of the band, and Beatriz is swiftly established. In the moments following the dance, Beatriz's primness is reinforced by her refusal to kiss her boyfriend, also a band member, Fernando (Carlos Larrañaga), on the grounds that to do so prior to marriage is wrong.

However, earlier in the dance sequence the band, whose members will come to have a significantly disruptive effect on village harmony, is only revealed to us after we have heard the music for some minutes and been introduced to the complex social relations apparent within the village laid bare by Angelines's dance solo. On another level, the modernity of the music – its modishness – clashes with the musicians' appearance. The 'Americanism' of the music is from the very beginning hammed up and comic. The band members wear floral shirts and play accordeons. This is further complicated when it is revealed that they come from Madrid. The props of their act, their *appearance* – in a variation on the use to which such paraphernalia has been put in other films discussed in this book, to reinforce a discourse of respectability – is in this instance intended to bolster a *performance* of cultural modernity that visually (and audibly) competes with traditional rural mores. It is a visually hesitant, faltering and incomplete performance: a mixed construct of Spanishness in which modernity mingles with tradition, the city with the countryside and masculinity is feminized in dress.

As the titles appear on screen, the camera pans over a magazine rack and we glimpse the kind of split ideological and geographical representation that characterizes the movie: *Time-Life* magazine, the Falangist *El Alcázar, La Codorniz*. We see Italian and American cover girls in the bikinis that will spur Angelines into action and the very historically specific headline: 'Franco Meets with Hussain'.[3] This collage reflects a kind of fragmentary plurality in its focus on fashion and geopolitical events. As will become apparent, it is also suggestive of how the public imaginary can operate piecemeal on the media, in ways not dissimilar to Villar del Río population's reading of the newsreel broadcast in Berlanga's *Welcome Mister Marshall!* Contemporaneous history and a different past national history merge. Even the name of the village club – *El Progreso* – resonates with echoes of the Second Republic or, indeed, the tradition of 19th-century liberalism.[4] Bakhtin, describing this process of combining disparate elements as 'refraction', writes: 'This varied *play with the boundaries of speech types*, languages and belief systems is one of the most fundamental aspects of comic style' (1996: 308).

Moments prior to the dance scene, following the shot of the newspaper stand, the action of the film begins with a shrill complaint concerning an item of clothing. In this very first sequence of the movie doña Teresa (María Luisa Ponte) bewails the theft of a corset from her haberdashery where Beatriz works. Teresa loudly complains to a group of other women who accompany her as a kind of female chorus who will voice traditional morality throughout the film. She then stalks across the square to the steps of the club to remonstrate with Beatriz. Teresa functions as a kind of moral cipher who directs a particular linear narrative from start to finish, one that becomes thoroughly undermined. Teresa is convinced that the 'loose' Angelines has stolen the garment. The precarious connection between apparent victim (Teresa) and alleged perpetrator (Angelines) is thus bound up in a vulnerable discourse concerning sexual mores that has clothing as its raw and binding material. Teresa is, after all, in a compromised position when it comes to frowning upon those who make use of such apparently *risqué* items of clothing as lace corsets; she sells them in her shop.

The film follows band member Fernando whose involvement with Ignacia Vidal (Tota Alba), the head of the most financially well-off family in the village and from whom Fernando hopes to extract money, evolves into him leading a double life. From the beginning of their relationship Fernando assumes the role of Ignacia's sartorial advisor. As time goes by he models female clothes for her in the secrecy of her bedroom each Saturday night after the band's performance. Fashion is something repeatedly described in their conversations as a means of breaking free from the constraints of village life and is associated with abroad – particularly France – and youth. With Fernando's help Ignacia plans to escape the village and the country – disposing of her brother, Venancio (Jesús Franco), and sister, Paquita (Rafaela Aparicio), *en route* – once she has sold the family's land and house. In the midst of a family fight Venancio intervenes to protect Paquita from Ignacia and unwittingly kills the elder sister with a bottle. Fernando, dressed as a woman, surprises them and helps dispose of the body before joining them in their flight. At the beach of Cabo de Palos he administers a sleeping draught to the champagne they drink, with a view to abandoning them but overestimates the dosage and mistakenly kills them.[5] As we shall see, consumption – in its most literal sense of eating and drinking – marks the central aspects of the film.

Clothes and a mutual loathing of life in the village are also what connect Ignacia with Angelines. Angelines is seduced by the audacious modernity represented by the bikini and dreams of becoming a model in the city. She detests the coarseness and lack of sophistication of the rural culture that surrounds her and its stultifying propensities. 'If you stay here you will end up as a fossilized piece of dried cod,' she tells Beatriz – allied to her by dint of the oppression by doña Teresa they share and their common interest in the band members – the day she abandons the village wearing fake leopard skin trousers. Meanwhile Ignacia sums up village life succinctly with the phrase: 'In this *pueblo* you are worn-out old clothing, but abroad you are something else'.

Ignacia, as a respectable woman of a certain age in the cloistered confines of the village, cannot be seen purchasing the items of provocative clothing that Fernando procures for her from doña Teresa's shop. Beatriz works in the same shop and they start up a relationship. Clothing – like music – functions as a conduit that connects Beatriz, Ignacia, Angelines and Fernando whose ramifications spread across and beyond the village, linking and mediating the relationship of the *pueblo* with abroad and Madrid. Aptly, in the context of the apparently closed world of the village, the haberdashery shop is called *La Parisien*.

Ignacia is a kind of closeted female dandy who, while yearning to travel and traverse borders, plays out her fantasies through the surrogate medium of Fernando. Being roughly the same height, Fernando walks the street disguised as Ignacia; indoors he performs as her model and mannequin. Their relationship commences with Fernando substituting for her desires in private and terminates with him quite literally replacing her – once dead – in public. One of the more remarkable features of Zunzunegui's essay on *The Strange Journey* is the absence of any detailed reference to the film's spectacular cross-dressing sequences. He restricts his comments to one brief phrase to justify a comparison with Hitchcock's *Psycho* (an undeniable influence on this film). Music and dress provide the modes of expression that exceed Zunzunegui's lines of discursive demarcation.

Fernando and Ignacia dance tango together in a scene that contrasts dramatically with Angelines's introductory sequence in the village club. Where Angelines is daringly public and shamelessly loud, Fernando and Ignacia's tango is private and notably silent; it is furtive. In this instance they are dressed in accordance with tango with Fernando wearing a suit and Ignacia a flowing and transparent white robe. The element of spectacle is exaggerated, as in drag performance, only this time Ignacia wears the costume that Fernando has previously modeled for her. The sequence is quite remarkable as a visual gag. The two protagonists dance, each with an auricular in one ear, the tape recorder slung over Fernando's shoulder in complete silence except for the shuffling of the couple's feet. We are party to a kind of mime – a soundless imitation of the movement of tango – just as previously we have been subject to Fernando's parody of femininity as he parades around Ignacia's bedroom in a white lace negligée. The substitutional tango – its musical presence established by its very absence – relates it to the film's cross-dressing sequences to further diminish the claims made in defence of a native Spanish tradition. Tango, like the twist, is not a Spanish dance. It helps turn the concept of *pueblo*, or any other form of *national* authenticity, inside out. At the heart of all of these issues – and they revolve around movement, dress and eating – is the consuming, dystopic body. Fernando invents a crippled and ailing brother first to stall Ignacia's plans to elope and then as an excuse not to marry Beatriz. This false brother is a convenient counterfeit that reflects other alleged 'essences': the artificiality of the family structure – sibling relations are central to the Vidals – and gender are just two instances.

Contrary to the movement and flight that distinguishes Fernando and Ignacia's relationship – whether through the unheard music or escape to another country – this fictious brother is always referred to in terms of his paralisis. He is nothing but an infirm, moribund body whose in-betweenness has the double sense of being both an obstacle to conventional comic happiness – articulated as an impediment to marriage – and as a half-developed figure inhabiting that Bakhtinian borderland between life and death. Physicality is also what establishes the sibling relation that connects him to Venancio and Paquita, to which Ignacia refers explicitly. When Fernando pleads with Ignacia and says, citing his false brother, 'But he is paralized', Ignacia retorts, 'And mine are fools, which is worse.'

It is precisely the comicity of this film that has been overlooked by Zunzunegui. His failure to lend more than cursory attention to clothing and music, to go beyond merely noting the film's antecedents, structure and intertextual features deprives *The Strange Journey* of its subversive quality. There is a logic to this: if the concept of *pueblo* is intimately related to nation and it is for the national tradition that Zunzunegui seeks to claim this movie, then it is little wonder that he avoids areas in which the entire concept might be subject to interrogation. Zunzunegui's approach betrays its own ideological premises. It is the humdrum comfort of belonging – 'timeless and unchanging' (Cook, 1996: 27) – that characterizes the *pueblo*; a togetherness that is similar, indeed, to that alluded to in the previous chapter regarding comedy itself.

In the introduction to their edited book on cinematic remakes, Andrew Horton and Stuart Y. McDougal refer to Julia Kristeva's definition of intertextuality to clarify Bakhtin's ideas on heteroglossia and refraction in the following terms: '[T]exts form what Kristeva calls a "mosaic of citations" each modifying the other, and many modern authors like Borges or T.S. Eliot in *The Waste Land*, have foregrounded this issue in their own work' (1998: 3).

Intertextuality figures prominently in this film and Zunzunegui is quite right to identify elements of Hitchcock's *Psycho* and *Rebecca* present in the movie. However, he simplifies the theoretical ramifications of such presences in pursuit of his own argument. As we have seen previously, for Zunzunegui the Spanish native tradition absorbs the foreign into its own canon. Such a view has much in common with that of Kinder, who writes of Berlanga and Bardem that they 'dialogized the neorealist aesthetic against the conventions of Hollywood melodrama' (1993: 6). For both these commentators, claiming certain directors as auteurs or insisting upon an authentic Spanish tradition, the popular is resoundingly excluded. Intertextuality becomes subversive when appropriation – such as that of Italian and Hollywood cinema – takes the form of cannibalization.

The idea of 'cannibalism' as a symbolic element – as well as a very real one in this film – ties in with the Gramscian idea of 'borrowing' that recurs throughout the films discussed in this book. The use made of Hitchcock by Fernán Gómez constitutes a reworking – almost a *re-dressing* – of the original films to produce what is very much a comic rendition of the original. Just as the florid costumes worn by the musicians in the band jar comically with the Americanized nature of the music they play, this is also a hammed up, spoofed version of Hitchcock.

In Chapter 1, I referred to Haro Tecglen's use of the concept of anthropophagy as a means by which apparent political enemies consume and absorb their opponents' discourses. In the same passage, I cited Landy's description of civil society's vulnerability to 'cannibalization' at the hands of the state (1994: 236). The film theorist Robert Stam, with extensive recourse to Bakhtin, has written on the function of cannibalism in Brazilian cinema. In *The Strange Journey*, moreover, anthropophagy is an issue that is directly relevant to the diegesis.

Cannibalism figures quite literally within the text of this film. Venancio, Paquita and Fernando hide Ignacia's corpse in the wine vat in the cellar of the house. The gaggle of old men who spend their days on the terrace of the bar in the main square and who – as Zunzunegui rightly points out – act as a *zarzuela* type chorus drink the new wine unaware of the fact that Ignacia is discomposing within it. The collectivization of agency – the making of the population complicit in Ignacia's murder – constitutes, in a sense, the cheerless underbelly of the festivities of *Welcome Mister Marshall!* It is still, nonetheless, a comedy, one that metonymically, mimes the nation as a totality. If Villar del Río is Spain in miniature, so too is the village here which, interestingly, in a parody of the nominative function of discourse, remains unnamed throughout the film.

There is also a direct link between this act of mass cannibalism and clothing. When Ignacia's body is eventually discovered it is because her body is blocking the tube through which the wine is pumped from its storage place to the bar. The comment of the bar owner's assistant, when asked what it is that is preventing the flow of wine, is illustrative: 'It seems like a rag' he says. The word 'rag' is also employed derogatively by Fernando in the course of his later testimony before the investigating magistrate to describe Ignacia's obsession with clothing. The same clothes which are used by Fernando as a disguise, as masquerade, for much of the film, prove the means by which Fernando is revealed. Cannibalism and cross-dressing are linking devices, expressed via the human body, that implicate the entire community. The Bakhtinian philosophy of the grotesque, marked by *up* and *down* positioning, reflects a bodily cosmology in which, 'The mask is related to transition, metamorphosis, the violation of natural boundaries' (Bakhtin, 1984: 40). This violation of frontiers connects the bodies of the individuals with spatial relations concerning the parameters of the body-politic of the village itself.

Chapter 2's discussion of Neville's *Life on a Thread* introduced the concept of thresholds as suggestive of articulating junctures – cross-over points – for spatial boundaries. In *The Strange Journey* there are a remarkable number of doorways, open windows, passages and key holes that function either as the means by which the characters surreptitiously move or as conduits to spy upon their neighbors. In both instances clandestinity contains the principle – or the promise – of pleasure but, significantly, also contributes to the later collectivization of agency. As we will see below, a dialectic is established between interior scenarios and the exterior. Paquita glimpses Fernando's silhouette through the crack in Ignacia's bedroom door, having previously peeped through the keyhole. The elderly men, who indulge in the collective wine drinking, are the same group who join Angelines on the dance floor in the earlier sequence. By night they spy on Angelines from behind a hay cart as she undresses and are witnesses to Fernando's nightly jaunts dressed as a woman. During the day, from their permanent spot in front of the bar, they maintain a running commentary on the goings-on in the Vidal household. Their choral function, which marks them as figures from *zarzuela*, also links to the skewed body-politic of the village, tellingly riven by gender division with the women gathered around doña Teresa on one side of the square, the men outside the bar on the other.

The Vidal family itself constitutes a example of the physical manifestations of the grotesque. Like the large, austere and looming house that the Vidals inhabit in topological contrast to the low-lying spread of the village, the bodies of the members of the family are marked by the same *up* and *down* relation. Ignacia is tall, rigid, and imposing: the black dress she wears in public throughout the film suggests perpetual mourning. In contrast, Paquita and Venancio are both short, dumpy and vivacious. Their movements are scampering. From their first appearance in the film we are aware of a gender disturbance: Ignacia is patriarchal, in that it is she who exercises disciplinary and financial control in the household. Her brother and sister, meanwhile, are forty-year-old infants. Hopewell describes them well when he writes that Venancio 'looks like a retarded cherubim, his sister has a tiny face perched on a pumpkin of a body' (1986: 61).

In Bakhtin's thought the notion of the hole – an aperture, like the threshold – is important. Holes breach frontiers. Bakhtin has in mind the bodily orifices of the 'rending, chewing mouth' (1984: 281) and the anal passage as dialogical elements of communication between borders. The porous borders in the case of *The Strange Journey* – and many other films discussed in this book – are those of genre (detective story, horror film and comedy), gender, and the boundary between the city and country that is ruptured by outsiders, who are frequently musicians or entertainers, like the travelling theater company in Mihura's *Aventure* or Lola Sevilla and Manolo in *Welcome Mister Marshall!* The channels that traverse such frontiers are also the means by which clandestine movement is conducted by and between the protagonists. Fernando passes through a labyrinth of passageways, entrances, doorways and different open windows in order to reach Ignacia's room unseen. His notion of concealment is reinforced by holes as well as by dress. The night of Ignacia's death sees a cluster of orifices combined with cross-dressing. Ignacia's body is dumped into a hole. This is an orifice, moreover, within a cellar; that is, in the *lower* bodily part of the same building which, when observed by the male chorus gathered in the square, looms *upwards* and which has attracted the notice of Zunzunegui for its similarity to that of the motel in Hitchcock's film. As already noted, the positioning of the house, dominating the village landscape, reflects the Bakhtinian schema of up and down in the internal relations behind the doors of the Vidal household.

This physical similarity between the Vidal family and the topology of the village draws attention to spatializing contrasts, particularly those borders that divide and connect the collectivity of the *pueblo* and its individual members. In the metaphorical body of the *pueblo* there are significant spatial differences between the dark, fetid holes through which Fernando passes and the open space of main square. While Fernando and the Vidal family members engage in unusual behavior, unseen and indoors, such individual agency becomes collectivized out in the open in the main square in the act of mass cannibalism. Bakhtin expresses the idea of the bodily cosmos by referring to drink, dress and that of the figure of the woman:

> The woman of Gallic tradition is the bodily grave of man. She represents in person the undoing of pretentiousness, of all that is finished, completed and exhausted. She is the inexhaustible vessel of conception, which dooms all that is old and terminated. Like the Sybil of Panzoult in Rabelais' novel, she lifts her skirts and shows the parts through which everything passes (the underworld, the grave) and from which everything issues forth. (1984: 241)

The blurring between genders has a corresponding effect on the divisions within the collectivity that constitutes the village population. The two choruses, occupying different sides of the square, are made complicit in the crimes committed. These two groups are defined and divided by gender but united by a mutual interest in consumption. The women who bemoan the moral demise of contemporary life do so in the shadow of the haberdashery, while the village bar acts as the center of operations for the group of elderly men. In this context it is of some comic importance that the three victims of 'murder' in this film are killed either by what they consume or by an implement directly connected to consumption. Venancio and Paquita die by drinking poisoned champagne, administered by Fernando, while toasting their escape and Ignacia is killed by her brother wielding a bottle of home-made liquor. It is appropriate that, once dead, she should be deposited in a wine vat and left to rot.

Consumption connects to cannibalism, which has already been connected by clothing to cross-dressing, to collectivize agency. The two choruses' division into genders is first interrogated by Fernando's cross-dressing and consequently transgressed wholesale when the village population consumes Ignacia's remains. Furthermore, cross-dressing is fundamentally comic. 'Comedians,' observes John Lahr in his biography of a more recent cross dresser, Barry Humphries (Dame Edna Everage), 'traditionally are the instinctive enemies of boundaries' (1992: 44). Boundaries, as I argued in Chapter 1, define the geographical area of political operations of nation-states. Transvestites – like comics themselves – are in-between genders, their transgression lies in the fact that they transcend dividing walls. The topology of the body – the very real bodies of the tall Ignacia/Fernando and the short Paquita/ Venancio – is reflected in the topology of the village, with the towering house in one corner of the square, from where its inhabitants are observed from below. At the end of the previous chapter, I suggested that the notion of the body was a traditional means of expressing a unified and utopian concept. In this film both the body and the village are exposed as dystopias. Given that both the body and the village should figure as important components in the construction of the utopian discourse of the nation, it is significant that it should be precisely by means of non-discursive elements that it becomes undone. Clothes – and to a lesser degree music in the form of the twist, the tango and the Madrilenian band – breach established borders and provide the material for what Bakhtin suggests is the function of *travesty*.

The Spanish word *travestí* – in popular use – means transvestite. The English word is more general, often used in connection with farce, but also containing pantomime elements. As Lahr points out, Dame Edna Everage is a character that has evolved from the music-hall tradition as the pantomime dame. Travesty, however, also has a popular association with the notion of fraud, of the counterfeit and the inauthentic. Fernando's drag is apparently economically inspired, with a view to exploiting Ignacia's money. He is not a vocational transvestite and, by cross-dressing, he creates an *erzatz* woman. Indoors he performs as a fashion mannequin who becomes a substitute for Ignacia outside. To escape in the company of Venancio and Paquita, Fernando dresses up as Ignacia so as to confuse the village gossips in the square. He quite literally replaces Ignacia both in the collective mind of the village chorus and as the authority figure who murders the two siblings as they always feared Ignacia would. In the tradition of the grotesque that concerns Bakhtin terror 'was turned into something gay and comic' (1984: 39). Herein lies the key element of the grotesque, which is the ambivalence of its comedy. The apparent divisions between the inner topology of the Vidal house and the open spatial precinct within which the village collectivity moves are once more reflected in the film. Just as the concept of death is linked to consumption in the collective act of cannibalism in the square, within the Vidal household laughter and consumption are also central features. Ignacia's bedroom is a sort of sacred chamber from which Venancio and Paquita are rigorously excluded. Once Ignacia is dead, the two siblings finally build up the courage to return to the scene of the crime. Although they profess to be terrified, they are also hysterical with laughter. They participate in the lengthy folk tradition of laughing at death. In this sequence they not only violate Ignacia's space but also discover their sister's illicit collection of erotic underwear, her store of chocolates and their childhood play things, among which is a hula-hoop. All the emblems of Rabelaisian grotesque come together in this sequence. The hula-hoop recalls the cartwheel, which Bakhtin refers to as a 'primeval phenomenon of popular humor [...] which by continual rotation [...] suggests the rotation of earth and sky' (1984: 353). Rotation is suggestive of unfinalizedness, of the relation in-between the body that links the mouth with the anus. It is significant that circular movement should be identified with these destabilizing characters; they know no boundaries.

This is further emphasized when in the same sequence Paquita discovers a very life-like doll hidden in her sister's wardrobe which she cradles as if it were a baby. This scene connects to another tradition in folk humor. One of Paquita's traits is that she is prone to fits of hysteria during which she stutters and splutters. Stuttering as an impediment is a distinctive feature of Harlequin in *commedia dell' arte*. Bakhtin relates this figure to that of childbirth: 'Harlequin's gesture is also quite obvious: he helps to deliver the word, and the word is actually born' (1984: 309). We have seen stutterers and stammerers before in *Welcome Mister Marshall!* and rarely are they submissive. In *The Strange Journey* Paquita is repeatedly associated with childbirth and yearning for a child. In the same vein, one of Venancio's distinguishing features is his tremulous tone of voice. In the moments following his murder of

Ignacia, the camera homes in to focus upon Venancio's trembling hands. If, as Bakhtin claims, tremors, quivering and stammering are linked to birth, then Ignacia's death heralds a new life. As with Fernando's cross-dressing, Bakhtin further connects all these elements to imitation. Throughout the film, the physical movements of Paquita and Venancio are symptomatic of what Bakhtin considers 'the three main acts in the life of the grotesque body': sex, death and birth. It is apt for the purposes of this book's argument that Bakhtin should not only relate 'bodily topography' to that of its cosmic and geographical counterparts, but also locate the physicality of folk humor – complete with its symbolism of circus tricks and children's games – within such a notion of mimicry:

> [T]hese three acts are transformed or merged into each other insofar as their exterior symptoms and expressions coincide (spasms, tensions, popping eyes, sweat, convulsions of arms and legs). This is a peculiar mimicking of death-resurrection; the same body that tumbles into the grave rises again, incessantly moving from the lower to the upper level. (1984: 354)

There is a set of references that, although scarcely perceptible, fly in the face of Francoist convention and have cumulative effect in the *travestying* of dominant discourse, particularly if we continue the analogy that commenced with *Welcome Mister Marshall!* in which the *pueblo* stands as a synecdoche for the nation. We have already seen the name of the village club associated with 19th-century liberal and republican traditions. Ignacia's desire to be free of the village and to explore the outside, *foreign* world is summed up by her telling phrase that makes clear the village is indeed metynomic of Spain: 'Egalité, fraternité, liberté'. This is echoed – mimicked – by Paquita on the beach as she toasts to 'liberty' before downing the champagne that will kill her. Such mimicry of dominant discourse – which Bakhtin has identified as based upon an imitation of 'sexual intercourse, death throes [...] and the act of birth' (1984: 353) – proves unruly. Doña Teresa, the guardian of Christian mores in the village, resorts to the priest in the course of her unfair persecution of Angelines. The priest is yet another amiable, overweight and Italian type priest who, when he declines to reveal what Angelines might have divulged in confession, is denounced by the outraged Teresa – like a parodic version of Franco's wife Carmen Polo (whose photo appears on the front page of one of the newspapers displayed in the introductory sequence) – as a 'Socialist!'. As with many other loyal followers of dominant discourse that have appeared in this book, Teresa proves an unreliable and contradictory conduit of ideology.

The character of Beatriz is interesting when viewed within the framework of comedy. Marriage as a traditional resolution of comedy is a utopian solution that we have seen violated and mocked in Berlanga, and particularly mocked by death. In this film, *travesty*, in Bakhtin's sense of the word as an inversion of convention and hierarchical values, plays a fundamental role in destroying Beatriz's utopian dream of marriage. The prevalence of clothing – including Beatriz's job in the haberdashery – consolidates the notion of travesty. Although never previously engaged, Beatriz confesses to Fernando that she has been building up her 'bottom drawer' – a collection of domestic items in preparation for family life – since childhood. This is not dissimilar to Ignacia's secret hoard of clothing and sweets. At one stage, alone and to the strains of the marriage waltz, she enshrouds herself in a sheet and enacts her private fantasy before the mirror. Just as Fernando covertly performs a travesty of a woman before Ignacia, Beatriz, to whom he is now betrothed, also acts out a travesty of the marriage ceremony, in front of the mirror, in the privacy of her own bedroom.

Privacy and its violation are key factors in comedy and relate to a pattern of interior and exterior relations, similarly to the corporeal schema of the grotesque. Ignacia's killing is committed in her bedroom in the heart of the house and the village, but Venancio's and Paquita's death occurs on a beach well outside of the village. Yet again frontiers and thresholds assume an importance. For Cook, citing Donald once more, the

> borders between self and other, inside and outside, are [. . .], insecure, permeable. The 'inside' is always fragmented and differentiated rather than pure and united, and the 'others' are never successfully expelled. The act of exclusion produces symptoms: the 'others' return in the form of grotesques to haunt the official culture. The struggle to oust this grotesque produces another, which can be described as 'a boundary phenomenon of hybridisation or inmixing, in which self and other become enmeshed in an inclusive, heterogeneous, dangerously unstable zone' (Donald, 1992, p. 58). This complex, hybrid fantasy emerges from the very attempt to demarcate boundaries. (1996: 37)

Ignacia's bedroom acts as an inner sanctum in relation to the rest of the house – particularly in excluding her siblings – in much the same way as the building in which the Vidals live is frontiered against the rest of the village. This is a reflection of the ambivalent relation of the two choruses with respect to the outside world. The women's chorus led by doña Teresa tend to regard outsiders and those who are influenced by them – like Angelines – as corrupt. The male chorus is more open and welcoming. Given that these are choruses that express themselves in the square, 'self and other' are read here as spatial entities. There are a series of concentric circles – spatially organized – that are turned inside out by means of travesty, by and through the body. The square is the point of arrival and of departure, the entrance and exit to the village where the bus awaits its passengers and the band's car habitually parks. It is the public arena in which newcomers and those leaving cross paths, which is what happens when the two characters most closely associated with clothing and whose lives have been changed by it pass one another: the villager Angelines, who leaves forever, and the city-dwelling Fernando, who returns to face the consequences of his relationship with Ignacia. It is significant that, just as the Vidal family house stands in one corner of the square, Beatriz's bedroom also overlooks the same square. The final shot of the film is a take from her point of view as she looks *down* to see Fernando – in the aftermath of his confession – being led across the square, the public esplanade of the *pueblo* that is a synecdoche of the nation, by members of the distinctive and nationally specific Civil Guard.

Conclusion

Chapter 2's discussion of *Life on a Thread* concerned movement while this film deals principally with stasis. However, as is explicit in its title, *The Strange Journey* also involves a voyage and if dandies are travellers then, according to de Certeau, so too are readers. Angelines is 'put in motion' (de Certeau, 1984: 105) quite literally by her reading of popular magazines in a context concerning clothes and abandons the village to pursue her ambition to become a model. It is apt, thus, in the context of the destabilizing of time-honored rigidities of tradition, not only of *pueblo* but also of genre, with which much of this chapter is concerned, that de Certeau should write the following: 'To read is to wander through an imposed system (that of the text, analogous to the constructed order of a city or of supermarket)' (1984: 169). For de Certeau,

> Far from being writers – founders of their own place, heirs of the peasants of earlier ages now working on the soil of language, diggers of wells and builders of houses – readers are travellers; they move

across lands belonging to someone else, like nomads poaching their way across fields they did not write, despoiling the wealth of Egypt to enjoy it themselves. (1984: 174)

In the same essay, de Certeau quotes Lévi-Strauss on *bricolage* in ways that beg comparison with Gramsci and clarifies the compatibility of the former with the Italian Marxist. Reading, says de Certeau in a point also emphasized by Cook,

> can be considered as a form of the *bricolage* Lévi-Strauss analyzes as a feature of 'the savage mind,' that is, an arrangement made with 'the materials at hand,' a production 'that has no relationship to a project,' and which readjusts 'the residues of previous construction and destruction.'. (1984: 174)

Like many other films discussed in this book *The Strange Journey* resists generic classification. It possesses all the characteristics of a *sainete* whose normal urban context has been shifted to that of a Castilian village. As with Neville's films – particularly those discussed in Chapter 3 – it combines elements of murder mystery with those of comedy. Fernán Gómez himself in interview has remarked on this confusion:

> I confess that *The Strange Journey* strikes me as a funny film, a horror story between country bumkins. People have said that it is like something out of Bergman mixed up with who knows what. In reality though it is a thing by Arniches called *La casa de Quirós*, which is a terrifying story, with a lot of ghosts, set in a house in a village. And I have always envisaged it as something typical of Old Castile, of ridiculous terror, with monsters and birds, but with village idiots. What a laugh! My idea was that the film was a *sainete*, and that all the old folk who appear should be like those in *sainete*. I thought that in this way the public would be entertained. What I never, ever achieved with this film was to persuade the public to actually see it. (Cobos *et al.*, 1997: 75)

Lahr writes that the grotesque 'is a species of confusion' (1992: 118). The attempts at generic enclosure, by which national-cultural discourse is most clearly distinguished, are undone by the mobility generated by the grotesque. While *The Strange Journey* serves Zunzunegui eponymously[6] as a paradigm that 'demarcates the boundaries' of the Spanish native tradition, I hope to have demonstrated that the film's non-discursive elements undo the very discourse that Zunzunegui seeks to sustain. 'Confusion' is unhelpful for the purposes of classification. Nominative practices such as those pursued by many of the critics – both Spaniards and otherwise – whose work I have sought to interrogate throughout this book are weakened by the apparently innocuous operations in all the films that have been analyzed.

According to Fernán Gómez, *The Strange Journey* originally ended with Beatriz alone and distraught before the hoard of domesticity she had been accumulating for married life. The film's producer considered that too despondent an ending and thus imposed the version in which Fernando is led across the main square by two uniformed members of the Civil Guard, having confessed to the crimes (Fernán Gómez in Cobos *et al.*, 1997: 75). Both endings are emphatically non-comic and both are laden with notions of broken romance and isolation. They also connect the 'space' of the village square with the idea of clothing that fills Beatriz's bottom drawer. These are arrestingly incongruous images of a hiccup at the heart of the utopian locus, that of the destroyed prospect of married life and the corrupted collectivity that constitutes the *pueblo*.

' "Home," ' writes Pam Cook, 'is [...] a haunted house' (1996: 39) and the symbolic home at the heart of the utopian Spanish national imaginary is frequently the *pueblo*. *The Strange Journey* constitutes a sort of *queering* of that national construct. This village is riddled with dysfunction, all frontiers are perforated and hierarchical relations up-ended.

From cross-dressing to cannibalism, agency moves from the individual to the collective. The *zarzuela*'s traditional play of couples and its accompanying choruses in the village square form the public, exteriorized expression of a variety of concomitant internalized – and covert – rituals in bedrooms of houses that are adjacent to the same square. The breaching of national borders is achieved by the material of music and dress, through *bricolage*, new combinations of indigenous elements with those from the United States, France and Italy. The construction of the *pueblo* as a parody and metonym for the nation – as a queered or dandified dystopia – is, moreover, further connected to the state by means of incongruity. While Fernando's subterfuge and flight in drag lampoons stable gender identity, dress also makes a mockery of national identity. Comedy thrives on the incongruous and the uniform of the Civil Guard with its accompanying three-cornered hat is both comical and nationally specific. It is perhaps of some note that once more the

Civil Guard – the clearest and most public appurtenance of state repression – intervenes in the final stages of this film, just as previously its members had made striking appearances in films like *Plácido, The Executioner* or *The Little Car*. On this occasion, though, the Civil Guard are filmed at the very center of the village square.

Conclusion: Gila's Telephone

Hello, is that the enemy?

– Miguel Gila, 2001: 25

The purpose of this book has not been to define comedy; neither has it asked why or what it is – either socially or psychologically – that makes people laugh; nor even has it sought to explore in depth those varied and competing theories concerning the nature of the comic mode. It has however, and rather in spite of itself, touched upon all these issues albeit tangentially. Its primary motive has been to adopt a theoretical approach to comedy as an ideological field within the specific cultural context of Spain and the Francoist dictatorship at an historical moment in which the importance of cinematic comedy is almost universally recognized; I refer to the early work of Berlanga, his contemporaries and his immediate predecessors. This book's principle interrogation has concerned itself with what *that* critical consensus really means in a context in which culture is defined by the complex relationship between the state and its people.

The argument of the final chapter suggested that cross-dressing was one means that served to lay bare the contradictions inherent in the Spanish village as a locus of the identificatory – and imaginative – process by which the nation constitutes an idea of its collective self. Indeed, Evans and Babington have observed that cross-dressing is a well-worn 'all-embracing device of comic deceit' (1989: 282). This book, while not specifically concerned with analyzing gender identity, has examined the ways in which the ideological effects of comedy inflect, weaken and occasionally menace the means by which the nation constructs itself around its varied and variable identities in ways that suggest reworking traditional forms from within. I have argued

189

that non-discursive practices, while ongoing within the spatial arenas of dominant discourses, are not synonymous with those discourses; that they maintain a dialogic relationship with them, akin in some ways to the connection of a shadow with the object of its reflection.

In conventional literary criticism it is often held that there are two traditions of Spanish humor: the lacerating wit of Quevedo and the kinder, more empathetic narrative comedy deriving from Cervantes. These two traditions recently achieved some kind of fusion when, in the year 2000, Spain's self-proclaimed heir to Quevedo, Francisco Umbral, was named winner of the Spanish-speaking world's most prestigious literary prize, the *Premio Cervantes*. The award convulsed the country's press. While *El Mundo*, the newspaper in which Umbral has been publishing his daily column since its launch in 1989, celebrated gleefully, his former employers on *El País* hinted darkly that the government had intervened to manipulate the jury. To this end *El País* published a long article by Juan Goytisolo condemning the award. Goytisolo, invoking the Fraga Iribarne of the period studied in this book, managed to write the entire article without once mentioning Umbral's name. For the author of *Señas de identidad* the jury's decision:

> proves conclusively [. . .] the putrification of Spanish literary life, the triumph of tribal and greasy croneyism, the existence of fraternities, nepotism, mutual back scratching, the grotesque apotheosis of the *esperpento*. If *Spain is different*, then it is beyond all redemption. (Goytisolo, 2001: 11)

The familiar terminology of Goytisolo's article re-emerged three months later – in rather more measured tones – when the pages of *El País* hosted a debate between novelist Antonio Muñoz Molina and film critic Ángel Fernández-Santos. The subject under discussion was the disconcerting popularity of current domestic cinematic products such as *Torrente: The Stupid Arm of the Law* (1997) and *Torrente 2* (2000), both directed by Santiago Segura. Considering these films' eponymous central character – a lumpen, fascistic ex-policeman obsessed with violence, a devotee of 1960s beach rumba star El Fari, whose main passion is Atletico de Madrid football club – the painfully earnest Muñoz Molina, disregarding the possibility of irony in Segura's movies and dismissive of the cinema-going public's capacity to discern it, warned that 'nostalgia [. . .] is a treacherous business' (2001: 15). Apparently oblivious to the contradiction, Muñoz Molina indulged in a spot of nostalgia himself when he lamented the current dearth of cultural offerings and the passing of the era which had given rise to films such as Victor Erice's 1973 art-house movie *The Spirit of the Beehive.* Fernández-Santos (who was one of the script writers on Erice's film), on the other hand, made a spirited effort to locate and celebrate the *Torrente* phenomenon within a national discourse. Nonetheless his comments proved tellingly reminiscent of previous commentators discussed in this book when he wrote: '*Torrente* unveils what remains of the sordid elements of Black Spain' (2001: 15). Muñoz Molina did not share Fernández-Santos's celebratory view of such 'blackness' and held that it represented the 'cavernous blackness of ignorance and backwardness' (2001: 15). This dispute over 'blackness' has marked a large part of the discussion in this book. Moreover, it proves suggestively ideological. In essence these writers share the concerns of their fellow contributor to *El País.* Despite his apparent cosmopolitanism, Goytisolo remains entrenched in the Spanish cultural and national discourse he critiques.

The primary impulse of this book has not been to hazard the kind of national, cultural evaluation that Goytisolo makes. As with the different views on 'blackness', its concern has been with highlighting and analyzing the contradictions inherent in hegemonic relations. In both these examples – the acrimonious Goytisolo polemic on Umbral and the more civilized Muñoz Molina/Fernández-Santos disagreement – Spain the nation, its cultural discourses and the politics of the popular are at the heart of critical debate. Irrespective of the virtues (or lack of them) of Segura and Umbral, Goytisolo, Fernández-Santos and Muñoz Molina maintain an elitist view of artistic production that excludes serious consideration of popular culture. It is, moreover, significant that, like those commentators whose work has been subject to critique in this book (Kinder and Zunzunegui), all these writers are associated with a 'progressive' discourse; one that is ideologically undone by the 'popular'. Such a discourse, which in post-dictatorial Spain dominates the outlets of the Grupo Prisa, has staked a inflexible (albeit often implausible) claim to hegemony of the Left. This book has sought to offer a more complex and mobile view of ideology. Just as dominant ideology finds expression among oppressed and exploited groups, progressive ideology is not necessarily incompatible with dominant discourse. Contradiction is the distinguishing feature of such relationships and exploration of such contradiction has informed the writing of this text.

In Hispanic film studies more has been made of melodrama than comedy, yet both represent broad areas of popular cultural consumption: the fields in which populism becomes relevant. Comedy is the cheerful relative of melodrama; both, by virtue of their populist quality, confound the discursive boundaries of history and ideology. This book has been written with the Gramscian view of ideology as mixed, conflictual and contradictory at its center. I have argued against notions of ideology either as a crude set of false ideas at the service of dominant groups or as a unifying body that seeks to resolve contradictions. Ideology, I have maintained, functions as one element among others in a dynamic hegemonic process. Eagleton puts it well when he describes dominant ideology in the following terms:

> It is neither a set of diffuse discourses, nor a seamless whole; if its impulse is to identify and homogenise, it is nevertheless scarred and disarticulated by its *relational* character; by the conflicting interests among which it must ceaselessly negotiate. (1991: 222)

This book has sought to disentangle the ideologies surrounding ludic populism by examining flippancy, fun and the means to which entertainment is put. Terms like escapism are commonplace in our critical vocabulary and form a part of the ideological arsenal with which popular culture is dismissed. I have tried to subject such discourse to the complexities and color of everyday life. Escapism, of course, is an epithet that has long been applied to comedy. Aristophanes's wartime comic drama, *The Birds*, was described as such (Aristophanes, 1961: 7). The fundamental and enduring element of comedy and particularly of its subaltern performers is that quality most alien to both academic commentators and newspaper writers: humility. The intelligent employment of humility has always undone elitist attempts at cultural codification and proved the most dangerous of subversive weapons.

The disruption of the structures of power that comedy poses is explicitly debated and analyzed throughout this book. Alfredo Bryce Echenique has recently repeated the commonly expressed claim that carnival is no longer a threat to hierarchical structures: 'The mythology of carnival these days is codified and archived [. . .] In the carnivals that I have seen the idea of subversion has been totally integrated by the authorities' (2001: 44). I have argued that this, in fact, is not the case. The body continues to consume and expel; Bakhtin's 'rending mouth', the comic's face-pulling, far from being incorporated within dominant culture often remain the only things left with which to do battle. It is ironic that claims which deny all power to consumption should be made contemporaneously with the proclamation of the inexorable ascendancy of the consumer society. Comedy is unavoidably material and it is with this materiality in mind that I have aimed to theorize upon comedy and sought to avoid the more mechanical pitfalls of traditional Marxism. To this end, I have been concerned not to reproduce the sentiments of Adorno and Horkheimer outlined in the introduction to this book; that of 'the people' as dupes of dominant cultural production. It is materialism that marks the substance of my disagreement with those who have labeled Berlanga a satirist. The use of the term 'satire', in the context of the filmmakers studied in this book, is an attempt to come to understand the 'political' nature of this kind of comedy. Nevertheless, it is one that falls short in its scope. Satire is too easy a classification, a means by which debate surrounding the politics of comedy can be codified. In keeping with Bakhtin, I have argued throughout this book that the materiality of comedy is affirmative and that this positive quality proves political. Berlanga's physical comedy – and this is something particularly marked in the bodies of his characters – contains what L.E. Pinsky, quoted by Bakhtin, describes as 'the very impersonation of laughter [. . .] The comic aspect of the spontaneous manifestations of sensuality' (Bakhtin, 1984: 141). This is something that I hope to have demonstrated is not only common to the work of all the film directors discussed here but is also a political attribute. Manolo Moran in *Welcome Mister Marshall!* and José Isbert in *The Executioner* are politically subversive because their comedy is bodily and affirmative. Bakhtin writing on Rabelais might have had Berlanga in mind when he wrote:

> He is not a satirist in the ordinary sense of the word. His laughter is by no means directed at the distinct purely negative aspects of reality [. . .] Laughter purifies the consciousness of men from false seriousness, from dogmatism, from all confusing emotions.
> (Bakhtin, 1984: 141)

In Chapter 7, I mentioned the deceptive presence of speech impediments in a number of films discussed throughout the book. In this context, it is of some significance that in Plato's *Symposium* Aristophanes's intervention is curtailed, initially by an attack of hiccups. When he is finally able to speak he says:

> Yes, it stopped, but not till I applied the sneezing treatment. I can't help wondering whether it is the virtuous love in my body which desires such noises and tickling sensations as a sneeze.
> (1951: 58)

While we have seen that Bakhtin has often been accused of utopianism, his notion of the body is also a site of dystopia. The body in Bakhtin while being the key to renewal is a permanent source of dysfunction. It is apt that the great dramatist of classical Greek comedy should be introduced – like Mamá Dolores in *Welcome Mister Marshall!* or Paquita and Venancio in *The Strange Journey* – in a philosophical text concerning physical love – the very meat of romantic comedy – and should be impeded from speaking by bodily dysfunction.

Bryce Echenique's argument above is reminiscent of the familiar view that carnival and its accompanying comedy provide a 'safety valve' in which popular resentment is vented and contained by the authorities. It has been suggested that Bakhtin's book on Rabelais was written as a rejoinder to sentiments of this nature expressed by the Bolshevik intellectual A.V. Lunacharvsky (Dentith, 1995: 73–79). However, Simon Dentith alludes to another possible interpretation of carnival, one which I have supported throughout this book: that the transformations of carnival make momentarily possible what would otherwise be inconceivable. In a book that has interrogated 'official' utopias of smooth and seamless atemporalities – whether they be of the humanist variety that Sir Thomas More mapped out, or the more negative brands portrayed by Swift, Welles or Orwell – such as the *pueblo* in the national imaginary disrupted by cross-dressing, Bakhtin offers what Dentith acutely describes as 'a malleable space' (1995: 75). This positive utopianism of 'the popular', that provides a glimpse of a different future, is also a critique of official utopias. As we have seen, Bakhtin has written of carnival that it is 'a second life of the people, who for a time entered the utopian realm of community, freedom, equality and abundance' (1984: 9).

Comics are measured by their failure. Melodrama and comedy in fact have more in common than the populism to which they have been harnessed by dominant groups; they share a darkness that is often confused with 'blackness'. While the great cinematic comics are distinguished by their physical movements they are also marked by the fact that they are losers. Groucho Marx, Charles Chaplin, Buster Keaton or Harold Lloyd create themselves bodily as a consequence of the fact that the body is all they have. They are bent-backed funny walkers or elastic acrobats. In part this is because they either emerged from the silent era, or (as with Groucho Marx and his brothers) their comedy makes reference to that period. They are also melancholic. It is this melancholy – something closely aligned with humility – that distinguishes a tradition of comedians and humorists that persists today. El Gran Wyoming,

Pablo Carbonell, singer-songwriter Javier Krahe, the mimic Carlos Latre and other contemporary Spanish comedians represent the intelligent humor of failure that connects politics to the popular. It is one of the unacknowledged strengths of the work of Pedro Almodóvar that he – like Berlanga before him – has known how to exploit this melancholy and its link to the popular without kowtowing to the state's political agenda. Both directors, moreover, have transformed the conventions of comedy in so doing. And, as a consequence, Almodóvar and Berlanga have been much sought after as objectives of dominant appropriation. Berlanga has been fêted at home as a representative of precisely the thing he has most exposed, Spanish *alegría*; meanwhile, Almodóvar has become an international item of cultural fashion and fatally labeled a postmodernist. Both filmmakers have also been accused of frivolity for the very same reasons that they have been celebrated: for their apparent reluctance to assume a clearly defined political affiliation. In fact this gives a clue to the subversive quality that relates them to one another. What Berlanga and Almodóvar have in common is the use to which they have put national stereotypes in order to unmask them. One need only observe the wry use of the utopian village in several of Almodóvar's films to see that both directors have drawn from the same sources: the nation's uneven development and the dominant cinematic production of their times: Italian and North American cinema. This, of course, is a very different thing to saying that Berlanga is a neorealist and Almodóvar a postmodernist. As I argued in Chapter 1, while uneven development and mixed cultural influence are given narrative expression by *esperpento*, the latter is patently not limited to Spain. Humor and comedy are repeatedly associated with nations and national characteristics – it is a commonplace to talk of a *British* sense of humor – yet comedians, buffoons, tricksters and clowns are distinctive for their international qualities. As this text has demonstrated, the circus is distinguished by its nomadism, by its lack of national affiliation.

'[I]t is the Fool', writes Jan Kott in his extraordinary essay on King Lear, 'who deprives majesty of its sacredness' (Kott, 1967: 131). Clowns move and relativize what authority maintains is rigid and inmutable. Lear and Gloucester 'desperately believe in the existence of absolutes', Kott adds and continues:

> They invoke the gods, believe in justice, appeal to laws of nature. They have fallen off 'Macbeth's stage', but remain its prisoners. Only the Fool stands outside 'Macbeth's stage' just as he stood outside 'Job's stage'. He is looking on apart and does not follow any ideology.

He rejects all appearances, of law, justice, moral order. He sees brute force, cruelty and lust. He has no illusions and does not seek consolation in the existence of natural or supernatural order, which provides for the punishment of evil and the reward of good. Lear, insisting on his fictitious majesty, seems ridiculous to him. All the more ridiculous because he does not see how ridiculous he is. (1967: 131–132)

In the context of the discussion of clothing and travesty that has pervaded this book, it is significant that on his first appearance in Shakespeare's play the Fool should offer the Earl of Kent his cap (1951: 1080).

The lack of critical consensus concerning approaches to high and low culture has never prevented political incursions and overtures across the barriers of 'the popular' in the cause of the nation. Exemplary of this is the case of stand up comedian Miguel Gila. In a much less publicized award than the *Cervantes*, Gila received the 1999 *Premio Gato Perich* for humor from the then Minister of Education and Culture and current leader of the main opposition PP, Mariano Rajoy. Two years later, following the death of the comedian, Manuel Vázquez Montalbán recalled the occasion when he observed dryly in *El País*, 'May the viewer compare the current humor of the PP, which erradicates his human condition, and the humor of Gila, who restored to him the role of a rational, albeit rather short, animal' (2001: 39).

Gila, who died in July 2001, perhaps sums up the bleak comedy of the downtrodden and certainly symbolizes an entire generation of losers: those, that is to say, who lost the Civil War. Gila certainly understood the power of humility. Some of his most celebrated monologues, published in a posthumous collection, have titles that might have served as chapter headings for several sections of this book: *The Marriage, The Journeys, The Apartments,* and *The Weddings.* Even more pertinently the biography of Gila stands paradigmatically on the margins Spanish 20th-century history. A combatant for the Republican forces during the Civil War and a member of the Socialist youth organization, Gila was captured in December 1938 by members of General Yagüe's Thirteenth Division, and ordered to be summarily executed. The drunken members of the firing squad miraculously missed their target and Gila fell into a ditch unscathed and later escaped. The impact of this would pervade his later comic stage work. His act – like Aristophanes's play 2400 years beforehand or the work of his contemporary and counterpart in comic failure, Spike Milligan – was a relentless reflection upon war.[1]

Gila, with the prop of a telephone, conducts imaginary negotiations across the lines of the battlefield and with world statesmen. In a sense Gila's monologues are dialogically alive. Gila always addresses an invisible someone.

Gila's professional career began while he was a political prisoner in the 1940s when Miguel Mihura published his cartoons in *La Codorniz*. In many ways his humor derives from that of Mihura, Jardiel Poncela and Neville. His disarming guilelessness is inherited from Chaplin. Vázquez Montalbán calls him 'the scourge of arrogance' (2001: 39). Just as Gila stands as a partialized figure in the wings of Spanish history, his stage act mocked the pretensions of the powerful by resort to a common, everyday item: the telephone. Gila's performative strength lay in his parody of the *paleto*: the po-faced, uncomprehending village idiot that pervades the history of Spanish literature and this book. He wore either, like Isbert's executioner, a yokel's beret or a footsoldier's period-piece tin helmet. Perhaps unsurprisingly Gila, who spent twenty years living in exile in Argentina during the dictatorship, would abandon Spain once more in 1986 – during the first of the post-dictatorship PSOE governments, the very administrations that sustained the 'progressive' discourse outlined at commencement of this chapter – because, in his own resoundingly Bakhtinian terms, 'Today's Spaniard doesn't practice dialogue, just monologue' (Mora, 2001: 39).

The word shadow recurs on several occasions in this book. Comedy is a form of shadow play. The areas that mark the spatial limitations of political authority – borders, twilight zones and the communicating orifices which turn power inside out rather than upside-down – are also the shadowy domains of clowns. Comics operate in the shadows, flickering in-between the shifting planes of discourse; they are a laterally slanted threat on the sidelines of history. Shadows are metonyms that mock the totalities they accompany and with which they are associated. They are the insubstantial products of movement and of displacement; the everyday menace lurking on the margins of regulated order. At the outset of this book, I stated that one of the principal objectives of its theoretical investigation was to identify the nature of subversion. The conventional pursuit of resolution and closure, of community or marital togetherness is very often ruptured on the outer flanks of discourse by such minor and apparently insignificant figures. Bakhtin's clowns and fools – 'life's maskers' – who populate town squares and whose 'entire being' is public and 'utterly on the surface' (Bakhtin, 1996: 159–160) are frequently and mistakenly cited – similarly to the comic dramas of Aristophanes whose characters are repeatedly accused of lacking depth

(Aristophanes, 1961: 10) – as evidence of superficiality. The most apparently simple things are often the most complex; the unresolved flecks, the appurtenances, the 'supplementary strokes', the shadows and the appendages; the Fool's cap, carnival noses, the helmet, the beret, Gila's telephone.

Notes

Introduction

1. Among those who participated in *Uninci* were PCE organizers Ricardo Muñoz Suay and Federico Sánchez (*nomme de guerre* of the future Minister of Culture [1988–1991] under one of the post-dictatorship Socialist governments, Jorge Semprún).

1 Comedy and the weakening of the state

1. Leo Bassi performed nightly at the Teatro Alfil in Madrid throughout the spring of 1997. He has returned to the city each year since and actively intervenes in political discourse, aptly (and uncontrolably) from the margins. In early 2004, shortly before the Government fell in the March 14 elections he led 350 people to the Valle de los Caídos (where Franco and the founder of the Falange, José Antonio Primo de Rivera, are buried) to protest the refusal of the then ruling party, the Partido Popular (PP), to condemn crimes against humanity commited by the Francoist dictatorship.
2. Canal Plus is owned by the media group Sogecable, which also controls the Prisa Publishing group, whose most prominent outlet is daily newspaper *El País*, as well as the chain of radio stations called La Ser among its many economic interests.
3. The Moncloa Pacts were a series of agreements concerning social and economic policy that were negotiated throughout 1977 which led to the legalization of independent trades unions in Spain and certain political parties.
4. Suárez, the former General Secretary of the Francoist 'Movimiento', was appointed by King Juan Carlos to steer the country towards democracy and became Spain's first democratically elected Prime Minister. Carrillo was at the time General Secretary of the Communist Party which remained illegal until 1978.
5. The Gramscian 'organic intellectual' is not, as has occasionally been suggested, an intellectual in the customary sense of the word, such as a university professor. It is somebody who has broken with the traditional way of thinking of his or her class and provides the collective within a commumity or workplace with a form of leadership that propagates these new ideas. Gramsci writes: 'This means working to produce *élites* of intellectuals of a new type which arise directly out of the masses but remain with them to become, as it were, the whalebone in the corset' (1971: 340). A 'traditional intellectual', on the other hand, such as a priest or school teacher, does indeed perform the ideological functions of dominant groups but is also susceptible to being 'turned' particularly in rural circumstances where the emergence of organic intellectuals is less likely.

6. Particularly so in the case of the *Naval Battle*, organized by the neighborhood associations since 1980 to jocularly demand recognition as a seafaring community (Madrid is, of course, landlocked). For several years during the 1990s the local PP councillor Eva Durán Ramos sought to ban the celebrations alleging they constituted an 'apology for terrorism'.

7. The construction of the towers was marred by one of the many corruption scandals that involved the government of the time and led to the jailing of the then KIO representative in Spain, Catalan financier Javier de la Rosa. Among those films which have used the towers are *La buena estrella* (Ricardo Franco, 1996), *Carne trémula* (Pedro Almodóvar, 1997) and *El día de la bestia* (Alex de la Iglesia, 1995).

8. Puerta de Alcala, Puerta de Hierro, Puerta de Toledo, etc.

9. TVE is constituted very differently to other public broadcasting organizations such as the BBC, in that there is little pretence of independence from the ruling administration. Its governing body reflects the party political composition of Parliament and its director general, together with its top staff (including some newsreaders), are appointed by the incumbent government.

10. This song was used as an anthem to launch the daily newspaper *Diario 16* in 1976. It was also played over loud speakers at the gates of Guadalajara Prison on 10 September 1998, the day José Barrionuevo and Rafael Vera, formerly Minister of the Interior and Secretary of State for Security Matters respectively, entered jail to begin their sentences for kidnapping. Theirs were the first convictions of members of PSOE governments for crimes committed in the name of Grupos Antiterroristas por la Liberación (GAL).

11. Their convictions were eventually overturned but only after twenty-three people had spent eighteen months in prison. Another person committed suicide the day before he was due to be taken into custody. HB, together with a number of other organizations and media outlets linked to radical Basque nationalism, has since been declared illegal.

12. Savater has been instrumental in the criminalization of those who do not share the position of the Spanish state in the Basque Country. His questionable influence on Spanish cultural life – and his fondness for protagonism – was perhaps most clearly exemplified recently both by his refusal to participate in Julio Medem's 2003 documentary on the Basque conflict, *Pelota vasca. La piel contra la piedra* (a film that disputed Savater's thesis on the issue) and the hasty manner by which he joined the PP in accusing ETA of the Madrid train bombings of 11 March 2004 (his article in *El País* appeared the following day, by which time it had emerged that the attacks had been carried out by an Islamic fundamentalist group). This has not prevented him being lavishly fêted by social democratic commentators both within Spain and abroad. While keen not to be seen as supportive of state terrorism, Savater has consistently campaigned for the PSOE (the party responsible for GAL).

13. Pemán (1898–1981) was a prolific poet, novelist and playwright of the dictatorship who specialized in exalting the virtues of Spain (and particularly

Andalusia where he was born). He is best known as the author of the words to the Francoist national anthem.

14. Sáenz de Heredia was, additionally, a cousin of Falangist leader José Antonio Primo de Rivera and had worked closely with Luis Buñuel at Filmófono.

15. The *chica ye-ye* was the title of Concha Velasco's 1965 hit that gave rise to a craze among young women, coinciding with the 1960s pop music boom in other parts of Europe and North America. In 1998 Velasco appeared in the stage production of Williams's *The Rose Tattoo* in Madrid.

16. The trilogy of films made by La Cuadrilla was a deliberate parody of the traditional obsessions of the Spanish public: bullfighting (*Justino, asesino de la tercera edad*, 1995) football (*Matías, un juez de linea*, 1996) and politics (*Atilano, Presidente*, 1998) and in doing so draws upon *costumbrismo* (local color).

17. This film concerns a man who is pursued by the ghost of his dead friend who doubles as a shadow.

18. *Peribañez y el comendador de Ocaña* by Lope de Vega is a key text of the honor code of 17th-century Spain.

2 Tactics and thresholds in Edgar Neville's *Life on a Thread* (1945)

1. Gramsci's 'dual perspective' refers to the *articulating* function of the revolutionary or Jacobin party in linking political action and theory, force and consent (1971: 169–173). In the style of de Certeau, he *poaches* or appropriates Machiavelli's image of the Centaur to express this idea.

2. I refer here principally to the 'dominant ideology' thesis of Marx's and Engels's *The German Ideology* and the 'false consciousness' theory that sustains it.

3. 'The two Spains' is a euphemistic term, originally coined by poet Antonio Machado, often employed to describe the relation between those who lost the Civil War and those who won.

4. Conchita Montes – Neville's muse and common-law wife from 1934 until his death in 1967 – and the lead actress in *Life on a Thread* had made her cinematic debut in *The Front of Madrid*. Neville had separated from his legal spouse Ángela Rubio Argüelles. Montes and he never married.

5. The term *castizo*, discussed more fully in Chapter 3, generally refers to that which is typically Spanish and is very much associated with the lower-class neighborhoods of central Madrid.

6. *Carnival Sunday* (1945).

7. It is perhaps worthy of note that Bakhtin cites the Roman tragedian Seneca as an example of a menippean satirist. Seneca, of course, was born in Córdoba in what is today southern Spain.

8. Spain's national lottery was first introduced by Carlos III in 1763 and remains a model for similar initiatives that were subsequently promoted in other countries often by the state itself.

9. Pedro Carvajal and Javier Castro have written, '*Life on a Thread* was a terrible failure: some spectators even asked for their money back' (Carvajal and Castro, 1999: 52).

3   Metropolitan masquerades: The destabilization of Madrid in the Neville Trilogy

1. All three films discussed here disturb Ortega y Gasset's notion of *populismo casticista* as discussed in his work on Goya (1987: 291–310). It is this text that Santos Zunzunegui cites in his discussion of the same films (1999: 102–107). More specifically, I am grateful to Tatjana Gajic for drawing my attention to the ideological closeness that existed between Neville and another erstwhile Falangist and later liberal intellectual, Dionisio Ridruejo.

2. Joseph Roach has written that traditionally the dead and the living have inhabited the same intimate space and cites the example of the Parisian charnel house in the Church of the Innocents in the rue St Denis, which was estimated to have contained around four million corpses when it was finally evacuated following the French revolution (1996: 50–51). The establishment of cemeteries on the outskirts of cities is a relatively recent phenomenon, one that coincided with the European bourgeois revolutions and the rise of modern medicine when close proximity to the dead came to be considered unhealthy and unhygienic.

3. The term *castizo*, as used throughout this chapter, refers to the popular slang, customs and culture of central Madrid. It is closely associated with *costumbrismo*.

4. Carrere's text constituted a high point in a tradition of popular – or pulp – fiction (known as the *folletín*) by which much of the Madrid bohemia earned its meager living during the 1920s.

5. Francisco Llinas dates the story of this film by reference to the soundtrack of the zarzuela *El año pasado por agua* by Chueca premiéred in 1889 (Llinas, 1999).

6. And not only in cinema. Gubern points out that the Spanish national football team was not permitted to wear its traditional red strip until 1948 and, likewise, Russian Salad was renamed National Salad (1997: 33).

7. May 2 is the official holiday of the Madrid region in commemoration of the failed uprising in 1808 in opposition to the French invasion. Among Goya's most celebrated work are his paintings of the following day's executions.

8. Joseph Bonaparte was appointed regent of Spain by his brother and was popularly dubbed both *Rey de Plazuelas* (King of the Squares) for the urban clearance he initiated and Pepe Botella for having 'freed alcohol from crippling taxes' (Thomas, 1988: 45).

9. Aptly to my own argument concerning estrangement, Michael Ugarte has remarked on Valle's Madrid that it 'is a world of strangeness and absurdity, a world in which language makes it possible to step beyond the immediate reality of the city ...' (1996: 143).

10. Lola's nickname *La Billetera* might be translated as lottery seller.

11. Augusto M. Torres is mistaken in referring to this location as the Café del Imperial. Apposite as it may be to Bhabha's post-colonial work, no such café existed. The Café Imparcial, however, did and seems equally apt in light of journalistic claims to impartiality at work in this film. *El Imparcial* was, moreover, the name of a major daily newspaper of the late 19th and early 20th centuries. It was from this daily that a group of journalists departed to found *El Liberal*.

12. *Chulapo/a* denotes those individuals who are Madrid's most typical representatives. On the other hand, *churrona*, *socia* and *mujerzuela* are insults loaded with class bias and suggestive of dubious sexual morality.
13. Once more there appears to be some kind of Jewish subtext here. Money lenders in Spain were, as elsewhere, traditionally Jewish. Indeed Carrere's original novel, *La torre de los siete jorobados*, opens with Basilio's visit to a Jewish money lender in the Rastro.
14. The government of Prime Minister Eduardo Dato (a former mayor of Madrid) was beset by leftist protests throughout 1917 in the form of riots and a general strike. The same year the military intervened to suppress the unrest. Dato was assasinated in 1921.
15. Traditionally nightwatchmen (*serenos*) working in Madrid came from northwestern province of Galicia.
16. The Masked Dance is clearly based on the dances held at Fine Arts Circle (*El Círculo de Bellas Artes*) in Madrid, which commenced in 1891 and were held annually in a variety of city theatres until the Civil War. These dances were renewed following the end of the dictatorship. However, even the democratic period, in its beginnings, proved fearful of Carnival. The prohibition on wearing masks was only lifted in 1980, five years after the death of Franco.
17. There is an echo here of one of the better-known articles by 19th-century Madrilenian chronocler Mariano José de Larra entitled 'El mundo todo es máscaras. Todo el año es Carnaval' ('The World is all Masks: All the Year is Carnival').
18. Perhaps the most celebrated representation of this particular battle is Pieter Breugel's 'The Fight Between Carnival and Lent' (1559).
19. For a thorough analysis of the influence of painting on the film see Dapena, 2001.
20. *La Pradera de San Isidro* (*San Isidro's Meadow*) is also the name of a *sainete* by Ramón de la Cruz (Sala Valladaura, 1996: 57–88).

4 Populism, the national-popular and the politics of Luis García Berlanga: *Welcome Mister Marshall!* (1952)

1. Rey was one of the directors of Uninci, the production company created by a group of recent graduates from Madrid's Escuela Oficial de Cine (among them Bardem and Berlanga) together with Ricardo Muñoz Suay allegedly with the backing of funds from the Soviet Union. Rey came from a family with Republican sympathies: his father, Colonel Casado, was the officer who negotiated the surrender of the Republican Army to the Francoist forces, and was imprisoned following the war.
2. Berlanga mentions the Austro-Húngarian Empire in each one of his films subsequent to *Welcome Mister Marshall!*, allegedly for reasons of superstition.
3. See Chapter 1's discussion of Mihura's films.
4. Gramsci writes: 'One of the most important characteristics of any group that is developing towards dominance is its struggle to assimilate and to conquer "ideologically" the traditional intellectuals, but this assimilation and conquest is made quicker and more efficacious the more the group in

question succeeds in simultaneously elaborating its own organic intellectuals' (1971: 10).

5. 'Noticiarios y Documentales' (NO-DO) was the name of the official newsreel that movie theaters were obliged by law to show before each screening from 1943 to 1975.

6. Susan Sontag writes of the widely held consensus that 'a society becomes "modern" when one of its chief activies is producing and consuming images' (Evans and Hall, 1999: 80).

7. The reference here is to the sequence in the de Sica film in which the residents of the Milanese shanty town mob Totó who has been granted magical powers to fulfill wishes.

8. The neorealist influence in this sequence is obvious: aside from the reference to de Sica's film, many of the actors here are non-professional which adds to the naturalism of the shooting. According to Berlanga himself, the extras recruited to populate the village during the filming were instructed to invent their responses in this sequence. (Comments made by the director at a seminar on Berlanga's work held at Madrid's *Circulo de Bellas Artes*, November 1993, which I attended).

9. By 'international' discourse I would include recent, often inspired, work by Kinder, D'Lugo and Vernon which has concentrated on 'transnationalism' as a means of deconstructing 'national' discourse. The problem with this approach, I think, is that it frequently overlooks 'local' historical specificities and takes as its starting point the 'globalization' of culture.

10. See Hopewell (1986), Kinder (1993), Rolph (1999) and Vernon (1997).

11. In a timely reminder of the importance of these figures, a recent poll conducted among Spanish critics by the film magazine *Nickel Odeon*, concerned with discerning the popularity of repertoire actors in the history of Spanish cinema, was topped by Isbert with Manolo Morán coming second (Nickel Odeon, 1996: 160–169).

12. The *director general* is played by actor José Franco who frequently plays Bakhtinian type comic characters – see, for example, don Matías in *The Bordadores Street Murder* – not dissimilar to those habitually played by Manolo Morán.

13. A convention that stretches from Theocritus to James Fenton. See Milton's *Lycidas* or James Fenton's *Children in Exile* for examples of the pastoral that uses the form to intervene in political discourse.

5   Humor and hegemony: Berlanga, the state and the family in *Plácido* (1961) and *The Executioner* (1963)

1. Interview with the film director in which Berlanga reports a private conversation with the former Minister Manuel Mora Figueroa, present at the cabinet meeting when Franco reportedly made this statement.

2. Quite literally in Berlanga's case. His 1980 film is entitled *National Patrimony*.

3. The comic 'sensibilities' of Britain, Poland, Austria, Jewish humor and so on could equally well be defined as 'black'. Indeed Azcona himself has frequently cited Kafka and Woody Allen as his central influences but not Valle-Inclán.

4. The film was shot in Manresa in the eastern province of Valencia.

5. Berlanga claims that this was the name of a real campaign in his home town of Valencia (Cañique and Grau, 1993: 36).

6. Roach describes a similarly tense moment in the 1991 Mardi Gras in New Orleans when rival parades coincided in the same street at the same time by mistake (19–21). Elsewhere in the same book, while detailing 'a revolutionary spatial paradigm: the segregation of the dead from the living,' he remarks, that 'In this light, modernity itself might be understood as a new way of handling (and thinking about) the dead' (48).

7. Like the Americans in *Welcome Mister Marshall!*, Carmen Sevilla is a promise that never materializes.

8. The long take is not, of course, by any means an invention of Berlanga's but perhaps his particular use of it is. The long shot in his cinema exploits traits of the *sainete* tradition that are limited in stage production.

9. This is also an echo of the Catalán nativity scene which invariably features the figure of the *caganer* defecating in one corner of the nativity scene something that also occurs in *The Executioner*.

10. This is very similar to de Certeau's view of 'time' as the field in which subaltern resistance is cultivated. '... a tactic depends on time – it is always on the watch for opportunities that must be seized "on the wing"' (1984: xix). See also the discussions of *Life on a Thread* and *Welcome Mister Marshall!*

11. See, for example, Arniches's *Una señora de Trevélez* and its filmic versions by Neville and Bardem (*Calle Mayor*).

12. In the very first sequence of the film Julián draws attention to the centrality of the infirm body and medical discourse in this film when Plácido asks him to lend him money to pay the installment on his motorized cart, Julián responds: 'You have got a trade. I am an invalid'.

13. The banquet, of course, has a lengthy historical presence in classical and Christian culture from Plato's *Symposium* to 'The Last Supper' and Beowulf, to mention just a few examples.

14. The tourist boom would give rise to an abundant number of films throughout the 1960s in which the male Spanish *juergista*, invariably played by Alfredo Landa or Manolo Escobar, preyed upon foreign females with an improbable degree of success. Berlanga would explicitly parody this sub-genre in his 1969 movie *¡Vivan los novios!*

15. The making of *The Executioner* coincided fortuitously with the executions of PCE member Julián Grimau and anarchists Francisco Granados Gata and Joaquín Delgado Martinez (the latter two were garroted) in 1963. Partly for this reason it was attacked by both Spain's ambassador to Italy Alfredo Sánchez Bella who saw in it a 'libel' of Spain, and by Italian Anarchist groups who regarded it as an apology for Francoism, when it was shown at the Venice film festival.

16. The *martinete* is a flamenco theme sung off screen with the singer unidentified. However according to Berlanga the singer is actually a non-gypsy, the actor Agustín González who plays Álvaro in *Plácido* (Cañique and Grau, 1993: 50). It is of note that the twist should merge with what is often claimed as the most traditional of 'Spanish' music; music whose origins purportedly lie in ethnic Otherness.

17. '[...] they came outdoors to recite the rosary so that they could be seen and in the churches they made great demonstrations of their faith, but everyone in Mallorca knew that this was nothing more than a mere façade that covered their real convictions' (Blázquez Miguel, 1988: 262). I am grateful to Jorge Aladro Font for first drawing my attention to this aspect of the film.

18. As in the Francoist *Movimiento's* ideal of *organic democracy*, framed within a sacred trinity of 'family-municipality-syndicalism'.

19. In similar vein, following the death of Franco, Berlanga was appointed President of the national Spanish film archive, the Filmoteca Española, only to fall foul of the 1982 Socialist government's appointed head of cinema Pilar Miró who forced his resignation.

6   'Making do' or the cultural logic of the *Ersatz* economy in the Spanish films of Marco Ferreri

1. The image of the body-politic has been used since antiquity and both Marx and Shakespeare refer to it, albeit with opposite motives in mind. Indeed it is worth looking at these two examples if only because they both refer to the same example of Menenius Agrippa. In *Coriolanus*, Menenius quells the citizens' revolt by recounting 'the fable of the Belly' in which the body's members rebelled against the Belly for being 'idle and unactive,/Still cupboarding the viand, never bearing/Like labour with the rest' (Shakespeare, 1951: 828). For Menenius, the Belly – 'the storehouse and the shop/Of the whole body' (1951: 828) – represents the senate, the administration of the state which is the body in its entirety. Likewise, both Shakespeare and Marx look to Plutarch for their source for this fable but whereas, for Shakespeare, it holds good as a means of demonstrating the need to maintain order in the fabric of civil society, for Marx it is evidence of alienation and 'makes man a mere fragment of his own body' (Marx cited in Harvey, 1990: 104), little more than an appendage of the machine with which he works. Man's humanity is physically amputated to a synecdoche.

2. Roach, a scholar of the stage, writes primarily about performance and surrogacy in the context of theatrical representation. I seek here to make use of both his insights and terminology to explore other avenues.

3. In the collaborative film *Las cuatro verdades* (1963), the script of the episode directed by Berlanga and entitled *La muerte y el leñador* was censored precisely for referring to the street as 'la Gran Vía' (Cobos *et al.*, 1996: 126).

4. 'Elimination' or 'extraction' is also what awaits the residents of the boarding house in the form of 'eviction'.

5. I am grateful to Justin Butler, a graduate student of mine at the University of Missouri, for drawing my attention to this aspect of the sequence.

6. This chapter's analysis of *The Little Car* revolves around the version of the film most frequently shown in Spain. Marsha Kinder's discussion of the same film concerns a version in which don Anselmo actually succeeds in killing his family.

7. The relevance of don Quixote to this shot is in its echo of the 'barber's basin' episode in Chapter XXI of Cervantes's novel, when Quixote mistakes the tin shaving dish with which a local barber covers his head to avoid getting wet

in the rain for 'Mambrino's helmet' (Cervantes, 1992: 258–269). Like Quixote, don Anselmo is clearly impressed by the sight. The shaving dish reference is also reminiscent of the earlier discussion of 'swabs'.

7   The *Pueblo* travestied in Fernando Fernán Gómez's *The Strange Journey* (1964)

1. *Objetivo* was a left-wing film magazine founded in 1953 by Bardem and Ricardo Muñoz Suay, among others. It was closely associated with the Spanish Communist Party. There is no doubt that the *Objetivo* group was indeed impressed with Italian neorealism. The magazine's articles have led Kinder to conclude: 'By 1955, neorealism may have been nearly dead in Italy, yet [...] the movement was still very alive as an influence in Spain' (1993: 26). It is my contention, however, that in spite of the enthusiasm of the *Objetivo* writers, there is very little sign of this influence to be seen in Spanish film production of the period.
2. Augusto Torres says of the first of these that 'it has always been considered the greatest of the Spanish silent films' (1996: 64).
3. The reference is to King Hussain of Morocco with whom Spain maintained a conflict over future sovereignty of its then colony Western Sahara, a dispute which continues today.
4. The entry in the *Historia de España Menéndez Pidal* for Salustiano Olózaga (1805–1873) reads as follows: 'As governor of Madrid under Mendizábal, in his fanaticism for progress, which he identified with democracy, he ordered the demolition of the ancient Merced convent in 24 hours, and gave it the name of the Plaza del Progreso' (Juretschke, 1989: 614). Following the nationalist victory in 1939 the Plaza del Progreso in the center of Madrid was renamed the Plaza Tirso de Molina. Interestingly, though, the cinema in the same square retained its original name of *Cine Progreso*.
5. Cabo de Palos is a coastal resort in the south-eastern Spanish province of Murcia. The real life discovery of the murdered corpses of a brother and sister was what originally inspired Berlanga's idea for this film.
6. The title of Zunzunegui's 1999 critique of North American critics of Spanish cinema is *El extraño viaje* (*The Strange Journey*).

Conclusion: Gila's telephone

1. Spike Milligan (1918–2002) fought in World War II and wrote a series of comic memoirs about the experience. Milligan was consistently denied British nationality for his refusal to swear an oath of allegiance to the Crown and died an Irish citizen a few months after Gila.

Bibliography

Adorno, Theodor and Horkheimer, Max (1993) [1973] 'The Culture Industry: Enlightenment as Mass Deception', in *The Cultural Studies Reader*, ed. Simon During (London and New York: Routledge), 30–43.

Aguilar, Carlos and Genover, Jaume (1996) *Las estrellas de nuestro cine* (Madrid: Alianza Editorial).

Alonso, Dámaso (1991) [1946] *Hijos de la ira*, ed. Fanny Rubio (Madrid: Espasa-Calpe).

Althusser, Louis (1972) *Politics and History: Montesquieu, Rousseau, Hegel and Marx* (London: NLB).

Álvarez, Joan (1996) *La vida casi imaginaria de Berlanga* (Barcelona: Editorial Prensa Ibérica).

Anderson, Benedict (1991) *Imagined Communities: Reflections on the Origins and Spread of Nationalism*, 2nd revised edition (London: Verso).

Aristophanes (1961) *The Birds*, trans. and intro. William Arrowsmith (New York: Signet).

Armero, Álvaro (1995) *Una aventura americana: Españoles en Hollywood* (Madrid: Compañía Literaria).

Auerbach, Erich (1971) [1946] *Mimesis: The Representation of Reality in Western Literature* (Princeton, New Jersey: Princeton University Press).

Azcona, Rafael (1999) *Estrafalario: Los muertos no se tocan, nene; El pisito; El cochecito* (Madrid: Alfaguara).

Bakhtin, Mikhail (1984) *Rabelais and His World*, trans. Hélène Iswolsky (Bloomington: Indiana University Press).

——(1996) *The Dialogic Imagination*, ed. Michael Holquist (Austin: University of Texas Press).

——(1997) *The Bakhtin Reader*, ed. Pam Morris (London: Arnold).

Barthes, Roland (1973) [1957] *Mythologies*, ed. and trans. Annette Lavers (St Albans: Paladin).

Baudrillard, Jean (1993) [1983] 'The Evil Demon of Images and The Precession of Simulcra', in *Postmodernism: A Reader*, ed. and intro. Thomas Docherty (New York and London: Harvester Wheatsheaf), 194–199.

Bergson, Henri (1999) [1911] *Laughter: An Essay on the Meaning of the Comic*, trans. Cloudesley Brereton and Fred Rothwell (Los Angeles: Green Integer).

Berlanga, Luis García (2001) Interview at the Málaga Film Festival in 'Homenaje a José Luis López Vázquez', Televisión Española (2 June).

Besas, Peter (1985) *Behind the Spanish Lens: Spanish Cinema Under Fascism and Democracy* (Denver: Arden Press).

Bhabha, Homi K. (1994) *The Location of Culture* (London and New York: Routledge).

Blázquez Miguel, Juan (1988) *Inquisición y criptojudaísmo* (Madrid: Ediciones Kaydeda).

Brandist, Craig (1996) 'Gramsci, Bakhtin and the Semiotics of Hegemony', *New Left Review*, 216 (March/April): 94–109.

Bryce Echenique Alfredo (2001) 'Diálogo sobre el humor con Julio Villanueva Chang', *Claves de Razón Práctica*, 115 (September): 44–48.

Burguera, María Luisa (1999) *Edgar Neville: Entre el humor y la nostalgia* (Valencia: Institució Alfons el Magnànim).

Butler, Judith (1990) *Gender Trouble: Feminism and the Subversion of Identity* (London and New York: Routledge).

Callinicos, Alex (1987) *Making History: Agency, Structure and Change in Social Theory* (Oxford: Polity Press).

——(1989) *Against Postmodernism: A Marxist Critique* (Oxford: Polity Press).

Camporesi, Valeria (1993) *Para grandes y chicos: Un cine para los españoles 1940–1990* (Madrid: Ediciones Turfan).

Cañique, Carlos and Grau, Maite (1993) *¡Bienvenido Mr. Berlanga!* (Barcelona: Destino).

Carr, Raymond (1980) *Modern Spain: 1875–1980* (Oxford: Oxford University Press).

Carrere Emilio (1998) [1924] *La torre de los siete jorobados*, prol. Jesús Palacios (Madrid: Valdemar).

Carroll, Noël (1991) 'Notes on the Sight Gag', in *Comedy/Cinema/Theory*, ed. Andrew S. Horton (Berkeley and Los Angeles: University of California Press).

Carvajal, Pedro and Castro, Javier (1999) 'El tiempo de Neville', *Nickel Odeon*, 17 (Winter): 50–55.

Certeau, Michel de (1984) [1980] *The Practice of Everyday Life*, trans. Steven Rendall (Berkeley and Los Angeles: University of California Press).

——(1988) [1975] *The Writing of History*, trans. Tom Conley (New York and Chichester: Columbia University Press).

Certeau, Michel de, Luce, Giard and Pierre, Mayol (1998) *The Practice of Everyday Life, Vol. II: Living & Cooking*, trans. Timothy J. Tomasik (Minneapolis and London: University of Minnesota Press).

Cervantes, Miguel de (1992) [1605] *Don Quijote de la Mancha*, Vol. I, ed. John Jay Allen (Madrid: Cátedra Letras Hispánicas).

Cobos, Juan, José Luis Garci; Antonio Giménez Rico; Miguel Marías and Eduardo Torres-Dulce, (1996) 'Berlanga: Perversiones de un soñador', *Nickel Odeon*, 3 (Summer): 36–150.

Cobos, Juan; Luis María Delgado; José Luis Garci; Miguel Marías and Eduardo Torres-Dulce (1997) 'Entrevista a Fernando Fernán Gómez', *Nickel Odeon*, 9 (Winter): 40–97.

Colón, Carlos (1996) 'La música en la "cocina americana": Música y comedia en España 1951–1975', *Nickel Odeon*, 5 (Winter): 214–226.

Cook, Pam (1996) *Fashioning the Nation* (London: British Film Institute).

Couto Cantero, Pilar with Fernández Colorado, Luis, eds (2001) *La herida de las sombras: El cine español en los años 40* (Madrid: Cuadernos de la Academia).

Dalle Vacche, Angela (1992) *The Body in the Mirror* (Princeton: Princeton University Press).

Dapena, Gerard (2001) '*Domingo de carnaval*: un cine de diversion y crimen', *Secuencias* 14: 29–39.

Deleyto, Celestino (1998) 'Love and Other Triangles: *Alice* and the Conventions of Romantic Comedy', in *Terms of Endearment: Hollywood Romantic Comedy of the 1980s and 1990s*, ed. Peter Evans and Celestino Deleyto (Edinburgh: Edinburgh University Press), 129–147.

Dentith, Simon (1995) *Bakhtinian Thought: An Introductory Reader* (London and New York: Routledge).

D'Lugo, Marvin (1991) *The Films of Carlos Saura: The Practice of Seeing* (Princeton: Princeton University Press).

Doane, Mary Ann (1992) 'Film and the Masquerade: Theorising the Female Spectator', in *Film Theory and Criticism*, ed. Mast, Cohen and Braudy (Oxford: Oxford University Press), 758–772.

Docherty, Thomas, ed. (1993) *Postmodernism: A Reader* (New York and London: Harvester Wheatsheaf).

Docker, John (1994) *Postmodernism and Popular Culture: A Cultural History* (Cambridge: Cambridge University Press).

During, Simon, ed. (1993) *The Cultural Studies Reader* (London and New York: Routledge).

Dyer, Richard (1998) [1979] *Stars* (London: British Film Institute).

——(1992) *Only Entertainment* (London and New York: Routledge).

Eagleton, Terry (1991) *Ideology: An Introduction* (London: Verso).

Evans, Peter, ed. (1999) *Spanish Cinema: The Auteurist Tradition* (Oxford: Oxford University Press).

Evans, Peter (2000) 'Satirizing the Spanish Christmas: *Plácido* (Luis García Berlanga 1961)', in *Christmas at the Movies: Images of Christmas in American, British and European Cinema*, ed. Mark Connelly (London and New York: I.B. Tauris), 211–221.

Evans, Peter and Bruce Babington (1989) *Affairs to Remember: The Hollywood Comedy of the Sexes* (Manchester and New York: Manchester University Press).

Evans, Peter and Celestino Deleyto, eds (1998) *Terms of Endearment: Hollywood Romantic Comedy of the 1980s and 1990s* (Edinburgh: Edinburgh University Press).

Fernández-Santos, Ángel (2001) 'Viejas caspas vivas', *El País* (April 22): 15.

Fillin-Yeh, Susan, ed. (2001) *Dandies: Fashion and Finesse in Art and Culture* (New York and London: New York University Press).

Filmoteca Nacional de España (1977) *Edgar Neville en el cine* (Madrid: Filmoteca de España).

Fiske, John (1989) *Understanding Popular Culture* (London and New York: Routledge).

Forgacs, David (1993) 'National-Popular: Geneology of a Concept', in *The Cultural Studies Reader*, ed. Simon During (London and New York: Routledge), 758–772.

Foucault, Michel (1984) *The Foucault Reader*, ed. Paul Rabinow (Harmondsworth: Penguin).

——(1990) [1976] *The History of Sexuality, Vol. I: The Will to Knowledge* (Harmondsworth: Penguin).

Galán, Diego (1997) *La buena memoria de Fernando Fernán-Gómez y Eduardo Haro Tecglen* (Madrid: Alfaguara).

Gila, Miguel (2001) *Siempre Gila: Antología de sus mejores monólogos* (Madrid: Aguilar).

Gillan, Jennifer (2001) ' "No One Knows You're Black": Six Degrees of Separation and the Buddy Formula', *Cinema Journal*, 40.3 (Spring): 47–68.

Goytisolo, Juan (2001) 'Vamos a menos', *El País* (10 January): 11.

Graham, Helen (1995) 'Popular Culture in "The Years of Hunger" '; in *Spanish Cultural Studies: An Introduction*, ed. Helen Graham and Jo Labanyi (Oxford: Oxford University Press), 237–245.

Graham, Helen and Jo Labanyi, eds (1995) *Spanish Cultural Studies: An Introduction* (Oxford: Oxford University Press).

Gramsci, Antonio (1971) *Selections from the Prison Notebooks*, ed. Quintin Hoare and Geoffrey Nowell-Smith (London: Lawrence & Wishart).

——(1985) *Selections from the Cultural Notebooks*, ed. David Forgacs and Geoffrey Nowell-Smith (London: Lawrence & Wishart).

——(1990) *Selections from Political Writings 1921–1926*, ed. Quintin Hoare (Minneapolis: University of Minnesota Press).

Grande, Felix (1987) *Memoria de Flamenco*, 2 vols (Madrid: Espasa-Calpe).

Gubern, Román (1997) *Viaje de ida* (Barcelona: Anagrama).

Gubern, Román, José Enrique Monterde, Julio Perucha Pérez, Esteve Riambau and Casimirio Torreiro (1995) *Historia del cine español* (Madrid: Cátedra).

Gutiérrez-Solana, José (1998) *La España negra*, ed. Andrés Trapiello (Granada: La Veleta).

Hall, Stuart (1998) [1981] 'Notes on Deconstructing "the Popular" ', in *Cultural Theory and Popular Culture: A Reader*, ed. John Storey (London: Prentice Hall), 442–453.

Haro Tecglen, Eduardo (1998) 'El caníbal', *El País* (4 March): 65

——(2001) 'Humoristas', *El País* supplement, *Babelia* (27 January): 14.

Harvey, David (1990) *The Condition of Postmodernity* (Oxford, UK and Cambridge, Mass.: Blackwell).

Harris, David (1992) *From class struggle to the Politics of Pleasure: The Effects of Gramscianism on Cultural Studies* (London & New York: Routledge)

Hayward, Susan (1996) *Key Concepts in Cinema Studies* (London: Routledge).

Hebdige, Dick (1998) [1986] 'Postmodernism and "The Other Side" ', in *Cultural Theory and Popular Culture: A Reader*, ed. John Storey (London: Prentice Hall), 371–386.

Hobsbawm, Eric and Terence Ranger eds (1984) *The Invention of Tradition* (Cambridge: Cambridge University Press).

——(1990) *Nations and Nationalism since 1780* (Cambridge: Cambridge University Press).

Higginbotham, Virginia (1988) *Spanish Film Under Franco* (Austin: University of Texas Press).

Hopewell, John (1986) *Out of the Past: Spanish Cinema After Franco* (London: British Film Institute).

Horton, Andrew, ed. (1991) *Comedy/Cinema/Theory* (Berkeley and Los Angeles: University of California Press).

Horton, Andrew and Stuart Y McDougal, eds (1998) *Play It Again, Sam: Retakes on Remakes* (Berkeley and Los Angeles: University of California Press).

Jameson, Fredric (1993) [1991] 'Postmodernism or the Cultural Logic of Late Capitalism', in *Postmodernism: A Reader*, ed. and intro. Thomas Docherty (New York and London: Harvester Wheatsheaf), 62–92.

Juretschke, Hans, ed. (1989) *Historia de España Menéndez Pidal, Tomo XXXV* (Madrid: Espasa-Calpe).

Kinder, Marsha (1993) *Blood Cinema: The Reconstruction of National Identity in Spain* (Berkeley and Los Angeles: University of California Press).

——ed. (1997) *Refiguring Spain: Cinema/Media/Representation* (Durham and London: Duke University Press).

Kott, Jan (1967) *Shakespeare Our Contemporary* (Bristol: Methuen).

Krutnik, Frank (1998) 'Love Lies: Romantic Fabrication in Contemporary Romantic Comedy', in *Terms of Endearment: Hollywood Romantic Comedy of the 1980s and 1990s*, ed. Peter Evans and Celestino Deleyto (Edinburgh: Edinburgh University Press), 15–36.

Labanyi, Jo, ed. (2002) 'Musical Battles: Populism and Hegemony in the Early Francoist Folklovic Film Musical', in *Constructing Identity in Twentieth Century Spain: Theoretical Concepts and Cultural Practice* (Oxford: Oxford University Press).

Laclau, Ernesto (1977) *Politics and Ideology in Marxist Theory: Capitalism, Fascism, Populism* (London: New Left Books).

Laclau, Ernesto and Chantal Mouffe (1985) *Hegemony and Socialist Strategy: Towards a Radical Democratic Politics* (London: Verso).

Lahr, John (1992) *Dame Edna Everage and the Rise of Western Civilization: Backstage with Barry Humphries* (London: Flamingo).

Landy, Marcia (1994) *Film, Politics and Gramsci* (Minneapolis: University of Minnesota Press).

Liehm, Mira (1984) *Passion and Defiance: Film in Italy from 1942 to the Present* (Berkeley and Los Angeles: University of California Press).

Llinás, Francisco (1999) [1992] 'Juan Orduña y Edgar Neville: El haz y el envés', Extract from a paper originally delivered at the 'I Encuentros de Cine e Historia' in Orihuela, May 1992 and reproduced by the Filmoteca Española on publicity leaflet for a screening of *La torre de los siete jorobados* (7 December).

López Rubio, José (1999) [1983] 'Discurso para una academia', *Nickel Odeon*, 17 (Winter): 22–31.

Lozano, José (1997) 'Edgar Neville, Madrid en Cinelandia', *Nickel Odeon*, 7 (Summer): 134–142.

Luque, Juan de Dios; Manjón Francisco José; Antonio Pamies (2000) *Diccionario del insulto* (Barcelona: Península Atalaya).

Madanipour, Ali (1996) *Design of Urban Space: An Inquiry into a Socio-Spatial Process* (Chichester: Wiley).

Madrid, Luciano de (1944) 'Edgar Neville y el sainete', *Primer Plano*, 198 (30 July): 3.

Marsh, Steven (1999) 'Enemies of the *Patria*: Fools, Cranks and Tricksters in the Film Comedies of Jerónimo Mihura', *Journal of Iberian and Latin American Studies*, 5.1: 65–75.

——(2001a) 'Negociando la nación: Tácticas y prácticas del subalterno en la comedia del cine español de los años cuarenta', in *La herida de las sombras: El cine español de los años cuarenta*, ed. Pilar Couto Cantero and Luis Fernández Colorado (Madrid: Cuadernos de la Academia), 99–113.

——(2001b) 'Cine for the Rest of Us', *InMadrid*, 6.2 (February): 8–9.

——(2003) 'The *Pueblo* Travestied in Fernán Gómez's *El extraño viaje* (1964)', *Hispanic Research Journal*, 4.2: 133–149.

——(2004) 'Villar del Río Revisited: The Chronotope of Berlanga's *¡Bienvenido Mister Marshall!*', *Bulletin of Hispanic Studies*, 81.1: 25–41.

Marx, Karl (1977) [1869] 'The Eighteenth Brumaire of Louis Bonaparte', in *Surveys from Exile: Political Writings*, Vol. II, ed. David Fernbach (Harmondsworth: Penguin).

Marx, Karl and Frederick Engels (1970) [1846] *The German Ideology*, ed. and intro. C.J. Arthur (London: Lawrence & Wishart).

Mast, Gerald, Marshall Cohen, Leo Braudy, eds (1992) *Film Theory and Criticism: Introductory Readings* (New York and Oxford: Oxford University Press).

Matthews, Nicole (2000) *Comic Politics: Gender in Hollywood Comedy after the New Right* (Manchester and New York: Manchester University Press).

Mendoza, Eduardo (1996) *Una comedia ligera* (Barcelona: Seix Barral).

Merchant, Moelwyn (1972) *Comedy*, Critical Idiom series 21 (London and New York: Methuen).

Mihura, Miguel (1998) *Mis Memorias*, Clásicos del humor series (Madrid: Temas de Hoy).

Montero Alonso, José Francisco, Azorín García, and José Montero Padilla (1990) *Diccionario General de Madrid* (Madrid: Méndez y Molina Editores, SA).

Mora, M. (2001) 'Muere Gila, el humorista que combatió la sordidez del franquismo con un teléfono', *El País* (13 July): 39.

Muñoz Molina, Antonio (2001) 'Cultura espongiforme', *El País* (22 April): 15.

Neila, Clara (1997) 'Dario Fo: Esta sentencia es muy peligrosa', *El Mundo* (3 December): 17.

Neville, Edgar (1977) 'La vida en un hilo según Neville', *Edgar Neville en el cine* (Madrid: Filmoteca Nacional de España), 37–39.

Newman, Robert (2000) 'Performers of the World Unite', *The Guardian* (7 August): 9.

Nickel Odeon (1996) 'Cien españoles y los actores de reparto', Poll published in *Nickel Odeon*, 3 (Summer): 160–169.

Ortega y Gasset, José (1957) [1921] *España invertebrada* (Madrid: Revista de Occidente).

——(1987) [1950] *Papeles sobre Velázquez y Goya* (Madrid: Revista de Occidente en Alianza Editorial).

Perales, Francisco (1997) *Luis García Berlanga* (Madrid: Cátedra).

Pérez Perucha, Julio (1982) *El cinema de Edgar Neville* (Valladolid: 27 semana internacional de cine de Valladolid).

——ed. (1999a) *En torno a Luis García Berlanga* (Valencia: Mitemas).

——(1999b) 'Homenaje a José Luis López Vázquez', Unpublished speech delivered at the VIII Congreso de la Asociación Española de Historiadores de Cine, Celanova, Ourense (18 December).

Petronius (1965) *The Satyricon and the Fragments*, intro. and trans. John Sullivan (Harmondsworth: Penguin Classics).

Plato (1951) *The Symposium*, intro. and trans. W. Hamilton (Harmondsworth: Penguin Classics).

Plutarch (1965) *Makers of Rome*, intro. and trans. Ian Scott-Kilvert (Harmondsworth: Penguin Classics).

Preston, Paul (1993) *Franco* (London: Fontana Press).

——(1997) Introduction to Manuel Aznar's interview with Francisco Franco, reproduced in *El País Semanal* (2 November): 114–115.

Riambau, Esteve, ed. (1990) *Antes del apocalipsis: El cine de Marco Ferreri* (Madrid: Cátedra/Mostra de Cinema Mediterrani).

Richards, Mike (1995) 'Terror and Progress: Industrialization, Modernity and the Making of Francoism', in *Spanish Cultural Studies: An Introduction*, ed. Helen Graham and Jo Labanyi (Oxford: Oxford University Press), 173–182.

Rigalt, Carmen (1997) 'Entrevista con *El Gran Wyoming*', *La Revista de El Mundo* (19 January): 30–33.

Ríos Carratalá, Juan A. (1997) *Lo sainetesco en el cine español* (Alicante: Universidad de Alicante Publicaciones).

Roach, Joseph (1996) *Cities of the Dead: Circum-Atlantic Performance* (New York: Columbia University Press).

Rodríguez Lafuente, Fernando (1999) 'Edgar Neville en el bazar del destino', *Nickel Odeon*, 17 (Winter): 36–43.

Rolph, Wendy (1999) '*¡Bienvenido Mister Marshall!* (Berlanga, 1952)', in *Spanish Cinema: The Auteurist Tradition*, ed. Peter Evans (Oxford: Oxford University Press), 8–18.

Ross, Andrew (1998) *Real Love: In Pursuit of Cultural Justice* (New York: New York University Press).

Said, Edward (1995) *Orientalism* (Harmondsworth: Penguin).

Sala Valladaura, José María, ed. (1996) *Sainetes* (Barcelona: Crítica).

Salaün, Serge (1990) *El cuplé (1900–1936)* (Madrid: Espasa-Calpe).

Salinas, Pedro (1998) [1941] *Literatura española siglo XX* (Madrid: Alianza Editorial).

Sánchez Dragó, Fernando (1997) *Diccionario Espasa España Mágica* (Madrid: Espasa).

Sanz de Soto, Emilio (1999) 'Edgar Neville: ni comunista, ni fascista, sino todo lo contrario', *Nickel Odeon*, 17 (Winter): 56–60.

Savater, Fernando (1997) 'Carta a Dario Fo', *El País* (6 December): 12.

Shakespeare, William (1951) [1623] *The Complete Works*, ed. and intro. Peter Alexander (London and Glasgow: Collins).

Stam, Robert (1989) *Subversive Pleasures: Bakhtin, Cultural Criticism, and Film* (London: The Johns Hopkins University Press).

Storey, John, ed. (1998) *Cultural Theory and Popular Culture: A Reader* (London: Prentice Hall).

Swift, Jonathan (1990) *Selected Poems*, ed. C.H. Sisson (Manchester: Carcanet).

Thomas, Hugh, ed. (1988) *Madrid: A Travellers' Companion* (London: Macmillan).

Todorov, Tzvetan (1977) 'The Typology of Detective Fiction', *The Poetics of Prose* (Oxford: Basil Blackwell), 42–52.

Torrecilla, Jesús (2001) 'Disfraces que persisten: La imagen andaluza de España en *Bienvenido Mr. Marshall*', Unpublished paper delivered at the conference '50 Years of Literature & Cinema in Spain', University of California, Irvine (22 February).

Torres, Augusto M. (1996) *Diccionario Espasa Cine Español* (Madrid: Espasa).

Torres-Dulce Lifante, Eduardo (1999) '*La vida en un hilo*: El azar de la felicidad', *Nickel Odeon*, 17 (Winter): 166–170.

Torrijos, José María, ed. (1999) *Edgar Neville 1899–1967: La luz en la mirada* (Madrid: Instituto Nacional de Artes Escénicas y de la Musica).

Ugarte, Michael (1996) *Madrid 1900: The Capital as Cradle of Literature and Culture* (Pennsylvania: Pennsylvania State University Press).

Umbral, Francisco (1998) 'Felipe como Pemán', *El Mundo* (3 March): 64.

Valle-Inclán Ramón del (1991) [1924] *Luces de bohemia*, ed. Alonso Zamora Vicente (Madrid: Espasa-Calpe).

Vázquez Montalbán, Manuel (1986) *Crónica sentimental de España* (Madrid: Espasa Calpe).
——(2001) 'El flagelo de la prepotencia', *El País* (13 July): 39.
Vernon, Kathleen (1997) 'Reading Hollywood in/and Spanish Cinema: From Trade Wars to Transculturation', in *Refiguring Spain: Cinema/Media/Representation*, ed. Marsha Kinder (Durham and London: Duke University Press), 35–64.
Williams, Raymond (1976) *Keywords: A Vocabulary of Culture and Society* (Glasgow: Fontana).
——(1977) *Marxism and Literature* (Oxford: Oxford University Press).
Zunzunegui, Santos (1994) *Paisajes de la forma: Ejercicios de análisis de la imagen* (Madrid: Cátedra).
——(1999) *El extraño viaje: El celuloide atrapado por la cola, o la crítica norteamericana ante el cine español* (Valencia: Episteme).

Filmography

Adventure (*Aventura*, 1942) Director: Jerónimo Mihura. Screenwriters: Miguel Mihura, Jerónimo Mihura, Alfredo Marquerie. Photography: Enrique Barreyre. Music: Manuel Parada. Actors: Conchita Montenegro, José Nieto, Juan Calvo, José Isbert. Production: CEPICSA. Nationality: Spanish. 79 minutes.

Castle of Cards (*Castillo de naipes*, 1943) Director: Jerónimo Mihura. Screenwriters: Miguel Mihura, Antonio de Obregón. Photography: Michel Kelber. Music: Juan Quintero. Actors: Blanca de Silos, Raúl Cancio, Manolo Morán. Production: Montagu Marks for Vulcano. Nationality: Spanish. 92 minutes.

The Way of Babel (*El camino de Babel*, 1945) Director: Jerónimo Mihura. Screenwriter: José Luis Sáenz de Heredia. Photography: Cecilio Paniagua. Music: M. Parada. Actors: Alfredo Mayo, Fernando Fernán Gómez, Manolo Morán, Guillermina Grin, Mary Lamar. Production: Chapalo Films. Nationality: Spanish. 80 minutes.

My Adored Juan (*Mi adorado Juan*, 1949) Director: Jerónimo Mihura. Screenwriter: Miguel Mihura. Photography: Jules Krüger. Music: Ramón Ferrés. Actors: Conchita Montes, Conrado San Martin, Juan de Landa, Luis Pérez de León, Alberto Romea, José Isbert. Production: Emisora Films. Nationality: Spanish. 116 minutes.

Life on a Thread (*La vida en un hilo*, 1945) Director: Edgar Neville. Screenwriter: Edgar Neville. Photography: Enrique Barreyre. Music: José Muñoz Molleda. Actors: Conchita Montes, Rafael Durán, Guillermo Marín, Julia Lajos. Production: Edgar Neville. Nationality: Spanish. 92 minutes.

The Tower of the Seven Hunchbacks (*La torre de los siete jorobados*, 1944) Director: Edgar Neville. Screenwriters: José Santugini, Edgar Neville. Photography: Enrique Barreyre. Music: Maestro Azagra. Actors: Antonio Casal, Isabel de Pomés, Guillermo Marín, Julia Lajos, Félix de Pomés. Production: Luis Judez for J Films, Germán López for España Films. Nationality: Spanish. 90 minutes.

Carnival Sunday (*Domingo de carnaval*, 1945) Director: Edgar Neville. Screenwriter: Edgar Neville. Photography: Enrique Barreyre. Music: José Muñoz Molleda. Actors: Conchita Montes, Fernando Fernán Gómez, Guillermo Marín, Julia Lajos. Production: Edgar Neville. Nationality: Spanish. 83 minutes.

The Bordadores Street Murder (*El crimen de la calle de Bordadores*, 1946) Director: Edgar Neville. Screenwriter: Edgar Neville. Photography: Enrique Barreyre. Music: José Muñoz Molleda. Actors: Manuel Luna, Mary Delgado, Antonia Plana, Julia Lajos, Rafael Calvo, José Franco, José Prada. Production: Manuel del Castillo. Nationality: Spanish. 93 minutes.

Welcome Mister Marshall! (*¡Bienvenido Mister Marshall!*, 1952) Director: Luis García Berlanga. Screenwriters: Juan Antonio Bardem, Miguel Mihura, Luis García Berlanga. Photography: Manuel Berenguer. Music: Jesús García Leoz. Actors: Lolita Sevilla,

Manolo Morán, José Isbert, Alberto Romea, Elvira Quintillá. Production: UNINCI. Nationality: Spanish. 78 minutes.

Plácido (1961) Director: Luis García Berlanga. Screenwriters: Rafael Azcona, José Luis Colina Luis García Berlanga. Photography: Francisco Sempere. Music: Manuel Asins Arbó. Actors: Castro Sendra Barufet 'Cassen', José Luis López Vázquez, Elvira Quintillá, Manuel Alexandre, Amelia de la Torre. Production: Alfredo Matas for Jet Films. Nationality: Spanish. 85 minutes.

The Executioner (*El verdugo*, 1963) Director: Luis García Berlanga. Screenwriters: Rafael Azcona, Luis García Berlanga, Ennio Flaiano. Photography: Tonino delli Colli. Music: Miguel Asins Arbó. Actors: Nino Manfredi, Emma Penella, José Isbert. Production Nazario for Naga Films (Madrid), Zebra Film (Rome). Nationality: Spanish and Italian. 95 minutes.

The Little Apartment (*El pisito*, 1958) Directors: Marco Ferreri and Isidoro M. Ferry. Screenwriter: Rafael Azcona. Photography: Francisco Sempere. Music: Federico Contreras. Actors: José Luis López Vázquez, Mary Carrillo, Concha López Silva, J. Cordero, Celia Conde. Production: Isidoro M. Ferry for Documento Films. Nationality: Spanish. 87 minutes.

The Little Car (*El cochecito*, 1960) Director: Marco Ferreri. Screenwriters: Rafael Azcona, Marco Ferreri. Photography: Juan Julio Baena. Music: Miguel Asins Arbó. Actors: José Isbert, Pedro Porcel, María Luisa Ponte, José Luis López Vázquez, José Álvarez 'Lepe', Antonio Requelme. Production: Pedro Portabella for Films 59. Nationality: Spanish. 88 minutes.

The Strange Journey (*El extraño viaje*, 1964) Director: Fernando Fernán Gómez. Screenwriters: Pedro Beltrán, Manuel Ruiz Castillo. Photography: José Aguayo. Music: Cristóbal Halffter. Actors: Carlos Larrañaga, Tota Alba, Lina Canalejas, Jesús Franco, Rafaela Aparicio, Sara Lezana. Production: Impala, Ízaro Films, Pro Artis Ibérica. Nationality: Spanish. 98 minutes.

Index